Mircea A. Tamas

THE CENTER AND

THE WORLD

ROSE-CROSS BOOKS

2016

RENÉ GUÉNON AND THE TRADITIONAL SPIRIT

THE METAPHYSICS OF
COSMOS – YEAR – MAN

This edition is published by **Rose-Cross Books**
TORONTO
www.rose-crossbooks.com

Cover design by *Imre Szekely*

Library and Archives Canada Cataloguing in Publication

Tamas, Mircea A. (Mircea Alexandru), 1949-, author
    The center and the world: René Guénon and the traditional spirit
/ Mircea A. Tamas.

ISBN 978-0-9865872-7-6 (paperback)

    1. Guénon, René. 2. Metaphysics. 3. Symbolism. 4. Civilization,
Subterranean. 5. Geographical myths. I. Title.

B2430.G84T33 2016   194   C2016-901137-2

CONTENTS

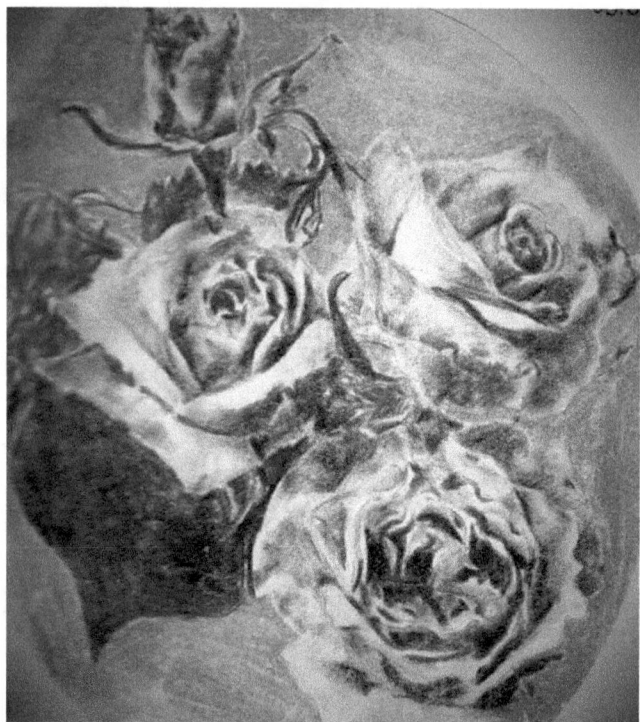

ONE

THE PRINCIPLE

WE WROTE IN our previous work, *A View of the Center*, that the Center of the World is the Principle's "location" and, in an absolute sense, there is no difference between the Center and the Principle. We may define the Principle as follows:

The blank page is not a print error, but an effort to underline the impossibility for our human mind to define or encompass, in a mere definition, the Principle.[1] The only thing we can do is to state some insights about the Principle, about Dao, about Godhead, about Brahma, in the same way the fundamental and primordial *Yi Jing* of the Far-Eastern tradition describes, through a net of changes, the unchangeable.

The Babylonian cosmogony, recorded in the *Enuma Elish*, starts with: "When in the height heaven was not named,/ And the earth beneath did not yet bear a name,/ And the primeval Apsu, who begat them,/ And chaos, Tiamat, the mother of them both/ Their waters were mingled together."

Apsu is the Abyss, which is a symbol for the Universal Possibility such as René Guénon defined it. The Universal Possibility, symbolized for our finite mind as an infinite valley or abyss, should be regarded as "the limit of all limits," "the integral of all integrals," containing by this supreme integration not only the manifestation but also the non-manifestation, the Being and the Non-Being. The Being is – as Guénon explained from a universal perspective – the principle of the universal manifestation, but it is not the absolute Infinity and does not coincide with the Universal Possibility.

The absolute Being, even though the source of manifesttation, does not belong to it, being itself non-manifested. Matgioi wrote, commenting on Lao Zi: "Dao is like the one who provides the design, the materials for a house and the workers to build it, but will not live in it." Guénon called this domain of the non-manifested possibilities, to which the Being belongs, the Non-Being. Yet the Non-Being is not the nothingness, the emptiness, the non-existence, the impossibility,

---

[1] "It is better to be silent than to reason about Dao. Dao cannot be heard with the ears; it is better to contemplate it in silence than to ask about Dao. This is what is called the Great Attainment. (…) The Principle is not reached with the eyes or the ears. We look for it, and there is no form; we hearken for it, and there is no sound. When they discuss Dao, they misrepresent it and prove that they don't understand it" (*Zhuang-zi*, 22, 5/E, 7/G).

but corresponds to the Supreme Principle, it is the Infinite Brahma or Dao.

"Then was not Non-Being nor Being: there was no realm of air, no sky beyond it. What covered in, and where? and what gave shelter? Was water there, unfathomed depth of water? Death was not then, nor was there aught immortal: no sign was there, the day's and night's divider. That One Thing, breathless, breathed by its own nature: apart from it was nothing whatsoever."[1] Then, the Non-Being appeared; then, "the Being, in the earliest age of Gods, from Non-Being sprang" (*asatah sad ajâyata*).[2]

"All things under heaven [the ten thousand beings] sprang from It as the Being (and named); that Being sprang from It as Non-Being (and not named)."[3]

"Beyond the senses is the mind, beyond the mind is the intellect, higher than the intellect is the Great Âtmâ, higher than the Great Âtmâ is the Unmanifest. Beyond the Unmanifest is Brahma, all-pervading and imperceptible. Having realized Him, the embodied self becomes liberated and attains Immortality."[4]

"He desired: many may I be, may I be born! He made *tapas*. Having made *tapas*, He sent forth all this, and what of this more. This having sent forth, into that very thing He then entered. That having entered, both the being and the beyond He became, the definite and the indefinite, the abode and the non-abode, the conscious and the unconscious; both the real (the truth) and the false did the Real (the Truth) become, and whatever else is there. That, they say, is the Real (the Brahma Truth). ... In the beginning all this was but the Unmanifested (Brahma). From that emerged the manifested. That Brahma

---

[1] *Rig-Vêda Samhitâ*, 10.129.
[2] *Rig-Vêda Samhitâ*, 10.72. It is no coincidence that Ananda K. Coomaraswamy studied precisely these Vedic hymns; see *A New Approach to The Vedas*, Munshiram Manoharlal Publisher, 1994.
[3] *Lao-zi, Dao De Jing*, XL.
[4] *Katha Up.* 3, 7-8.

Mircea A Tamas

produced Itself by Itself. Therefore It is called the self-producer."[1]

It seems that the Non-Being is above the Being, the former enclosing the latter, yet we may see the Infinite or the Universal Possibility as an assembly of Non-Being and Being.[2] The Being is One[3]; the Non-Being is the metaphysical Zero, and as the Silence envelops the Word, likewise the Non-Being encases the Being; the Word is uttered Silence, the One is the metaphysical Zero affirmed,[4] but, conversely, this Zero is more than non-affirmed One, and so is the Silence – more than the Word non-uttered. If we distinguish the Non-Being and the Being as two separate domains, then they could be considered two facets of the Universal Possibility: the non-manifestation and the

---

[1] *Taittirîya Up.* 2, 6, 7. Shankarâchârya's commentary says: "*Asat vai idam agre âsît*, in the beginning all this was but the unmanifested (Brahma). By the word *asat* is meant the unconditioned Brahma as contrasted with the state in which distinctions of name and form become manifested. Not that absolute non existence is meant, for the existent cannot come out of the non-existent." *Brahma-nirguna* is therefore not nothingness, non-existence, but Non-Being.

[2] In the Hindu tradition this assembly has different names: *martyâmartya* (mortal-immortal), *niruktanirukta* (explication-complication), *shabdashabda* (sound-silence), *vyaktâvyakta* (manifested-unmanifested), *kalakala* (temporal-eternal), *sakalâsakala* (discrete-continuous); Heraclites the Obscure offers another formula: "Immortal mortals, mortal immortals, living the death of those, dying the life of those."

[3] "The One is all things and no one of them; the source of all things is not all things; all things are its possession – running back, so to speak, to it – or, more correctly, not yet so, they will be. (…) Seeking nothing, possessing nothing, lacking nothing, the One is perfect" (Plotinus, *Fifth Ennead*, II, 1). In the Far-Eastern tradition, the initiate strives to "obtain the One" (*deyi*), and the Daoist meditation is called "to guard the One" (*shouyi*).

[4] "The book of the Yellow Emperor (*Huang di*) says: 'When a shape stirs (becoming determinate), it begets not a shape but a shadow. When a sound stirs (becoming determinate), it begets not a sound but an echo. When the Non-Being stirs (becoming determinate), it begets not no-being but the Being'" (*Lie-zi, Heaven's Gifts*, 4). "As the spider sends forth and draws in its thread, as plants grow on the earth, as hair grows on the head and the body of a living man – so does everything in the universe arise from the Imperishable" (*Mundaka Up.*, I, 7).

manifestation.[1] However, we may consider the Universal Possibility itself as the feminine aspect of the Infinity, in which case we mastermind a supreme pair, Qian and Kun, the active and passive perfections, as Matgioi and Guénon named them. Far-Eastern tradition tells that the first emperor was Fu Xi, and he is described with horns (like Matsya-Vishnu, Phanes or Moses), a sign of spirituality and royalty.[2] Fu Xi witnessed the divorce of Heaven and Earth, and then he noticed a Dragon emerging from the waters of a river, with its back marked by some curious diagrams, called "the river chart," composed of round points, black and white, diagrams the emperor used as a model to draw the eight primary *guas*. Fu Xi contemplated the sky, then he looked down to the earth, observing its particularities, considering the appearance of the birds and of the earth's products, the characteristics of the human body and of all things, and only then did he begin to draw the eight primary trigrams. The trigrams were conceived combining two fundamental traits: a straight continuous line, symbolizing Heaven, Qian, the Active Perfection, Yang, and a straight discontinuous line, symbolizing Earth, Kun, the Passive Perfection, Yin. The eight primary *guas* were arranged in a circle and then, once more, in another circle, concentric with the first one. By rotating the two circles in opposite directions the 64 hexagrams (or double trigrams) were generated.[3]

---

[1] We may give examples, for the possibilities of non-manifestation, silence, non-action, quietness, peace, immutability, void; this void is different from the Daoist Void, which represents the Universal Possibility, but each possibility of non-manifestation could symbolize the Principle (the non-action, for example, describes "the unchangeable change").

[2] The archaic ideogram for "prince" represented the prince's hair as horns (Léon Wieger, *Caractères chinois*, Kuangchi Cultural Group, 2004, p. 9).

宛 君

[3] "It is said that 'before tracing the trigrams, Fu Xi looked at the Heaven, then lowered his eyes to the Earth, observed its details, considered the characteristics of the human body and of all external things.' This text is especially interesting in that it contains the formal expression of the 'Great Triad':

The 64 hexagrams wove the texture of the oldest sacred scripture, the *Yi Jing*, "The Book of Changes"; of course, emperor Fu Xi, as an individual, was not the author of the *Yi Jing*, and we should rather consider Fu Xi representing an "intellectual aggregate" (like Hermes – Matgioi specified) or an Age that inherited the Tradition transmitted on the Dragon's back. Following the 64 hexagrams, one by one, all changes are generated, preserved and corrupted (in an Aristotelian sense).

The indefinity, Matgioi affirmed,[1] is suitable to symbolize the idea of infinity, the best representation being the straight line of indefinite length, which explains why Fu Xi chose the straight continuous line as the Principle's token. Nicolaus Cusanus has also symbolized God by an indefinite straight line, into which all the geometrical figures merge and all the contraries are resolved. The indefinite straight line suggests well the idea of non-determination, of non-definition, and it is appropriate to symbolize Active Perfection. With respect to Passive Perfection, affected by our individual rationality anchored into multiplicity, it is proper that it be represented by the discontinuous straight line. The production of the universal manifestation means then to double the line, replacing it with the *digram*, and to triple it, explicating the offspring. The *trigram*

Heaven and Earth, or the two complementary principles from which all beings spring, and man, who, by his nature partaking of both, is the middle term of the triad, the mediator between Heaven and Earth. Here we should specify that we refer to 'veritable man,' that is, he who having reached the full development of his higher faculties 'can assist Heaven and Earth in the maintenance and transformation of beings, and by that very fact constitutes a third power along with Heaven and Earth.' It is also said that Fu Xi saw a dragon emerge from the river, uniting in itself the powers of Heaven and Earth, and bearing the trigrams inscribed on its back, which is another way of expressing the same thing symbolically. Thus the whole tradition was first contained essentially and as if in germ in the trigrams, symbols marvelously adapted to serving as support for an indefinitude of possibilities; it only remained to draw from them all the necessary developments, whether in the domain of pure metaphysical knowledge itself, or in its diverse applications to the cosmic and human orders" (René Guénon, *Aperçus sur l'ésotérisme islamique et le Taoïsme*, Gallimard, 1978, p. 105).
[1] Matgioi, *La Voie métaphysique*, Éditions Traditionnelles, 1991.

The Principle

obtained, following a universal law, will appear as double, since all that is in Heaven replicates on Earth, and so the *hexagram* was born.[1] The ideogram for Dao is a synthesis of everything we described above.[2] We notice the two ends of the Dragon, of the Universal Man, and implicitly of the Principle: the head with the three hairs corresponds to Heaven and its three lights; the foot with the three footprints corresponds to Earth and its three

---

[1] In the Hindu tradition there are the three lights of Purusha and the three *gunas* of Prakriti.

[2] René Guénon said: *Un exemple remarquable de la pluralité des sens nous est fourni par l'interprétation des caractères idéographiques qui constituent l'écriture chinoise: toutes les significations dont ces caractères sont susceptibles peuvent se grouper autour de trois principales, qui correspondent aux trois degrés fondamentaux de la connaissance, et dont la première est d'ordre sensible, la seconde d'ordre rationnel, et la troisième d'ordre intellectuel pur ou métaphysique, ainsi, pour nous borner a un cas très simple, un même caractère pourra être employé analogiquement pour designer à la fois le soleil, la lumière et la vérité, la nature du contexte permettant seule de reconnaître, pour chaque application, quelle est celle de ces acceptions qu'il convient d'adopter, d'où les multiples erreurs des traducteurs occidentaux. On doit comprendre par la comment l'étude des idéogrammes, dont la portée échappe complètement aux Européens, peut servir de base à un véritable enseignement intégral, en permettant de développer et de coordonner toutes les conceptions possibles dans tous les ordres; cette étude pourra donc, à des points de vue différentiels, être reprise à tous les degrés d'enseignement, du plus élémentaire au plus élevé, en donnant lieu chaque fois à de nouvelles possibilités de conception, et c'est la un instrument merveilleusement approprie à l'exposition d'une doctrine traditionnelle* (Introduction générale à l'étude des doctrines hindoues, Guy Trédaniel, 1987, p. 137) ("A remarkable example regarding the plurality of meanings is given by the ideograms of Chinese writing: all the significances of these characters could be organized into three main groups, which correspond to the three fundamental degrees of knowledge, corporeal, rational, and pure intellectual or metaphysic, thus, to limit us to a very simple case, the same character could simultaneously be used analogically for designating the sun, the light and the truth, with only the nature of the context allowing one to identify, for each application, which of these meanings it is advisable to adopt, and this dilemma caused the multiple errors of Western translators. Consequently, one must realize how the study of the ideograms, so misunderstood by the Europeans, can be used as a basis for an integral teaching, while allowing the development and coordination of all of the possible meanings in all the orders; this study could be done from different points of view and at all the levels of teaching, from the most elementary to the most high, giving place each time to new possibilities of understanding, and it is an extraordinary instrument fit to expose a traditional doctrine").

13

tendencies. Inside the head, in non-manifestation, there is the duality hiding in unity and the unity hiding in non-duality.

The *Yi Jing*, as a synthesis, accommodates the Far-Eastern traditional doctrines, yet to try to decipher this scripture without any knowledge about Tradition or without the support of a spiritual master is a waste of time; and, even if such support exists, like in Matgioi's case, the comprehension of the Book of Changes would be extremely difficult due to these very changes generated by the "current of forms."[1] The *Yi Jing* is an opportunity for meditation and profound study from all viewpoints, for which reason we can receive enlightenment, better than following profane instruction, even by contemplating the Book's form, a changeable form, in accordance to the development of the cosmic cycles: at the beginning, the Book was a series of trigrams, essential and compressed ("complicated") symbols, the vision of which allowed the realization of everlasting Truth; then, the cosmic decline forced an explication and explicit description of these symbols, thus the succinct forms were born; eventually, the escalation of spiritual decadence imposed more and more elaborated commentaries.[2] This is the natural way from quality

[1] Comprehension of the Far-Eastern doctrines is extremely difficult for an outsider, as Coomaraswamy admitted. René Guénon said: "even the inferior steps to the status of a perfect seer are not accessible but with efforts that very few are capable of. The Daoism methods are extremely difficult to follow and their support is far too reduced in comparison with the one accorded by the traditional teaching of other civilizations, like India for example; however, they are almost impracticable for people belonging to other races. (...) Daoism is a very 'confined' doctrine and exclusively initiatory, aiming at an elite. (...) It is said that Lao Zi intrusted his teaching to two disciples (who, in their turn, educated ten disciples), and after he composed the *Dao De Jing* he disappeared toward the West, in Tibet" (*Taoïsme*, p. 121).
[2] The succinct formulas belong, in accordance to tradition, to Wen Wang, Fu Xi's son-in-law, and to his son, Zhou Gong. The commentaries belong to

to quantity, from essence to substance: Silence – Word – words. This is the way followed also by the Hindu tradition, where the *Upanishads* represent the explicit vision of the kernel that dwells in the *Vêdas*.[1] The *Logos*, Matgioi stated, is precisely the Dragon of the *Yi Jing*: "hidden dragon, non-action"[2]; "dragon appearing in the

---

Kong Fu Zi (Confucius), Zheng Zi ("the traditional commentary") and Zhu Xi ("the primitive sense").

[1] Coming back to the Far-Eastern tradition, it is interesting to observe that, as the *Upanishads* emerged from the *Vêdas*, so Daoism and Confucianism have a common origin – the *Yi Jing*. Matgioi wrote: "from Wen Wang's tetragram, that is, from the very marrow of the *Yi Jing*, Daoism was born. (...) Wen Wang was Lao Zi's predecessor." Guénon said also: "There is thus no cause to be astonished that the teachings contained in the *Yi Jing*, which Fu Xi himself claimed to have drawn from a very ancient and difficult to date past, should in turn have become the common basis of the two doctrines in which the Chinese tradition has been maintained to the present, and which, by reason of the completely different domains to which they relate, seem at first sight to have no point of contact, namely Daoism and Confucianism" (*Taoïsme*, p. 107). Daoism refers to metaphysics, stressing the importance of knowledge, while Confucianism deals with the social and practical applications. René Guénon illustrated the hierarchic difference between these two traditional branches using the following story: "'Hast thou discovered Dao?' asked Lao Zi. 'I have sought it twenty-seven years,' replied Kong Zi (Confucius) 'and I have not yet found it.' Whereupon Lao Zi gave his visitor these few precepts. 'The sage loves obscurity; he does not throw himself at every comer; he studies times and circumstances. If the moment is propitious, he speaks; otherwise, he keeps silent. Whoever possesses a treasure does not display it before the whole world; in the same way, one who is truly a sage does not unveil his wisdom to the whole world. That is all I have to say to you; make what profit you can out of it!' On returning from this interview Kong Zi said, 'I have seen Lao Zi; he is like the dragon. As for the dragon, I know not how it can be borne by winds and clouds and raise itself to Heaven" (*Taoïsme*, p. 109).

[2] Lao Zi affirmed: "Therefore the sage manages affairs by non-action (*wu-wei*), and conveys his instructions without the use of speech" (*Dao De Jing*, II); "When there is this abstinence from action (*wu-wei*), good order is universal" (III). Zhuang Zi also said about the sage: "He reached the perfect impassibility. Death and life are great considerations, but they could work no change in him. Though heaven and earth were to be overturned and fall, they would occasion him no loss. His judgment is fixed regarding the universal Principle in which there is no element of falsehood; and, while other things change, following their destiny, he changes not, sitting immobile in the center

15

field." The Silence is the hidden Dragon, the Word is the visible Dragon, the Judaic Kabbala names the Thinking (*Mahasheba*) "the hidden point," and the Word (*Memra*) is "the tangible point"; from this point, six directions of space radiated – another symbol for Logos and for the Universal Man. These six directions, reorganized from another perspective as six horizontal lines, define the first *gua* or hexagram of the *Yi Jing*, symbolizing the Principle as Active Perfection, Qian. We may note that we are able to identify the six lines due to the empty spaces that separate them, empty spaces representing the Void, while the line illustrates the One, the uttered Void. "The Word (*Memra*) has produced all things through its name One" (*Sepher Yetsirah*); the Word is One, and the Dragon is One, and the All is One, yet this truth, evident in the past, was lost during the advancement of the cycle, and therefore the *Yi Jing* had to have commentaries and the commentaries had to have more

---

of all things. (…) The external sign of this inner state is the imperturbability; take the result of this – how the heroic spirit of a single brave soldier has been thrown into an army of nine hosts. If a man only seeking for fame can produce such an effect, how much more (may we look for a greater result) from one whose rule is over heaven and earth, and holds all things in his treasury, who simply has his lodging in the six members of his body, whom his ears and eyes serve but as conveying emblematic images of things, who comprehends all his knowledge in a unity, and whose mind never dies! If such a man were to choose a day on which he would ascend far on high, men would (seek to) follow him there. But how should he be willing to occupy himself with other men?" (*Zhuang-zi*, 5, 1/A, quoted also by René Guénon, *Le symbolisme de la croix*, Guy Trédaniel, 1984, p. 53). "The softest thing in the world dashes against and overcomes the hardest; only the Non-Being, the Void enters where there is no crevice. I know hereby what advantage belongs to doing nothing (non-action, *wu-wei*). There are few in the world who attain to the teaching without words, and the advantage arising from non-action" (*Dao De Jing*, XLIII). "He who devotes himself to learning increases from day to day; he who devotes himself to the Dao diminishes from day to day. He diminishes and again diminishes, till he arrives at doing nothing. Having arrived at this point of non-action, there is nothing which he does not do" (*Dao De Jing*, XLVIII). "The utmost in speech is to be rid of speech, the utmost of doing is non-action. What common knowledge knows is shallow" (*Lie-zi*, The Yellow Emperor (*Huang di*), 11). "Heaven does nothing, and thence comes its serenity; Earth does nothing, and thence comes its rest. By the union of these two inactivities, all things are produced" (*Zhuang-zi*, 18, 1/A).

commentaries. Therefore, in the Islamic tradition, it was necessary to state a doctrine of Unity (*Et-Tawhîd*), in order to explicate what *ab origo* did not need any explication. The commentary of the *Yi Jing* affirms: "The Abyss is the resting abode of the Dragon. Sometimes the Dragon jumps, sometimes it does not."[1] The Dragon is "the omniscient master of the right and left ways."[2] Here it is the legend of the Dragon, as Matgioi told it: "The terrestrial waters mirrors the clouds flying in the sky. Their nature is similar; only their appearance is different. ... If their actions are not united, the celestial waters are powerless with regard to the earth; the terrestrial waters have no power upon the clouds. Thus, the fish in the earthly waters, the bird Hac (the crane[3]) in the celestial waters, they live separately and are imperfect. But if the storm rises the waters or the heat vaporize them; and if the clouds rain toward the earth, then the union of the terrestrial and celestial waters occurs; the bird Hac descends towards the earth, like the clouds; the fish ascends toward heaven, like the water of the river[4]; when they

---

[1] "The traditional commentary" says: "Sometimes the dragon jumps, sometimes it stays; ascending or descending, its position is not the same. Sometimes it advances, sometimes it retreats; coming closer or going away, the dragon follows the proper right way." This illustrates also the development of the cosmic cycles, never a linear progression.

[2] *Phankhoatu*, I (see Matgioi, *La Voie métaphysique*, p. 39). About *Phankhoatu*, "the Book of the returning things" see also Matgioi, *La Voie rationnelle*, Éditions Traditionnelles, 1984, p. 169.

[3] The ideogram for "flying" (indicating the super-invidual states) represents a crane:

飛 飛

[4] The ideograms describing the two movements show Heaven and Earth and their influences:

下 下 上 上

17

meet, the bird Hac lends its wings to the fish; the fish lends to the bird its body and the scales: in the middle of lightning and thunders, among the stormy waters, emerges the Great Fish with the secrets of the Law written on its back. This is the Dragon."[1]

In the Hindu tradition, this Dragon is Ananta, the master of the Abyss, the dwelling of the sleeping Vishnu.[2] The Abyss is the Babylonian Apsu, the Daoist Void, the synthesis of the waters, of the clouds and of the river.[3] The Abyss is the resting place of the Dragon, yet from a metaphysical perspective there is no difference between the Abyss and the Dragon. The Abyss is, in a way, the feminine aspect of Infinity, the Passive Perfection, Kun; the Dragon is the masculine aspect, the Active Perfection, Qian.

Nevertheless, to define the Abyss or the Void means systematization, limitation, and determination, but the Principle cannot be limited in any mode; therefore, to translate metaphysical notions into human language the negative way is used (*neti, neti*).[4]

---

[1] The famous Daoist treatise, *Zhuang-zi*, begins with "In the Northern Ocean there is a fish, the name of which is Kun, I do not know how many li in size. It changes into a bird with the name of Peng, the back of which is ..."

[2] Lie Zi told about the Abyss and the Dragon: "who knows how many thousands of millions of miles, there is a deep ravine, a valley truly without bottom; and its bottomless underneath is named 'The Entry to the Void.' The waters of the eight corners and the nine regions, the stream of the Milky Way, all pour into it, but it neither shrinks nor grows. (...) To the North of the utmost North there is an ocean, the Lake of Heaven. There is a fish there, several thousand miles broad and long in proportion, named *kun*. There is a bird there named *peng*, with wings like clouds hanging from the sky, and a body big in proportion" (*Lie-zi, The Questions of Tang*, 2). The Wallachian traditional data named the Abyss *Vidrosul* ("otterly," masculine) and the Dragon *Vidra* ("the otter," feminine), stressing the two aspects of the Infinity.

[3] "The highest excellence is like (that of) water. The excellence of water appears in its benefiting all things (the ten thousand beings), and in its occupying, without striving (to the contrary), the low place which all men dislike. Hence (its way) is near to (that of) the Dao" (*Dao De Jing*, VIII).

[4] Nicolaus Cusanus said that by negating something about God we get closer to the truth than when we affirm something. Meister Eckhart used the

The Principle

Meister Eckhart said in his sermons: "Beware! God has no name,[1] since nobody can talk about Him, nor can understand Him. If I say, 'God is good,' this is not true. I am good, God is not good. I would say even more: I am better than God; because what is good can become better, but God, since He is not good, cannot become better and neither the best, these terms being far away from God. He is above all. If I say also: God is wise, this is not true, I am wiser than God. If I add: God is a being, this is not true. He is the supreme Being and a superessential Void (Nothingness). Saint Augustine affirms about this: 'the best a man can say about God is to be silent because of the wisdom of the divine richness.' Therefore, be silent and don't chat about Him, because you would lie and sin. If you want to be perfect and without sins, don't chat about God. Don't try to understand anything [in a rational way] about God, because God is above [discursive] understanding. A master said: If I had a God that I understand, I would not consider Him God anymore. You must get rid of yourself and melt in Him, and your self with His Self must become so completely a 'mine,' such that you understand forever, with Him, His primordial being and His unnamed Void."

"A cicada and a little dove laughed at it, saying, 'We make an effort and fly towards an elm or sapan-wood tree; and sometimes before we reach it, we can do no more but drop to the ground.' (…) What should these two small creatures know about the matter? The knowledge of that which is small does not reach to that which is great; (the experience of) a few years does not reach to that of many. How do we know that it is so? The mushroom of a morning does not know (what takes place between) the beginning and end of a month; the short-lived cicada does not know (what takes place between) the spring and autumn. These are instances of a short term of life. Don't ask the ephemeral beings about the great turtle, which lives five centuries, or about the tree that lives eight thousand years"

---

negative way: "It is no good, no being, no truth, no One, then what is It? It is the Void ("Nothingness"), it is not this, not this."

[1] "Dao is forever nameless" (*Dao De Jing*, XXXII).

19

(*Zhuang-zi*, 1, 1/A); similarly, the finite individual mind cannot understand the Infinity, the individual one cannot comprehend the universal one.[1]

Lao Zi stated: "The Dao is hidden, and has no name; but it is the Dao which is skilful at imparting (to all things what they need) and making them complete" (*Dao De Jing*, XLI).

In the Islamic tradition, Allâh, in His Essence, is without names and qualities; Ibn 'Arabî affirmed: "Allâh is without resemblance, without pair, has no helper or adjutant, has no associate, no minister, and no adviser. He is not body, nor substance, nor accident, nor composition, He cannot be defined. He is no star, nor darkness that manifests, nor light that shines."

He is no light. He is no darkness. He "is" not, therefore the idea of nothingness, of void. He is indestructible, non-confinable, immovable, without ties, *non aliud* (as Nicolaus Cusanus would say). He is the Mysterious Anonymous, Ain Soph (*Zohar* III, 26 b).[2]

---

[1] "There are three types of knowledge," Meister Eckhart said; "one is the sensitive knowledge, and the second is the rational one, higher. The third is a noble power [the intellect] of the soul, so high and noble that it comprehends God intuitively, in Its essential simplicity. This power has no connection with anybody, it does not know about yesterday and tomorrow, because in eternity there is no yesterday and tomorrow but only the eternal present. This power is One in Unity. My eye [the eye of the heart] and God's Eye are the same eye and the same vision, the same knowledge and the same love." Muhyddin Ibn 'Arabî underlined: "The Seal of Sanctity, Khâtim al-Wilâyah, the pole and prototype of the sages, knowledgeable and ignorant, knows (as a synthesis) and, at the same time, doesn't know (rationally), sees and doesn't see, contemplates and doesn't contemplate."

[2] Saint Dionysius the Areopagite said: "Unto this Darkness which is beyond Light we pray that we may come, and may attain unto vision through the loss of sight and knowledge, and that in ceasing thus to see or to know we may learn to know that which is beyond all perception and understanding (for this emptying of our faculties is true sight and knowledge) and that we may offer Him that transcends all things the praises of a transcendent hymnody, which we shall do by denying or removing all things that are – like as men who, carving a statue out of marble, remove all the impediments that hinder the clear perceptive of the latent image and by this mere removal display the hidden statue itself in its hidden beauty. (...) For the more that we soar upwards the more our language becomes restricted to the compass of purely

The Principle

"Lao Zi said, «The Dao does not exhaust itself in what is greatest, nor is it ever absent from what is least; and therefore it is to be found complete and diffused in all things. How wide is its universal comprehension! How deep [abyss] is its unfathomableness! It contains everything and does not have a bottom»" (*Zhuang-zi*, 13, 9/G).

From a metaphysical perspective, the Infinity is identical with the Abyss, an Abyss identical with the Void as absolute Plenitude. "Dao is a void, used but never filled. An abyss it is,

---

intellectual conceptions, even as in the present instance plunging into the Darkness which is above the intellect we shall find ourselves reduced not merely to brevity of speech but even to absolute dumbness both of speech and thought. Now in the former treatises the course of the argument, as it came down from the highest to the lowest categories, embraced an ever-widening number of conceptions which increased at each stage of the descent, but in the present treatise it mounts upwards from below towards the category of transcendence, and in proportion to its ascent it contracts its terminology, and when the whole ascent is passed it will be totally dumb [mute], being at last wholly united with Him Whom words cannot describe. (...) We therefore maintain that the universal Cause transcending all things is neither impersonal nor lifeless, nor irrational nor without understanding: in short, that It is not a material body, and therefore does not possess outward shape or intelligible form, or quality, or quantity, or solid weight; nor has It any local existence which can be perceived by sight or touch; nor has It the power of perceiving or being perceived; nor does It suffer any vexation or disorder through the disturbance of earthly passions, or any feebleness through the tyranny of material chances, or any want of light; nor any change, or decay, or division, or deprivation, or ebb and flow, or anything else which the senses can perceive. (...) It is not knowledge or truth; nor is It kingship or wisdom; nor is It one, nor is It unity, nor is It Godhead or Goodness; nor is It a Spirit, as we understand the term, since It is not Sonship or Fatherhood; nor is It any other thing such as we or any other being can have knowledge of; nor does It belong to the category of non-existence or to that of existence; nor do existent beings know It as it actually is, nor does It know them as they actually are; nor can the reason attain to It to name It or to know It; nor is it darkness, nor is It light, or error, or truth; nor can any affirmation or negation apply to it; for while applying affirmations or negations to those orders of being that come next to It, we apply not unto It either affirmation or negation, inasmuch as It transcends all affirmation by being the perfect and unique Cause of all things, and transcends all negation by the pre-eminence of Its simple and absolute nature-free from every limitation and beyond them all" (*The Mystical Theology*, II, III, IV, V).

from which all things come" (*Dao De Jing*, IV); the "never filled" observation means that the Void is the Infinity and "it is the nature of the Dao, that even though used continuously, it is replenished naturally, never being emptied, and never being over-filled," the Principle being unchangeable and immutable.

"Chun Mang, on his way to the ocean, met with Yuan Feng on the shore of the eastern sea, and was asked by him where he was going. 'I am going,' he replied, 'to the ocean'; and the other again asked, 'What for?' Chun Mang said, 'Such is the nature of the ocean that the waters which flow into it can never fill it, nor those which flow from it exhaust it. I will enjoy myself, rambling by it'" (*Zhuang-zi*, 12, 12/L). Sometimes, this "ocean" is called "the Great Valley" and it represents the image of the Principle, as Léon Wieger stated in his translation.

The Great Valley is another name for the Universal Possibility, its symbolism being present in the Christian and Judaic traditions: "I will also gather all nations, and will bring them down into the valley of Jehoshaphat, and will plead with them there for my people and for my heritage Israel, whom they have scattered among the nations, and parted my land" (*Joel* III, 2); "Let the heathern be wakened, and come up to the valley of Jehoshaphat: for there will I sit to judge all the heathen round about" (*Joel* III, 2); "Let the heathen be wakened, and come up to the valley of Jehoshaphat: for there will I sit to judge all the heathen round about" (*Joel* III, 12).[1] "The valley spirit never dies. It refers to the dark and mysterious female (mother). The gate of the mysterious female is the root of Heaven and Earth. Continuous, seeming to remain" (*Dao De Jing*, VI). "The valley spirit never dies" is an ancient Chinese dictum; the dark mother is the Universal Possibility (the Abyss) and the valley spirit is the Dragon.

Nevertheless, in the Western world, the Universal Possibility of the Far-Eastern tradition is better known as Void than Valley. Yet for Daoism, the Void is not only the supreme Principle, the Infinity or the Universal Possibility, but it descends on "Jacob's ladder," projecting its reflections at

---

[1] In Masonry, the Lodge is an equivalent of the Valley.

The Principle

different levels, the universal manifestation being, if we can say so, imbued with a void that is its invisible support. The void could be a symbol of the feminine pole, in correlation with the plenitude as the masculine pole[1]; the void is also a token for the intermediary world (Hindu *antariksha*), "the Atmosphere" (Hindu *Bhuva*); it is the median void, which, in another sense, is the central void inside the heart cavity.[2] For modern man, the void is completely different from the Daoist void, and is regarded from such a narrow and materialistic

---

[1] In this case, the Mountain is the masculine principle and the Valley the feminine one. "To be 'male' (rooster) and appear as 'female' (hen) is to act as the world's ravine [the Abyss]. To act as the world's ravine, treat virtuosity [*De*] as constant, and avoid separating is to return to infancy. To be 'white' but appear as 'black' is to act as the world's paradigm. To act as the world's paradigm, treat virtuosity as constant and avoid lapses is to return to Non-Being. To be 'glorious' but appear as 'disgraced' is to act as the world's valley [The hexagram no. 3, Zhun, of the *Yi Jing*, having the first trait, the inferior one, a continuous line, signifies – Zheng Zi explained – "the symbolic image of nobility and a voluntarily descent under what is humble"]. To act as the world's valley, treating virtuosity as constant is sufficient to return to uncarved wood [simplicity]" (*Dao De Jing*, XXVIII). The Valley or the Abyss represents here *coincidentia oppositorum*, the land of perfection, of simplicity, of infancy (attributes characterizing the spiritual realization). We note the triads: ravine – valley – paradigm (Hindu *Dharma*) (the Principle's triad); cock and hen – white and black – glory and humility (the Yin-Yang's triad); infancy – infinity – simplicity (the triad of spiritual realization).

gua Zhun (Kan, water, up; Zhen, thunderbolt, down)

[2] *Gua* Ding (no. 50)'s commentary affirms: "Up, it is the clarity of gua simple Li, with the inner void, which represents the symbolic image of ears and eyes hearing and seeing with clarity."

23

perspective that the void is confused with nothingness and non-existence.

The Void, as we stressed, is void only in the sense of being non-manifested, but it presents a formidable symbolic richness of perfect plenitude. The Void is the infinite and abyssal Plenitude, of the Non-Being and the Being in non-duality, it is specifically the ambiance of the sages: "The perfect men of old trod the path of benevolence as a path which they borrowed for the occasion, and dwelt in Righteousness as in a lodging which they used for a night. Thus they rambled in the vacancy of Untroubled Ease [the Void]" (*Zhuang-zi*, 14, 5).

Gua Zhong Fu, no. 61, identifies the middle void with inner truth, perfect sincerity and absolute trust. The two middle traits (broken) represent this inner void, but the middle traits of the trigrams are continuous lines and designate the plenitude. Therefore this *gua* is the symbol for inner void and plenitude at the same time.[1]

gua Zhong Fu

Projected on the being plane, the void stands for the heart cavity: there dwells *jivâtmâ*, "the living soul," a reflection of the

---

[1] The Zhong Fu ideogram is:

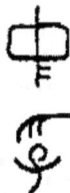

The upper sign is the ideogram for "middle"; the lower one represents the "blessing," the protective heavenly hand that is completely trusted by the emperor (as a newborn), whose heart is emptied of the worldly things and full with sincerity and trust.

immortal Self, *Âtmâ*; from a cosmic viewpoint, the cave is an empty space, therefore the feminine principle (womb, cup, container, bell, calyx) refers to this empty space, the void becoming more tangible due to a particularization that amputates its supremacy but offers an aspect accessible to the human mind.[1] Similarly, "the median void" that ties the elements of the manifestation and mediates the link between Heaven and Earth, is the free space, is the Atmosphere, translated in the corporeal world as an elusive emptiness.

In the *Yi Jing*, the symbolic image for the median, intermediary void is *gua* no. 27, Yi, built of Gen (mountain) up and Zhen (thunderbolt) down, that is, having at each extreme a continuous line and in the middle four discontinuous lines. "Up," Zheng Zi said, "is fixed, down is mobile; the outside is solid and the middle is void; it is the symbolic image of the jaws of the human mouth. (…) The divine man, establishing the *guas*, examines the meaning of the word 'to feed' (*yi*), applying it to Heaven and to Earth, which feed, that is, produce and sustain the ten thousand beings."

---

[1] The antagonist projection, in conformity with the reverse analogy, of the Principle on the plane of manifestation, at *principial* level, causes the supreme Void to appear as feminine vacuity. Such a projection is noted in the *Yi Jing*, in the case of the hexagrams no. 7 and 8, called Shi and Bi. Shi is built of Kun (earth) up and Kan (water) down, that is, of five discontinuous lines and a continuous one – the second line (counted as usually from inside towards outside); Bi consists of Kan up and Kun down, that is, of five discontinuous lines and a continuous one – the fifth. The continuous line of Bi has as reflection the continuous line of Shi, corresponding to each other in a reverse analogy, the former symbolizing the emperor (the Principle's vicar, always the fifth position being that of the emperor) and the latter signifying the army general, the temporal power (the token of the feminine principle).

gua Shi

gua Bi

gua Yi

The comparison of *gua* Yi with the human mouth is highly beneficent; yet even higher benefit is obtained in considering the mouth a symbol for the Principle, the Far-Eastern sages exclaiming, while they admired the work of Heaven and Earth: *"Gua* Yi designates huge circumstances!"* Heaven up, immutable; Earth down, changeable; between the two principles, the median void that nourishes and sustains the universal manifestation. The trigram Gen is considered to represent immobility (the upper jaw, fixed), and the trigram Zhen mobility (the lower jaw, mobile). Thus, the two jaws, specified by the continuous lines, symbolize the masculine and feminine principles, the Active and Passive Perfections; between them – the median void, which nourishes the universal Existence, the void that gives birth to the *Logos*, the primordial Sound (the Hindu *Parashabda*), the Mouth as a Whole being the epitome of the Principle.[1] "Now then, as regards the meditation on the manifestation. The Earth is the first letter [the lower jaw]. Heaven is the last letter [the upper jaw]. The Wind (Vâyu, prâna, Atmosphere) is the union-place. Then the meditation with regard to Âtmâ follows. The lower jaw is the first letter. The upper jaw is the last letter. Speech is the union-place. The tongue is the link" (*Taittirîya Up.*, *Siksha Valli*, III, 2-4).

The Mouth produces all the beings and also the Mouth swallows back all the beings. From an initiatory point of view,

---

[1] In the Hindu tradition, Purusha's mouth represents the Brâhmana caste; the symbol of the mouth, René Guénon indicated, illustrates the teaching function and the transmission of the traditional lore (*Introduction*, p. 196). The hands represent the Kshatriya caste, and there is a Chinese ideogram showing the mouth and hands together between Heaven and Earth (Wieger 28):

the Dragon's mouth swallows the neophyte and then expels him; not by chance, in the Hindu tradition, the *Brahmana* caste came from the Principle's mouth. Interestingly enough, there is another *gua*, which refers explicitly to Mouth – *gua* no. 21, Shi He, built of Li (fire) up and Zhen (thunderbolt) down; the only difference, in comparison to *gua* Yi, is the fourth trait, which is a continuous line instead of a discontinuous one, a fact Zheng Zi commented on as follows: "Outside, energetic hardness, inside, void; it is the symbolic image of the jaws of the human mouth. Yet in the middle of the intermediary void there is another trait that indicates the energetic rigidity and represents the symbolic image of an object between the jaws. Having something in the mouth, this something separates the upper jaw from the lower jaw, which cannot get united. This something has to be bitten with the teeth and then the reunion of the jaws occurs. (…) In the universe, violence, falsehood and disarray will oppose this reunification." Regardless if it is about the Cosmos, empire, or family, the obstacle that divides causes unhappiness. During the decadence of the cycle, the division between Heaven and Earth is more and more accentuated; therefore there occurs also the separation between father and son, emperor and vassal, between friends, or between relatives. From an initiatory viewpoint, the obstacle that separates the being from the Principle is the ignorance.

gua Shi He

It is understandable now why the traditional doctrines are incompatible with simplist interpretations, with systems and rigid frames, a notion such as the void accepting a diversity of symbolic meanings is a very unpleasant situation for the profane mind.

The human mind functions using images and forms (the form, Sanskrit *rupa*, is one of the existential conditions of the human world); therefore, it is "inhuman" to ask one to imagine the void, and the rational mind has to conclude that the void is nothingness. The mistake, even though understandable, is not less serious, since the formal world represents only a tiny "part" of the universal manifestation, the celestial and informal world, and then the Non-Being, defining the vastest domain of the Universal Possibility; and, only the sage, the veritable man, following the initiatory way to perfection, could surpass the formal manifestation, this strip, so narrow and so unjustly treasured, a strip that, in fact, constitutes a redoubtable obstacle, since the human mind is imbued with restless images, boiling swirls and turbulent eddies, generated by the formal world, all the initiatory ways, regardless of their traditional origins, stressing the fundamental importance of taming the mind and liberating it beyond the forms ("trans-forming" it). For this reason, the Buddhist schools, for example, stubbornly insist upon the void as "non-form," and the traditional symbolism uses formal supports to help the comprehension of the void and, at the same time, with quieting of the mind.

Related to the void, the Tibetan masters affirmed that the invisible state could be obtained when all mental activities have ceased. The neophyte, after a long initiatory training, succeeded to realize the void, by emptying his mind, and thus establishing a state of invisibility with regard to the vicinity; this state of "insignificance,"[1] of emptiness (of forms and images), of extinction, of non-action, is, in fact, a state of supreme spiritual activity, otherwise the void would be just nothingness. In the state of invisibility, the sage empties his mind of images, of forms, ceasing any action (physical and psychical), but at the same time he is steadfast in the center of the *swastika*, of the wheel, and by his spiritual and pure intellectual activity he shines with a blinding light that will make everybody sightless.

What is this emptiness of forms? It is the primordial state, which Isaiah the prophet announced: "Prepare ye the way of

---

[1] "In-significance" means with "no sign," that is, with no name.

the Lord, make straight in the desert a highway for our God. Every valley shall be exalted, and every mountain and hill shall be made low: and the crooked shall be made straight, and the rough places plain" (*Isaiah* 40:3-5). And St. Luke said also: "Every valley shall be filled, and every mountain and hill shall be brought low; and the crooked shall be made straight, and the rough ways shall be made smooth" (3:5); the emptiness disappears, the plenitude disappears, the void and the plenitude are the simple Infinity, without any attributes, without forms. In other words, the void, as an informal state, could be symbolized by an unlimited, smooth and flat surface, a monotonous desert; but, this image is only a helpful support in the early stages of the novitiate.

Meister Eckhart, in a famous sermon, explained the Gospel's episode regarding the cleansing of the Temple. "And the Jews' Passover was at hand, and Jesus went up to Jerusalem, and found in the temple those that sold oxen and sheep and doves, and the changers of money sitting: and when he had made a scourge of small cords, he drove them all out of the temple, and the sheep, and the oxen; and poured out the changers' money, and overthrew the tables; and said unto them that sold doves, Take these things hence; make not my Father's house a house of merchandise" (*John* 2:13-16). The cleansing of the Temple, Meister Eckhart said, epitomizes the emptying of forms, the realization of a pure heart cavity, of the void. In different traditions, the "forms" (with all the mental and psychic waves) are called demons or devils. The "vacuity" means the victory against these devils, the peace obtained by annihilating the demons and following the cleansing of the Temple. This emptiness means to dismantle the arrogance and the ignorance in believing that the ego is independent and has a separate and self-sufficient existence.[1]

---

[1] Dalai Lama Tanzin Gyatso, Gyalwa Rimpoche, describes a tactic used to dismantle the ego. Any being (anything related to "to be") has a name, and when we seek deeper to find what corresponds to this name, we will find different components and attributes that describe this being, but the being is not one of these components or attributes. We conclude that we will not find

"Someone asked Lie Zi: 'Why do you value the void?' 'In void there is no valuing, but you value the state you obtain. The state of silence and peace in the void is ineffable. In stillness and void, we find where to abide. Taking and giving we lose the place'" (Lie-zi, *Heaven's Gifts*, 9).

The vacuity, the void is a state that cannot be imagined, and no one can think of it in a rational way. Zen knew very well how to express this inexpressible state. For example: "Sekkio asked one day one of his monks: 'Could you notice an empty space?' 'Yes master, I can,' the monk answered. 'Show me.' The monk extended his arms, embracing the void. 'So, that is how you do it?' Sekkio asked. 'Yet, you don't embrace anything.' 'What is then your way?' the monk inquired. The master replied

---

the being and what is left is the vacuity, yet this vacuity is not the nothingness but the void; this void does not mean that an existent entity is emptied of another existent entity, but that an independent existence does not have reality, being a vacuity. If a being is intrinsically real, the more we analyze it, the more real it will become; on the contrary, if a thing is illusory, the more we study it, the more unreal it will become and eventually it will disappear completely. Nâgârjuna said: "The form seen from far away becomes clear if we come nearer; a mirage disappears when we are closer. Why? If we are far away, the world appears real; if we come closer, it becomes less and less visible and at the end it will disappear like a mirage." We can define a table as an object made of wood, with a brown colour, etc. Yet the table is not the wood itself, not the brown. Where is the table? Only the name remains. A tree, in order to have its own existence, should be independent, that is, its fruits should not fall, its leaves should not fall. Nâgârjuna said: "Since there are no independent beings, there are no beings that are not 'void.'" The Vacuity though doesn't make the beings void, since the beings themselves are the Vacuity. Meister Eckhart affirmed: "We say that the man has to be so poor that he should have no place where God could operate. While he reserves a place for Him, he keeps a distinction (that is, in Buddhist terms, an intrinsic existence). Therefore I pray God to liberate me from 'God,' because my essential being is above 'God,' when we perceive God as the principle of creatures." The liberation from God is the Vacuity, beyond creation, beyond manifestation, beyond any ties. "A good traveler leaves no tracks (...), and a well made door is easy to open and needs no locks. A good knot needs no rope and it cannot come undone" (*Dao De Jing*, XXVII). Ramana Maharshi asked the famous question: "Who am I?" Am I the current of forms, the changes or the modifications? Of course not. What remains after emptying and discarding the ephemeral elements is the Self, the Vacuity of Meister Eckhart and of the primeval Buddhism.

The Principle

instantly by grabbing the monk's nose and strongly squeezing it. 'Oh, how this hurts!' the monk complained. 'This is how you can notice the void,' the master concluded." One day, when the emperor asked Bodhi-dharma, the first Zen patriarch of China, about the sacred doctrine, he received this answer: "An immense void and nothing inside that could be called sacred." The Principle is the immense void. The Principle does not have a name, it cannot be defined,[1] and all our endeavors to understand it as Valley, or Void, or Abyss are just methods to shake our mentality and our prejudices, to start healing our blindness.[2]

"Dao," Matgioi affirmed, "is the series, the sum and the result of all the modification in the universe, or, of the various states of the manifested Qian." The beginning of the *Yi Jing* tells about Dao in relation to Wen Wang's tetragramatic formula: "It is the origin of all things, it is the whole Heaven; it is the initial cause; the initial cause of activity expresses, generally and completely, Dao of Heaven. Dao of Heaven's Activity produces all beings. A great light illuminates Dao's beginning and end,

---

[1] In his commentary about *gua* no. 20, Guan, of the *Yi Jing*, Zheng Zi said: "Dao is what is most spiritual (*shen*). (…) This Way of a supreme intelligence cannot be named. The divine man, alone, conforms silently to it, mysteriously fixed by knots."

[2] In the Hindu tradition, *avidyâ* means "ignorance" and it is the main cause of our disarray, the main obstacle on the way to Liberation. The profane world is supported by this "blindness." In the *Yi Jing*, the fourth perfect *gua* is Meng, built of Gen (mountain) up and Kan (water) down, and "illustrating the blindness and the lack of discrimination." The word *meng* means "the lack of light" and symbolizes the ignorance, the mountain signifying the obstacle in the way of the creek, which doesn't know where to go. In the Hindu traditon, as well as in the Islamic one, the ability to discriminate has an important role in the process of spiritual realization.

gua Meng

31

thus we see the six situations of *gua* [the six continuous lines of the hexagram Qian, the first hexagram] appearing each one in time. The first and the last lines of *gua* are Dao of Heaven's beginning and end. (...) Dao means change and transformation, due to activity, it generates all beings; big or small, high or short, each one, following its own species, conforms exactly to its nature and destiny. What Heaven confers, it is destiny[1]; what the beings receive, it is their nature. (...) Maintaining the total harmony, it means to follow the good and the perfection; Dao of Heaven and Earth is permanent and everlasting; it maintains the total harmony" (Zheng Zi's traditional commentary). The four terms of Wen Wang's formula are indissolubly related to Dao: Dao produces them, Dao supports them, Dao watches them, and Dao harvests them. Wen Wang, Zheng Zi stressed in his commentary, considered Dao, the Way of Activity, as expressing the greatness of intelligence and the supreme rectitude, that is, exactly the determinative formula, the tetragram; and Zhu Xi underlined: the meaning of Qian can be clarified with the help of the immutable Way of Heaven, Dao. Dao of Heaven, it is also said in the *Yi Jing*, is the perfect sincerity, namely, the pure Truth.

---

[1] The ideograms *ling* and *ming* (Wieger 47) describe how the heavenly mouth confers to man the celestial mandate and his destiny between Heaven and Earth:

吞 介

TWO

THE DUALITY

TO PRODUCE THE SPACE, the point as center duplicated itself and became two points, which to be distinct must have a distance, even an infinitesimal one, between them; this distance is the "space." Similarly, the world was produced, not from One but from Two, even though there is no "two" but only "one" or, even better, only the "non-duality."

"To fix the principles of the tradition, Fu Xi made use of linear symbols that were both simple and at the same time as synthetic as possible, that is, the continuous line and the broken line, respectively signs of *yang* and *yin*, the two principles, active and passive, which, proceeding from a sort of polarization of the supreme metaphysical Unity, give birth to the whole of universal manifestation. From the combinations of these two signs, in all their possible arrangements, are formed the eight *gua* or 'trigrams,' which have always remained the fundamental symbols of the Far-Eastern tradition" (Guénon, *Taoïsme*, p. 104).

The Far-Eastern tradition specifies that the world exists due to the indefinite combinations of *yang* and *yin*, each being having in its composition a *yin* component and a *yang* one (the proportions are different for each being, in conformity with the law of uniqueness).[1] In the Hindu tradition, Prakriti, the feminine principle, nurses three tendencies (*gunas*), which are the primordial qualities and attributes of all the beings, existing at different levels of manifestation, tendencies that are in a perfect equilibrium within the fundamental undifferentiated Prakriti. Any manifestation signifies breaking this equilibrium and each being coalesces its nature using an always different and unique combination of the three *gunas*. The three tendencies are: *sattwa*, light thundering upwards (*yang*); *rajas*, breezy expansion (*yang* and *yin*); *tamas*, obscurity falling downwards (*yin*). "Scholars of the highest class, when they hear about the Dao, earnestly carry it into practice. Scholars of the middle class, when they have heard about it, seem now to keep it and now to lose it. Scholars of the lowest class, when they have heard about it, laugh greatly at it. If it were not (thus) laughed at, it would not be fit to be the Dao" (*Dao De Jing* XLI).

Lao Zi's saying illustrates very well the three tendencies. We may add that Purusha, the masculine principle, nurses in a similar way three tendencies, which are the three lights that, with their presence and invisible activity, force the *gunas* to break the equilibrium.[2] The six tendencies can be found in the *Yi Jing*, in *gua* Pi (no. 12),

---

[1] Only the "veritable man"'s nature has *yang* and *yin* in a perfect equilibrium (Guénon, *La Grande Triade*, p. 84). Moreover, even if Fu Xi, as "Lord of the Earth," used the square, "in himself he is Yin-Yang, being reintegrated in the state and nature of the 'primordial man'" (*La Grande Triade*, p. 132). "The gift of Heaven is the nature received at birth" (*Zhuang-zi*, 6, A). Related to this we should mention that, in reality, the nature of each being determines the "astral influences" and not the other way around (*La Grande Triade*, pp. 117-8). "[Yan Hsiung] answered: 'The astrologer foretells what the effects of the heavenly phenomena will be on man; the Sage foretells what the effect of man's actions will be on the heavens.' Or, as Tung Chung-shu puts it: 'The actions of man, when he reaches the highest level of goodness or evil, will flow into the universal course of heaven and earth, and cause responsive reverberations in their manifestations'" (J. C. Cooper, *Chinese Alchemy*, The Aquarian Press, 1984, p. 87).

[2] The ideogram for the three lights (as sun, moon, and stars) is (Wieger 312):

The Duality

a hexagram symbolizing the divorce between Heaven and Earth, between Purusha and Prakriti, a favorable situation allowing the ten thousand beings or the universal manifestation to "become." The manifestation cannot exist without duality, without separation. "Hence the sayings, 'Shall we not follow and honour the right, and have nothing to do with the wrong? Shall we not follow and honour those who secure good government, and have nothing to do with those who produce disorder?' show a want of acquaintance with the principles of Heaven and Earth, and with the different qualities of things. It is like following and honouring Heaven and taking no account of Earth; it is like following and honouring the Yin and taking no account of the Yang. It is clear that such a course cannot be pursued. To try to consider these two inseparable correlatives as distinct entities proves a weak judgment; Heaven and Earth are One, Yin and Yang are One; and so are all the contraries" (*Zhuang-zi*, 17, 5/A).

The two poles separated, superior and inferior, determine the whole manifestation, that is, the universal Existence, and therefore, everything belonging to Existence is marked by duality, doubt,[1] fear, contingency, and is ephemeral[2]; therefore,

---

[1] The word "doubt" is etymologically related to "duality."

[2] "The changeable change" characterizes the manifestation, which means that history does not repeat itself, that "the eternal return" is a false label, that all Existence, being an indefinite change, is defined by relativity, perishability and equivocation, that, "depending on time and circumstances, the result of the same actions is not the same" (*Zhuang-zi*). "There is no end or beginning to the Dao. Things indeed change, die and are born, not reaching a perfect state which can be relied on. Now there is Non-Being, and now there is Being; they do not continue in one form. The years cannot be reproduced; time cannot be

35

everything is relative in manifestation, and there are controversies and contradictions; therefore, it is impossible to transpose the metaphysical truth in the inferior plane of manifestation without alteration and error, the only efficient way being silent transmission ("the man of Dao keeps silent," Zhuang Zi stressed).[1] In comparison to silence, which is the divine way to reveal metaphysical knowledge, oral transmission seems like an inferior modality,[2] but it is still superior to "bookish" instruction, since written ideas are less rich in essence than those transmitted orally, which, in their turn, are less rich in essence than thoughts.

The *Yi Jing*'s commentaries affirmed: "The writing cannot exhaust the speech; the speech cannot exhaust the thought; yet, how the sage's thoughts could be manifested? Confucius said: The sage establishes symbols to exhaust the thoughts; he institutes the hexagrams." The symbols are the silence expressed beyond the words. "What is transmitted through words," Zhu Xi said, "is superficial, while what is learned through symbols is profound. Only considering the continuous line as unity and the discontinuous line as duality can we encompass completely the modifications and the transfor-

---

arrested. Decay and growth, fullness and emptiness, when they end, they begin again. It is thus that we describe the method of great righteousness, and discourse about the principle pervading all things. The life of things is like the hurrying and galloping of a horse. With every movement there is a change; with every moment there is an alteration. What should you be doing? What should you not be doing? You have only to be allowing this course of natural transformation to be going on" (*Zhuang-zi*, 17, 6/A).

[1] "One who knows does not speak; one who speaks does not know. Block the openings; shut the doors" (*Dao De Jing*, LVI); about blocking the openings see also chap. LII.

[2] We should mention Pratardana's doctrine about the inner sacrifice *Agnihotra*, which allowed the melting of words in the meditative breathing: "So long as a man speaks, he cannot breathe [ritually], he offers all the while his prâna (breath) in his speech. And so long as a man breathes, he cannot speak; he offers all the while his speech in his breath. These two endless and immortal oblations he offers always, whether waking or sleeping" (*Kaushitaki Up.*, II, 5).

mation, and it is obvious that those have no end and cannot be exhausted."[1]

Traditional doctrines, even though dressed in various clothes, have a common speech, that of symbols, which represents the fundamental modality to translate metaphysical truth to the individual world, the science of symbols being at least as rigorous and precise as Mathematics. A symbol, in a traditional sense, is a physical or cosmic "support" that expresses, analogically, a superior truth, usually belonging to a metaphysic or spiritual order. To explain the reality of the symbols, we must remember that all the "ten thousand beings" draw their reality from the Principle (otherwise, there is just vacuity), each thing being an emblem of the Principle, a reflection, a print, or a signature of Dao in the universal manifestation; and therefore, we should not be surprised if, looking around us, we notice that all the world's components could play the role of a symbol or of a "support," since the whole world is nothing else than an "image" of the Principle, everything being in conformity with That One. The language of the symbols is the closest to "silent speech," surpassing all the particular speeches.

One fundamental symbol of the Far-Eastern tradition is the figure of Yin-Yang.[2] From a cosmic point of view, the pure

---

[1] We find in the *Yi Jing*: "In the ancient times, strings with knots were used to transmit the rules; later, the sages replaced them with the writing." The knots along a string represented a symbolic and "complicated" way to transmit knowledge; we employ the expression "complication" as Nicolaus Cusanus understood it, equivalence for synthesis. With regard to the written instruction, we signal a frequent error of the modern world, which, ignoring the traditional mentality, wrongly believed that by dating the scriptures or a manuscript they could establish the very date of birth of a doctrine. In fact, oral transmission existed far before written. Hocart rightly said: "the first appearance of a custom in the texts is seldom, if ever, its first appearance in the world. It is often not recorded until it begins to decay" (A. M. Hocart, *Caste*, Methuen & Co, London, 1950, p. 22).

[2] The ideograms for *yang* and *ying* present the Three Worlds as three bricks and respectevly the light and the darkness:

Being appears as double, as two poles, Heaven and Earth, and Yang, the luminous principle, is the active, masculine and celestial pole, while Yin, the obscure principle, is the passive, feminine and terrestrial pole.[1] However, we must not forget that, in fact, the two poles are One, therefore the obscure part hosts a luminous point and the luminous part an obscure point. The circular figure or Yin-Yang is symbolically similar to the Cosmic Egg of Greek Leda, Castor and Pollux representing the pair luminous-obscure, immortal-mortal, yin-yang, Pollux being

[1] Heaven is completely *yang*, and Earth is completely *yin*. Between Heaven and Earth, the whole manifestation and the "ten thousand beings" participate in the celestial and terrestrial natures at the same time; therefore, in manifestation, *yang* is never without *yin* and *yin* without *yang* (that is one of the reasons why the figure presents a white point in the dark half and a black point in the luminous one, but, also, it is suggested that duality is rooted in unity); we could say that every being is somehow "androgynous," and every man, for example, has a masculine and a feminine component that influence his character (At the end of time, there is a flagrant disaccord between the result of the two components and the individual as a psycho-physical "organism." This disharmony and disorder generate tragedies that the modern science tries to solve in an artificial and materialistic way). "There is no assassin greater than the Yin and Yang, from whom nothing can escape of all between Heaven and Earth. But it is not the Yin and Yang that play the assassin; it is the mind and the appetites that cause them to do so" (*Zhuang-zi*, 23, 4/D). Matgioi indicated another significance for Yin-Yang: the circle is a spire of the vertical helix, representing a state of existence for the being, the helix symbolizing the integral being, as a geometric locus of all the states; on the plane of this particular state are projected the "anterior" (dark) states and the "posterior" (luminous) states, Yin-Yang appearing as a projection on the plane of a cylinder (or a double cone) of infinite length. Yin-Yang is thus "the circle of individual destiny," "birth" and "death" being two points, which don't belong to the horizontal circle, but to the vertical helix, obeying the Will of Heaven.

The Duality

yang, divine, that is, pure *sattwa*, essence, light, and Castor being *yin*, terrestrial, that is, pure *tamas*, substance, darkness.[1]

The projection on a plane of the two hemispheres of the Cosmic Egg leads to another fundamental symbol, the double spiral. The double spiral is related to the Yin-Yang, designating the two phases: expiration-inspiration, explication-complication, *solve-coagula*, evolution-involution, birth-death, that is, Heaven's Activity under its double aspect,[2] or, better yet, the double spiral illustrates, like Yin-Yang does, the Principle as twofold

---

[1] In Aristotelian language, Yang is pure activity and Yin pure potentiality. "When the state of Yin was perfect, all was passive and tranquil; when the state of Yang was perfect, all was active and productive. The fecund activity came forth from Heaven; the tranquil passivity issued from Earth. The two states communicating together, a harmony ensued and things were produced. Someone regulated and controlled this, but no one has seen his form. Decay and growth; fullness and emptiness; darkness and light; the changes of the sun and the transformations of the moon: these are brought about from day to day; but no one sees the process of production. Life has its origin from which it springs, and death has its place from which it returns. Beginning and ending go on in mutual contrariety without any determinable commencement, and no one knows how either comes to an end. If we disallow all this, who originates and presides over all these phenomena? The action (*yang*) and reaction (*yin*) of Heaven and Earth are the unique motor of this movement" (*Zhuang-zi*, 21, 4/D).

[2] The two branches of the double spiral correspond also to the alternate phases *katabasis_anabasis* (descent_ascension); *genesis_phthora* (Aristotelian terms meaning generation and corruption); day_night (*Kalpa_Pralaya* of Brahmâ); action_reaction. The *yin_yang* alternation, pacified and solved in Dao, is the World Motor, and the World cannot be otherwise understood. Life and the Cosmos, Plutarch said, are composed of two opposite principles, and of two antithetic powers, one guiding to the right, the other bending backwards, the whole of nature being a mixture of these powers. The one who seeks perfection and the absolute in this world proves to be a malign ignorant, because, in reality, the world cannot exist but with the manifestation of oppositions, of the alternations, of relativity and the ephemeral: after night, day follows, and again the night; if you want to understand joy, you must first experience sadness and vice-versa. "When one is about to take an inspiration, he is sure to make a (previous) expiration; when he is going to weaken another, he will first strengthen him; when he is going to overthrow another, he will first have raised him up; when he is going to despoil another, he will first have made gifts to him: this is the subtle vision of the world" (*Dao De Jing*, XXXVI).

(*ayam Âtmâ Brahman, Âtmâ* is *Brahma,* "the Principle is the Principle"), the two spirals symbolizing the celestial (*yang*) and terrestrial (*yin*) forces which govern the whole manifestation.[1] On the other hand, the double spiral describes, by a simultaneous illustration, the cosmogonic process (when the spiral is expanding from the center to the periphery) and the initiatory process (when the spiral is compressing from the periphery to the center).[2] Also, the continuous voyage from one center to the other depicts a complete cycle of manifestation – the development from the pole and the absorption into the pole (*Pralaya*), which is equivalent to the two opposite rotations of the *swastika*.

The double spiral journey corresponds to Nicolaus Cusanus' pair "explication-complication." The explicative branch of the double spiral produces the universal manifestation (the centrifugal aspect), and the complicative branch implies an initiatory voyage (the centripetal aspect). With respect to this journey we would like to mention an anecdote: "Lie Zi liked to travel. Hu Zi asked him: 'What is it you like so much about travel?' 'The joy of travel is that the things which amuse you never remain the same. Other men travel to contemplate the sights, I travel to contemplate the way things change. There is travel and travel, and I have still to meet someone who can tell the difference!' 'Is not your travel really the same as other men's? Would you insist there is a difference? Anything at all that we see, we always see change. You are amused that other things never remain the same, but do not know that you

---

[1] The two centers of the double spiral correspond to the white and black points of Yin-Yang.

[2] It could be compared to Saint Dionysius the Areopagite's saying, quoted in our previous chapter: "Now in the former treatises the course of the argument, as it came down from the highest to the lowest categories, embraced an ever-widening number of conceptions which increased at each stage of the descent, but in the present treatise it mounts upwards from below towards the category of transcendence, and in proportion to its ascent it contracts its terminology, and when the whole ascent is passed it will be totally dumb [mute], being at last wholly united with Him Whom words cannot describe"; we are facing the image of a double cone.

yourself never remain the same. You busy yourself with outward travel and do not know how to busy yourself with inward contemplation. By outward travel we seek what we lack in things outside us, while by inward contemplation we find sufficiency in ourselves. The latter is the perfect, the former an imperfect kind of traveling.' From this moment Lie Zi never went out any more, thinking that he did not understand travel. Hu Zi told him: 'How perfect is travel! In perfect travel we do not know where we are going, in perfect contemplation we do not know what we are looking at.¹ To travel over all things without exception, contemplate all things without exception, this is what I call travel and contemplation. That is why I say: How perfect is travel!"² (*Lie-zi, Confucius*, 7).

The double spiral is the seal of changes, changes that take place and permit the "current of forms," or the universal manifestation, to exist; but to find total pleasure and delight in these changes means to remain outside, on the circumference, while the true journey is about the veritable Way, Dao, the inner way of the Self, *sadhana* of the Hindu tradition.³ Thus the unchangeable and immutable motor of changes is reached.⁴

---

¹ "The primitive men acted in conformity to Dao, without knowing the Way. (…) From the moment they became conscious that the Way exists and tried to follow it, each in his style, they would lose it, since they used their individuality to follow the Way" (Matgioi's commentary on the *Dao De Jing*); therefore, the seer has to be like a child.

² In Masonry, the initiatory journey is hidden under the ritual expression: *to travel in foreign countries*, the quality of "pilgrim" being associated with that of "foreigner"; in the Islamic esotericism, the Sufi masters are "pilgrims" and "foreigners" (al-Jîlî wrote about "the foreigners" that are the only ones who have access to Knowledge).

³ "The inner way" is not easily available for everyone and the ignorance obstructs us from seeing it: "The brightness of the Dao seems like darkness" (*Dao De Jing*, XLI).

⁴ A well-known example with regard to this subject is Somerset Maugham's book, *The Razor's Edge*, in which the author trumpets his preference for the string of changes. "Maya is only a speculation devised by those ardent thinkers to explain how the Infinite could produce the Finite. Shankara, the wisest of all, decided that it was an insoluble mystery. You see, the difficulty is to explain why Brahma, which is Being, Bliss and Intelligence, which is unalterable, which ever is and forever maintains itself in rest, which lacks

nothing and needs nothing and so knows neither change nor strife, which is perfect, should create the world. Well, if you ask that question the answer you're generally given is that the Absolute created the world in sport without reference to any purpose. But when you think of flood and famine, of earthquake and hurricane and all the ills that flesh is heir to, your moral sense is outraged at the idea that so much that is shocking can have been created in play. (...) Nothing in the world is permanent, and we're foolish when we ask anything to last, but surely we're still more foolish not to take delight in it while we have it. (...) We can none of us step in to the same river twice, but the river flows on and the other river we step into is cool and refreshing too. (...) It was not for me to leave the world and retire to a cloister, but to live in the world and love the objects of the world, not indeed for themselves, but for the Infinite that is in them. If in those moments of ecstasy I had indeed been one with the Absolute, then, if what they said was true, nothing could touch me and when I had worked out the karma of my present life I should return no more. The thought filled me with dismay. I wanted to live again and again, I was willing to accept every sort of life, no matter what its pain and sorrow; I felt that only life after life could satisfy my eagerness, my vigor and my curiosity." As a reply, we may quote Julius Evola: to resist on the way of the supreme truth (*paramâtha*) "it is necessary a triple armor"; facing the Way, the profane one trembles and cries: "Better samsâra! (*varam samsâra evâvasthanam!*)" (*Bodhi-charyâvatâratîkâ*). "If, indeed, facing such a doctrine and facing such an exposition (like "That one, which was declared existent, for this very reason was declared non-existent, and so it is declared existent"), the thinking of the one aspiring illumination does not deviate and does not sink into the abyss, does not become confused and his mind is not captured, if he is not as if he would have his spinal column broken, if he does not feel the terror, if he is not seized by disarray – then he can be instructed about the perfect transcendent knowledge, prajnâpâramitâ" (*Prajnâpâramitâ*). For this reason the profane people yell: "Better samsâra!" The Tibetan lamas stated without equivocation: the individuals, who did not reach a high degree of (spiritual) knowledge, who live like animals, influenced by their impulses, are like the travelers wandering around the world, without a precise goal. Such a man notices a lake in the East, and rushes thirsty for water. Arriving close to the shore he smells smoke, which means a house or a tent is nearby. He forgets about the lake and starts north, where the smoke is. On his way, before finding the house, terrible phantoms make their appearance. Terrorized, the wanderer turns around and runs southward. After covering a safe distance, he rests. Other travelers, passing by, will tell him about a rich and happy land and the drifter enthusiastically will follow them towards the west. On the road, he will be many times tempted to change direction, before reaching the wonderful region. Thus, wandering all his life, he will never reach the goal. Death will take him, and the conflicting forces of his disorganized actions will spread towards the four cardinal points. On the contrary, the seers are like a conscious traveler who knows his target, well informed with regard

The Duality

Everything in the world is change, but the neophyte embarked on the spiritual way ennobles the change seeking transformation and the ancient commentaries of the *Yi Jing* said: "Dao of Heaven (Qian) is the change and the trans-formation; modification means a progressive transformation; the transformation is the perfect accomplishment of change; the change is the process producing all the ten thousand beings; (...) the transformation is the process of retrieving (re-absorbing) the beings; it is the good and the perfection" (the change refers to the first branch of the double spiral, the transformation to the second one).

The *Yi Jing* is a difficult scripture. Other traditional writings are also obscure for the profane mentality, but the *Yi Jing* is a synthesis, it is compact and "complicated," belonging to an Age when there was no need for too many words, when silence could be understood, while the *Dao De Jing*, for example, is more explicit, though still not easy to be comprehended. It is problematic to understand the *Yi Jing*, since it contains innumerable meanings, from the metaphysical to the divinatory one, and in the last centuries this latter was predominant, as expected, genuine and fake diviners using Fu Xi's scripture to read the destiny of the world and individuals.

It is impossible to try to decipher the whole *Yi Jing*. What can be done is to underline sections that enlighten the primordial Tradition, while many elements will remain in obscurity.[1] This unique book – it is said – is sufficient for learning everything, but often the text's mystery persists untouched and many tedious years are needed to study this scripture, not to say that at one moment the book itself becomes an obstacle on the path to spiritual realization, as

---

to the geographical situation and the roads to take. Strongly concentrated upon his goal, indifferent to the various mirages and temptations found along the road, this man controls the forces generated by his mental concentration, as well as his corporeal actions.

[1] Matgioi said: "The divinatory tradition of the *Yi Jing* became more and more obscure; and we can say that today it is completely lost. And we cannot be so naïve to try to rebuild it: the texts of the Book are almost unintelligible without the oral tradition."

Kitano Gempo suggested. "Kitano Gempo, a Zen master, was twenty years old when he traveled together with a merchant who used to smoke. When they took a break, under a tree, the merchant offered to Kitano some tobacco. 'What a pleasure to smoke!' he remarked. At the end of the journey, Kitano received from the merchant a gift: a pipe and tobacco. Kitano started to think: 'the pleasant things could distract me from my meditation! I have to renounce them before it is too late.' And he gave up smoking. When he was 23 years old, Kitano began to study the Yi Jing, the most profound doctrine of the universe. One day, worried about a letter he did not receive from his master, Kitano used the Yi Jing, which contained also the art of divination. He discovered that the letter has been lost, a fact confirmed later. 'If I can do such things with the help of the Yi Jing, I am in danger of neglecting my meditation,' Kitano thought. And he gave up this extraordinary science."[1]

The *Yi Jing* starts, naturally, with the hexagram Qian,[2] built of *gua* Qian up and the same *gua* down, that is of six continuous horizontal lines, one above the other, symbolizing the Principle,

---

[1] "The study of the scriptures – Shankarâchârya explained in his *Vivekaçûdâmani* – is useless so long as the highest Truth is unknown, and it is equally useless when the highest Truth has already been known. The scriptures consisting of many words are a dense forest which merely causes the mind to ramble. Hence men of wisdom should earnestly set about knowing the true nature of the Self. For one who has been bitten by the serpent of ignorance, the only remedy is the knowledge of Brahma. Of what avail are the Vedas and (other) scriptures, mantras and medicines to such a one? A disease does not leave off if one simply utters the name of the medicine, without taking it; similarly, without direct realization one cannot be liberated by the mere utterance of the word Brahma. (...) As a treasure hidden underground requires (for its extraction) competent instruction, excavation, the removal of stones and other such things lying above it and (finally) grasping, but never comes out by being (merely) called out by name, so the transparent Truth of the Self, which is hidden by Mâyâ and its effects, is to be attained through the instructions of a knower of Brahma, followed by reflection, meditation and so forth, but not through perverted arguments" (59-65).

[2] The initial sense of the word *qian* is "high," an attribute of the Principle. The ideogram for *qian* suggests the sun rising and the vapours or the fog ascending – therefore the idea of altitude (see Wieger, *Caractères chinois*, p. 273).

Heaven, divine Activity, the celestial Way (Dao), in conformity with the traditional commentary of Zheng Zi, who stated: "When we talk about Heaven, in an absolute sense we understand Dao, the celestial Way. (...) The Activity expressed by the word *qian* is the origins and the beginning of all ten thousand beings; therefore this *gua* represents Heaven, the positive, the father, the emperor. (...) Heaven is the ancestor of all ten thousand beings; the emperor is the stem to which all the provinces are connected. The Activity Way is prior to the multitude of beings and the thousands of varieties develop freely. The Dao of the emperor signifies to supervise, from the height of his exceptional rank, the plan of the Providence, while everything contained inside the four cardinal points follow its government and obey him; if the emperor realizes and operates the celestial Way (Dao), all the provinces enjoy the peace."

"The Dao in its regular course does nothing (*wu-wei*), and so there is nothing which it does not do (*Dao De Jing*, XXXVII), and the *Yi Jing* neatly stated that Dao is "the Activity Way," that Qian is "the activity without rest," therefore we have to understand that the Principle has as "effect" the activity, and Qian, even though used as an appellation for Heaven, or for the Principle, is the expression that defines the effect.[1] The immutable motor, without action, is the very activity, the warranty of the universal Existence; the Principle is the residence of the supreme activity; what appears as laziness and apathy for the profane view, is in fact maximum diligence and plenary activity, or better said, a metaphysical activity and a divine diligence, purely intellectual, thoroughly spiritual, and it would be a huge error to believe that *wu-wei*, non-action, is the Principle's passivity, when this passivity belongs to the feminine pole, the Mother.[2]

---

[1] "'Non-action' is not inertia, but on the contrary implies the fullness of activity, but an activity that is transcendent and altogether interior, non-manifested, in union with the Principle, and thus beyond all the distinctions and appearances that common people mistakenly take for reality itself, whereas they are only more or less distant reflections of it" (Guénon, *Taoïsme*, p. 114).

[2] Mircea Eliade made a similar error, though somehow subtler, when he wrote about *deus otiosus*, confusing non-action with idleness. "Non-action (makes its

Metaphysic activity belongs to non-manifestation, and the action is just a weak reflection of that in our world, the same way as modification is a reflection of transformation. "Dao, the Activity Way, means modification and transformation," the *Yi Jing* states, but the *Yi Jing* itself signifies "the Book of Changes" and we could doubt that such a book is of real help in our endeavour to understand the Principle, since change is a characteristic of Existence and the immutability of the Principle, but this Book represents the integration of all modifications and transformations, it is the very Activity. Now we understand better why Matgioi said: "Dao is the series, the sum and the result of all the modification in the universe," that is, the *Yi Jing* is the tale of Dao as the Principle of all transformations and modifications, as modification and then as transformation, as a reintegratory and initiatory way, which means that the *Yi Jing* is the tale of Dao as double spiral.[1] It is important to highlight the

---

exemplifier) the lord of all fame; non-action (serves him as) the treasury of all plans; non-action (fits him for) the burden of all offices; non-action (makes him) the lord of all wisdom. The range of his action is inexhaustible, but there is nowhere any trace of his presence. He fulfils all that he has received from Heaven, but he does not see that he was the recipient of anything. A pure void is what characterizes him" (*Zhuang-zi*, 7, 6). Huge difference between non-action and idleness! Vasile Lovinescu wrote: "Mircea Eliade was a promising thinker, which gave us the right to ask from him to be more than just a scholar. His modern mythological investigation did not find for the *principial* immutability but the ridiculous and insulting term *deus otiosus*, the idle god. (...) The silent point in the center of the musical spheres, *Deus otiosus!* The Daoist wu-wei, non-action, the supreme term of the Way, *Deus otiosus!* What was left to sully in this world?"

[1] With respect to the traditional interpretation, "change" in the *Yi Jing* has more than one meaning: the main sense, *bu-yi*, "the unchangeable change," corresponding to the supreme Void; the cosmologic sense, *jian-yi*, "the change," corresponding to the Being; the worldly sense, *bian-yi*, "the changeable change," corresponding to the multiplicity and the contingencies of the world. Saint John Damascene said: "All the existent things are created or uncreated; if they are created, they are without doubt also changeable, either by destroying themselves, or by changing in a free mode. If they are uncreated, they are without doubt also unchangeable; ... even the angels change, suffer modifications. (...) But the Creator has to be uncreated. Therefore, the Creator being uncreated, without doubt He is also unchangeable." And Muhhyiddin Ibn 'Arabî stated: "Allâh is the only one that

correspondence between one of the most ancient and profound sacred symbols and the most ancient scripture, since if we succeed in accepting that the double spiral is an insignia of the *Yi Jing*, we could perceive more sharply how the Book of Changes instructs about the Principle, concealing a metaphysical meaning, not only a divinatory one, we could grasp better how the *tuan*, the determinative formula, placed by Wen Wang at the beginning of the Book, translates into words (although, only four words) the double spiral, constituting the synthesis of the *Yi Jing*, the manifested kernel of Fu Xi's trigrams.

The double spiral is the quintessence of wisdom, it concentrates everything known from the metaphysical viewpoint and it is no wonder why the *Yi Jing* is in conformity with such a symbol, being a way to express discursively what is inexpressible. In short, the double spiral reveals the following: the Principle, Way and Activity, through a determinative transformation produces the manifestation – a chain of changes and modifications, the liberation from these bonds being realized through a transformation that leads to the Principle; that is why the *Yi Jing* is the Book of Changes!

The four words that compose Wen Wang's determinative formula and enhance the symbolism of the double spiral are: *yuan, heng, li, cheng*, at the head of the *Yi Jing*, where, after the six continuous lines, is written: "Qian; initial cause, freedom, good, perfection." Zhu Xi, whose famous commentary on the *Yi Jing* is known as "the primitive sense," illustrated the determinative formula by an apparent poetical image, but which contains one of the most suggestive and penetrating symbols of the primordial Tradition. Zhu Xi narrated: "The leaves of the tree, starting to grow, this is the activity of the initial cause; the flowers blooming, this is the freedom of expansion; the fruits

---

has the power to produce the essences and to modify the states. (…) The beings are doomed to disappear, to appear, to change, to be destroyed and to pass from a situation to another. They exist due to 'other one than themselves' and the existence is for them a loan, a transfer. (…) Without doubt, everything is illusory but Allâh. Everything is changeable and perishable but His Face."

budding, this is the good; the fruits developing and ripening, this is the purity or the perfection."

Everything we have mentioned is a cause for amazement: Fu Xi's trigrams, an overwhelming example of synthesis, silence and "complication," amaze us with their simplicity capable of hiding a maximum richness of meanings; Wen Wan's formula amazes us with its profound significance completely concentrated in four words; eventually, Zhu Xi's commentary is equally amazing. The symbolic image Zhu Xi depicted is perfect: the tree is a well-known symbol of *Axis Mundi*, the Axis being the Activity Way of the Principle and, in the end, representing the very Principle, Dao, because the tree, regardless of whether it has leaves or not, it has flowers or not, or it has fruit or not, is always the same in itself, it is immutable, and for this reason is a suitable emblem of the Principle, all the transformations and modifications that occur (the birth of leaves, etc.) being without effect on the tree itself, in the same way as the birth of the *principial* duality, of the manifestation and of the multiple changes could not affect the Principle.

On the other hand, the leaves, the flowers and the fruit are not able to exist without the tree, just as the manifestation has no reality without the Principle. A leaf that thinks about itself as independent and self-sufficient – this is something ridiculous, and here we must recall the definition of Vacuity (*Shûnyatâ*) as the ultimate nature of the beings that cannot have a self-sufficient existence. The tree itself is a central column of void, emptied of all the perishable accessories ("Dao is a void, used but never filled. An abyss it is, from which all things come").[1]

---

[1] If we extend the symbolic representation, we could consider the tree as something ephemeral, as Lama Tenzin Gyatso does, who says that for a fruit tree to be self-sufficient it has to have everlasting leaves and fruit. In Zhu Xi's symbolization, the very perishability of the leaves and fruit allows to illustrate the determinative formula, this image being also found in Shankarâchârya's *Vivekaçûdâmani*: "If a leaf falls in a small stream, or a river, or a place consecrated to Shiva, or in a crossing of roads, of what good or evil effects is that to the tree? (…) It does not affect the Âtmâ, the Reality, the Embodiment of Bliss – which is one's true nature. That survives, like the tree" (559-560).

The Duality

The great spiritual master Shankarâchârya offers a similar image: the ocean with its foaming waves. The waves, the foam and the drops of water represent the innumerable changes and modifications, perishable and without their own reality, while the ocean is the Principle (as Universal Possibility). Although the waves seem to have their own reality and their own form, in fact they are ephemeral creations, nor for a moment different from the ocean itself from which they draw their reality, not as separate parts, since the ocean is one, without parts and components.

There is no tradition where the tree as the Axis of the World – the locus of the Principle's invisible activity – is not present. In some traditions, this tree is described as reversed, with the roots implanted in Heaven, this picture being even more suggestive, more explicit, because the tree is Qian, the celestial Activity, it is Dao, the celestial Way. The tree produces twigs, leaves and flowers, which are the degrees of the manifestation, and, often, the flower itself is a symbol of the universal Existence. The first part of Zhu Xi's image coincides with the first branch of the double spiral; it is the evolvement and the explication of the Principle towards the world, it is the expansion from the Center to the periphery. The second one, the fruits budding and ripening, symbolizes the initiatory journey towards the Principle, commencing with the astonishing moment when "the fruit buds" in the heart cavity, when the seed of wisdom, *luz*, or the grain of the Eleusian Mysteries sprouts. The ripe fruit is wisdom itself, metaphysical knowledge, in various traditions, the golden apples, or the pomegranate,[1] symbolizing exactly this initiatory knowledge; Jason's Golden Fleece, the goal of his initiatory journey, was found in a tree, as its ripe fruit.

Yet the ripe fruit is more than that: it is the key for the union with the Principle, and we should say that as the apple designates both the fruit and the tree, so Zhu Xi's ripe fruit is a

---

[1] The word "pomegranate" comes from Latin *pomum* "fruit, apple." In classical Latin, the fruit was known as *malum granatum*, *malum* means "apple" and *granatum* derives from *granum* "grain."

second image of the tree, corresponding to the center of the
double spiral's second branch, on which the voyager advances
in an "enveloping" and "complicative" sense.

Zhu Xi's symbolic image unveils one more aspect: the
periodicity of manifestation. The leaves come out, grow and
then fade away and fall, after which a new cycle follows;
similarly, the deer's horns fall each year, and grow again richer
and with more branches, the deer symbolizing the Principle and
the horns the skeleton of the manifestation. The periodicity of
the universal manifestation, with its macro- and microcosmic
cycles, is imitated by the periodicity of the seasons, to which the
vegetal and animal life conforms, in the *Yi Jing*, the most
significant hexagrams referring to the four gates of the seasons,
the solstices and the equinoxes. The first *gua*, Qian, the active
and masculine Perfection, guards the summer solstice; the
second *gua*, Kun, the passive and feminine Perfection, watches
the winter solstice, the two solstices being in a natural way the
tokens of the superior and inferior poles, the regents of the
manifestation; in the Hindu tradition, the winter solstice
represents "the gate of gods" (*dêva-yâna*), and the summer
solstice "the gate of the ancestors" (*pitri-yâna*).[1]

[1] "The Year [the cosmic cycle] indeed is Prajâpati, and there are two paths
thereof, the Southern and the Northern. Now those who here believe in
sacrifices and pious gifts as work done (*ishtâpurta*), gain the moon only as their
(future) world, and return again (into manifestation). Therefore the Rishis who
desire offspring go to the South, and that path of the Fathers is the Substance
(Rayi). But those who have sought the Self by penance, abstinence, faith, and
knowledge, gain by the Northern path Aditya, the sun. This is the home of the
Essence (Prâna), the immortal, free from danger, the highest. From thence
they do not return, for it is the Liberation" (*Prashna Up.*, I, 9). Zhuang Zi
mentioned the two ways (gates): "What is it that we call the Dao? There is the
Dao, or Way of Heaven; and there is the Dao, or Way of Man. The noble
concentration in wu-wei, this is the Way of Heaven; doing and being
embarrassed thereby is the Way of Man. It is the Way of Heaven that plays
the part of the Lord; it is the Way of Man that plays the part of the Servant.
The Way of Heaven and the Way of Man are far apart. They should be clearly
distinguished from each other" (*Zhuang-zi*, 11, 7/F).

It seems strange that passive Perfection corresponds to "the gate of gods" and active Perfection to "the gate of the ancestors," but in the Far-Eastern tradition the superior point was the South and not the North, the *Yi Jing* using a "terrestrial" symbolism. "To close the gate – said a *Yi Jing* commentary – is named Kun; to open the gate is named Qian," where Qian and Kun represent the *potestas clavis* (*potestas ligandi et solvendi*).

Gua Tai represents the spring equinox and *gua* Pi the fall equinox – two consecutive hexagrams, no. 11 and 12.

gua Tai   *gua* Pi

Tai is built of Kun up and Qian down, that is, of three discontinuous lines (the passive Perfection) above three continuous lines (the active Perfection), while Pi is built of Qian up and Kun down, the spring equinox's *gua* suggesting the ascending spiral and the fall equinox's *gua* the descending spiral.

The two *guas* underline, among other things, the error of the modern world in believing all those theories about progress and evolution, when, in fact, because the law of the cycles governs the manifestation, after an ascendant phase, when the prosperity is obtained (*gua* no. 11), there must follow a declining phase (*gua* no. 12); more obvious is the "opposition" in the case of the solstitial *guas*, Qian and Kun, no. 1 and 2, these two symbolizing the primordial dyad, Qian being, at the same time, the legitimate exponent of the supreme Principle.

From a special viewpoint, Qian could be related to time and Kun to space, but, in fact, there is a combined influence of time and space, similar to that of Yang and Yin.

René Guénon attributed time to Cain and space to Abel: Cain is "the principle of compression, represented by time";

Abel is "the principle of expansion, represented by space."[1] In this case, Cain illustrates the dissolution of universal manifestation, which follows the way of the double spiral's compressive branch (the absorption back into non-manifestation); Abel illustrates the production of universal manifestation (the double spiral's expansive branch). At the same time, Guénon noted,[2] Abel's oblation means the smoke rising vertically (similar to dragon's flight in Qian), even if Abel as "a keeper of sheep" covered the space horizontally (the mare's movement); Cain's oblation was spread horizontally over the earth (similar to mare's movement in Kun), even if Cain as "a tiller of the ground" built vertically in time and grew plants vertically (the dragon's flight). The law of compensation, the law of action and reaction, of Yin-Yang, must be present when we refer to the universal manifestation.[3]

The two tendencies, compressive and expansive, represented by Cain and Abel, have to balance each other's influence, like Yang and Yin, otherwise the end of the world will occur soon. The obvious concerted effect of time and space is movement,[4] an Existence in repose being impossible; movement's cessation happens only when the sun and moon come together, or when the ten suns unite, or when time and space are absorbed in their principle.

---

[1] René Guénon, *Le règne de la quantité et les signes des temps*, Gallimard, 1970, p. 200.

[2] *Le Règne*, p. 203.

[3] Regarding Abel's oblation, we may quote the *Maitrâyanîya Upanishad*: "Now this is the channel to increase the food, which makes what is offered in the fire ascend to the sun. The sap which flows from thence rains down as with the sound of a hymn. By it there are vital breaths, from them there is offspring. And here they quote: 'The offering which is offered in the fire, goes to the sun; the sun rains it down by his rays; thus food comes, and from food the birth of living beings.' And thus he said: 'The oblation which is properly thrown on the fire goes toward the sun; from the sun comes rain, from rain food, from food living beings'" (VI, 33). The Hindu tradition describes the ladder that unites Heaven and Earth; it is the Dao of the Dragon. The rain symbolizes the spiritual influences.

[4] This movement can be considered change, modification or transformation.

The Duality

Fabre d'Olivet considered that Seth, Cain and Abel's younger brother, symbolized the movement; Seth is, indeed, Noah's ancestor and so, the ancestor of the produced beings after the flood. In the Hindu tradition, there is Trimûrti similar to the three brothers: Brahmâ produces the ten thousand beings, Vishnu represents space (measured by his three steps[1]), and Shiva is time. Guénon alluded to this correspondence (*Introduction*, p. 225), which deserves to be detailed. We will see that the traditional symbolism does not mean systematization. Vishnu is the conserving principle and, similar to space, he fixes and condenses; Shiva is the transforming and destroying principle and, similar to time, dissolves and changes. Vishnu is the Lord of the Three Worlds, Shiva is the Lord of the Triple Time. Vishnu is a solar god, related to agriculture, Shiva is a lunar god, related to nomadic and pastoral life (he also is Pashupati, the Lord of animals). Shiva is Vinâdhara, the lord of music, and Nataraja, the king of dance, producing the world by rhythm. Vishnu is Kûrma, the immutable pivot in the middle of the milk-ocean, producing the world during his cosmic sleep; at the same time, Vishnu is Mahakâla, the Great Time, who manifests in a cyclic mode through the *avatâras*; and his shell produces the primordial sound. Also, Shiva is the Lord of the Three Worlds, his flame producing the visible light.

In the *Mahâbhârata*, Hiranyakashipu, the king of the demons, deprived Shiva of his kingdom of the Three Worlds for a million years, which suggests that at the end of times even time is devoured, and Vishnu, as Narasimha-avatâra, restored the Gold Age. Similarly, Abel's death is compensated by Seth's birth; Seth combines his brothers' attributes and appears as the regent of a new cycle. In a way, Brahmâ also represents the movement, combining space and time, and he is "life," as a specific type of movement applied to our world, producing and

---

[1] The ideogram for these symbolic three steps of the one-footed is (Wieger 265):

vivifying the beings, which makes him the Vivifier (El-Hay of the Islamic tradition). In the Islamic tradition, El-Hay is precisely Seth, who restores the order, and there is a tradition saying that Seth recovered the Holy Grail (lost by Adam during the fall) in the terrestrial Paradise.

The Islamic tradition says, "man was serpent once," and Fu Xi and Niu Wa are described as dragons. The serpent with his two symbolic aspects, beneficent (luminous) and maleficent (tenebrous), could be compared to Yin-Yang.[1] The serpent, Guénon affirmed, is connected to the idea of life, and in Arabic the serpent's name is *'el-hayyah* (*el-hayâh* means "life"; in Hebrew, *hayah* means life and animal); this vivifying aspect of the serpent is related to Brahmâ and Seth.

On the other hand, the Egyptian god Set, identical to the dragon Typhon, is the destructive principle, and so, we could envision a strange pair: Seth – life and beneficial, and Set – death and maleficent[2]; as Cain killed Abel, so Set killed Osiris, and as Seth is born to replace Abel,[3] so Horus is born from Osiris. In fact, both Seth and Set contained, initially, the two opposite aspects. The name of Seth means "stability, fundament," but also "ruin, disorder"; Set has the serpent as

---

[1] In the Christian tradition, the two serpents are Christ and Satan; also, Hermes' two serpents are well known and they correspond to *yang* and *yin*, symbolizing the celestial and terrestrial influences. The Chinese ideograms for these influences are perfect symbols (see as well Guénon, *La Grande Triade*, p. 34):

$$\perp \quad \top$$
$$\underline{\underline{\Box}} \quad \overline{\overline{\Box}}$$

[2] This pair is only apparently "syncretic." For Set as *yin*, fighting the Sun (*yang*), see Ananda K. Coomaraswamy, *Ātmayanjna: Self-Sacrifice* (Selected papers, *Metaphysics*, Princeton Univ. Press, 1977, pp. 145-147).

[3] "And Adam knew his wife again; and she gave birth to a son, and called his name Seth: For God, said she, hath appointed me another seed instead of Abel, whom Cain slew" (*Genesis* 4:26).

The Duality

symbol, but it does not have only a maleficent meaning, since *uraeus*, the royal serpent, was an imperial sign.[1] The tiger is another emblem for Set, which brings us to Nimrod, whose name refers to a tiger's (or leopard's) skin.[2] The Islamic tradition stressed the role played by Abraham to promote pure spirituality and fight the illegitimate Nimrodian claim to supremacy, which could allude to the relation between Abraham (Ibrahim) and Ishmael (Ismail), the latter representing *kshatriyas*, like Nimrod.[3] There is a tradition saying that Seth, the son of Adam, built the primordial Kaabah as a pyramid (tent), and this one was destroyed by the flood. Abraham (Ibrahim) rebuilt it as a cube (*ka'bah*). If Abraham appears comparable to Seth, Ishmael's subordinate role in this Masonic work[4] could enhance his similarity with Set, but the law of Yin-Yang imposes, in manifestation, interactive relations and not absolute situations.

Abraham and Ishmael change their attributes (like Fu Xi and Niu Wa), and Abraham becomes the one who measures with the square, while Ishmael is elevated to the rank of tradition's sacerdotal keeper. Tha'labî said that "the Most High inspired in each one the other's tongue." As Guénon underlined, Fu Xi and Niu Wa changed their attributes, but they were represented with dragon's tails interlaced in a hierogamic union[5]; in fact, Niu Wa accomplished the stabilization of the world and, for her, the cubic form is a good insignia. A change of attributes could be found in the Tarot's third and fourth cards, where the Empress has the star (heaven) and the Emperor the cube (earth) as

---

[1] Guénon, *Symboles*, p. 158.
[2] Guénon, *Symboles*, p. 157. Guénon compared Set to Nimrod (*ibid.*, p. 158).
[3] Ishmael is described as a hunter. Also "he will be a wild man" (*Genesis* 16:12), but the original text alludes also to the Egyptian Set.
[4] Ishmael is sent to find the fundamental stone, but Abraham receives the black stone himself as Noah's heritage. Michel Vâlsan considered Abraham the invisible Word and Ishmael the visible Word.
[5] As Guénon said, the hierogamy refers to couples of complementaries regarded as masculine-feminine, even though there is a similar situation for other pairs (time-space, compass-square) (René Guénon, *La Grande Triade*, Gallimard, 1980, p. 76).

emblems. Similarly, Abraham built a cubic temple and Ishmael was sheltered in the semicircular *hijr*, a celestial symbol.

In manifestation, the actions and reactions of Yang and Yin are endless. For this reason the *ba guas* were *yang* and *yin* too, even if the continuous line is regarded as *yang* and the discontinuous one as *yin*. Tradition says that Fu Xi considered *yang* the trigrams having a continuous trait toward the inside and *yin* those with a broken trait toward the inside (when the eight trigrams were arranged in a circle); consequently, Qian, Dui, Li, and Zhen are *yang*, and Xun, Kan, Gen, and Kun are *yin*. It is also said that Wen Wang changed the arrangement, considering *yin* the trigrams with an odd number of broken traits (Xun, Li, Kun, Dui) and *yang* the trigrams with an odd number of continuous traits (Qian, Kan, Gen, Zhen); this second arrangement was related to the magic square, but also to the *swastika*,[1] which shows the indefinite rotation of the couple Yin-Yang and its influences in the universal manifestation.

---

[1] Marcel Granet, *La pensée chinoise*, Albin Michel, 1968, pp. 155-156, 163.

THREE

THE WORLD

THE PRESENT WORK, as a continuation of the previous one (*A View of the Center*), aspires to show how the Center and the World are connected, how the World develops from the Center and how the Man can find his way back to the Center. In fact, there is a "triad" describing perfectly all this: Cosmos-Year-Man.

It is interesting that the English word "world," which comes from Old English *weorold*, means the "age of man," which is an allusion to the other two components of the "triad," Year and Man, while the word "world" itself should not be view as the very limited "world" we are living in but as universal manifestation (the metaphysical view) or in a more specific sense as the Cosmos. In Latin, the corresponding word is *mundus*, which translates the Greek *cosmos*, "order," a word indicating the production of the universal manifestation, but especially viewed as emerging from the Inferior Pole, from Prakriti; similarly, in the Romanian language, the word *lume*, meaning "world," derived from Latin *lumen*, light.

In the Far-Eastern tradition, the production of this "order," of this "light," of this "world" is expressed as the production of the *guas*.

From the oldest times, Zheng Zi said, the seer traced the *ba guas*: Dao of the Great Triad was now completed.

The eight *guas* are:

Qian[1] (heaven)	Kan (water)	Dui (marsh)	Xun (wind)

Li (fire)	Gen (mountain)	Zhen[2] (thunderbolt)	Kun[3] (earth)

---

[1] Qian symbolizes pure activity, without action (*wei wu-wei*). The Qian ideogram seems to depict the sun's invisible activity upon a plant and the seed of life sheltered in non-manifestation; but we have to consider also the dragon's journey and the interaction between Earth (where the possibilities of manifestation are dormant) and Heaven (the sun rising and leaving *Axis Mundi*); the ideogram also suggests the vapours' elevation caused by sun's invisible activity, illustrating Heaven's attraction.

[2] We notice in the Zhen ideogram the superior horizontal line (Heaven) and the vertical line (thunderbolt, spiritual influence) in the middle of rain; the semicircle represents the cloud but also Heaven that covers. We also observe the one-foot and a bent man, who can see only the Principle's footprint.

[3] The Kun ideogram shows two hands and a middle vertical cord, which symbolize, from a viewpoint, Heaven's attraction (see Matgioi, *La Voie métaphysique*, chapter VI); the left side describes the production of the universal manifestation (symbolized by a plant), as a result of the celestial activity upon Earth (we have to consider, as usually, the interaction Heaven-Earth); the middle vertical line is sometimes considered the thunderbolt.

If we meditate upon these simple eight trigrams (*ba guas*), we understand how perfect and total they are. The elements appointed to the eight trigrams permit us to express symbolically, for our human comprehension, everything. The eight *guas* correspond to "the rose of the winds" and, therefore, govern the whole manifestation, in which case the universal Existence could have four pairs of contraries as a spinal column, made of the eight trigrams and underlining the duality: Qian-Kun, Kan-Li, Dui-Gen, Xun-Zhen, couples that take into consideration the reverse analogy of the *guas'* traits. These four pairs are hexagrams and in a similar mode others can be formed, up to sixty-four of them. The sixty-four hexagrams could be placed in a circle, a celestial figure representing "the circle of the rotary changes," or in a square, a terrestrial figure designating terrestrial modifications, an analogy of celestial modifications. The square with the hexagrams is an equivalent to the chess board, with its white and black tiles, the generation of the hexagrams reproducing the chess board geography: if we place the eight *guas* along the vertical and horizontal sides of the square, starting with Qian and ending with Kun, the first tile of the chess board will be the combination Qian-Qian, that is, the hexagram Qian, and the last tile will be the combination Kun-Kun, that is, the hexagram Kun; between them the other sixty-two perfect *guas* name the other tiles.

Each tile of the chess board, that is, each hexagram, white or black, will signify a state of universal manifestation, or, in particular, a modification of the World. "The words Qian and Kun designate, in a very precise mode, the mysterious essence of the *Yi Jing*, and Kun determines the order of the situations, and the change (*yi*) that occurs between these two. Qian and Kun destroyed; there would not be any change [the illusory duality having been destroyed]. (...) Heaven and Earth determine the situations, the mountain and the marsh mix freely their influences; the thunderbolt and the wind hit each other and make contact; the water and the fire don't annihilate each other; the eight simple *guas* combine together."

Various elements of the World are ascribed to each of the eight *guas*, stressing the fact that they are the fundament of the universal Existence. For example, the sun, the round shape, the precious stone, the prince, the gold, the stallion, etc. correspond to Qian. Some traditional texts were even more categorical, stating that the trigrams generated all the elements of a traditional civilization. For example: the hexagram Sui taught men horseback riding and the use of oxen for transportation; the hexagram Guai gave birth to the art of writing; the art of masonry and architecture were a result of the hexagram Da Zhuang.

The greatest mysteries, from an individual point of view, regard the production of the manifestation from non-manifestation, how the human form was generated, how the crafts and the arts were invented, all the traditional doctrines giving symbolic answers, concentrated in the following assertion: all that exist on earth have their archetypes and paradigms in heaven. Each métier, for example, has its archetype in heaven, the Principle being architect and peasant and fisherman. The *Yi Jing* offers hexagrams as explanation; these ones, of divine origin, contain the universal wisdom and they are the archetypes that have allowed the World to function. For the Jewish tradition, these archetypes were letters; for Pythagoras, they were the numbers; for the Hindu tradition, Purusha's parts. The "civilizatory hero," the "emperor" (like Fu Xi), or the "solar hero," activated the archetypes. The determinative formulas of *gua* no. 31, Xian, illustrate very well the correspondence hexagram-microcosm.

gua Xian

They say: "The first line, broken; to influence the big toe. The second line, broken; to influence the calves of the legs. The third line, continuous; to influence the thighs. The fourth line, continuous; to influence the heart. The fifth line, continuous; to influence the muscles of the spine. The superior line, broken; to influence the jaws, cheeks, and tongue." Or: "Qian is the head, Kun the stomach, Zhen the legs, Xun the thigh, Kan the ear, Li the eye, Gen the hand, and Dui the mouth." We note, among many other things, that Li, the fire (light), is related to the eye, and Qian and Kun correspond to the head and stomach; Coomaraswamy stressed that, in the Hindu tradition, the beheading of the dragon means to transform the head into the sun (that is, Qian as Principle), while the dragon's body becomes man's intestines.

But there is also a correspondence hexagram-macrocosm: "A commentator says: Here are the locations of the eight *guas*, following Fu Xi's teachings: Qian at South, Kun at North, Li at East, Kan at West, Dui at South-East, Zhen at North-East, Xun at South-West, Gen at North-West. Consequently, the combinations of the eight simple *guas* are generated, forming the 64 perfect *guas* or, what is called the study of 'what precedes heaven.'"

Combining the eight simple *guas*, in pairs, in order to encompass all the modifications of the Universe, the perfect *guas* of six traits were obtained, like the perfect *gua* Qian, for example, which was born by duplicating the simple *gua* Qian. Qian expresses Heaven (Tian), and also Qian is the activity *qian*; the activity without rest and pause is called Qian, Zheng Zi explained. When we consider Heaven (Tian) in an absolute mode, then we refer to Dao. The full trait, Zheng Zi added, is called *ji*, unity; and it is the number of "positivity." Fu Xi looked at the Heaven, then lowered his eyes to the Earth, observing its details: he saw that negativity and positivity[1] have

---

[1] We have to be very cautious when we use words like "negative" and "positive," since the real meaning of what is translated here has nothing to do with philosophical concepts or modern ones. The positive, from one of many points of view, is equivalent to plenitude, the mountain and the masculine; the negative is emptiness, the valley and the feminine. In the Oglala Sioux's tradition, the women that "lament" for a divine vision "go up on a hill in a

duality and unity as numbers. Fu Xi traced the simple line to symbolize positivity and a double (broken) line to symbolize negativity. He noticed that pure activity is the inner nature of positivity and its most grandiose expression is Heaven; therefore, the *gua* composed of three simple traits was called Qian and it was accredited to Heaven. And Zheng Zi concluded: "The initial cause, liberty, good, and perfection are what are called the four virtues. The first, expressed by the word *yuan*, is the beginning of all ten thousand beings[1]; the second, expressed by the character *heng*, means the development of all ten thousand beings; the third, expressed by the character *li*, is the faculty to satisfy the needs of each being, in conformity with its nature; the fourth, expressed by the word *cheng*, means the normal and perfect fulfillment of all."

Only the *guas* Qian and Kun have these four virtues; in all the other hexagrams they change, in accord with the subject. Matgioi called these "virtues" integrant qualities and we have to take into account for the future that Wen Wang's "virtues" are in fact essential and determinative "tendencies" and "attributes." The four "virtues" or "tendencies" render Dao explicit, with regard to the universal manifestation, and they are related to Lao Zi's De. Guénon wrote: "De, which we prefer to translate as Rectitude rather than Virtue (as it is sometimes translated), because we don't want to give it a moral interpretation, which is in total disaccord with Daoism; De, we said, is what we could call a 'specification' of Dao with respect to a particularized being, as, for example, the human being: it is the direction this being has to follow in order to have its existence (in this state in which the being was born) in concert with Dao, or, in other words, its existence to be in conformity

---

valley, for they are women and need protection." The men who "lament," they "go up to the high mountain" (Black Elk, *The Sacred Pipe*, Univ. of Oklahoma Press, 1989, pp. 46, 56).

[1] In the Hindu tradition, the initial cause is *kârana-sharîra*, the *principial* or causal form, non-manifested, Ishwara's residence. "That omniscient, omnipotent cause from which proceed the origin, subsistence, and dissolution of this world, that cause, we say, is Brahma" (*Vedânta-Sûtras*, I Adhyâya, I Pâda, 2, Shankarâchârya's commentaries).

with the Principle."[1] "All things are produced by Dao, and nourished by De. They receive their forms according to the nature of each, and are completed according to the circumstances of their condition. Therefore all ten thousand beings without exception honour Dao, and exalt De. (…) Thus it is that Dao produces (all things), nourishes them, brings them to their full growth, nurses them, completes them, matures them, maintains them, and overspreads them. It produces them and makes no claim to the possession of them; it carries them through their processes and does not vaunt its ability in doing so; it brings them to maturity and exercises no control over them; this is called its mysterious 'virtue,' De." (*Dao De Jing*, LI).

We may note that, for Matgioi, this apothegm above is "the great formula of Daoism. It is the direct explanation of Wen Wang's tetragram, the key of the *Yi Jing*. We can see again how Daoism came to light directly from the primordial Tradition. (…) Dao produces: it is the principle of activity; it is the Non-Being willing to be Being; it is One, the positive determination of Zero. (…) The Two, passive and feminine principle, came out of De, the Rectitude." The Virtue, or rather the Rectitude, De, is the reflected image of the Principle, Dao, carrying various aspects into the World, all in compliance with Dao. "If Dao is cultivated in the individual, then his virtue will become genuine. If it is cultivated in your family, then virtue in your family will be great. If it is cultivated in your community, then virtue will go a long way. If it is cultivated in your empire, then virtue will be splendid. If it is cultivated in the World, then virtue will be with everyone" (*Dao De Jing*, LIV). "He who is filled with (Rectitude) Virtue is like a newborn child. Wasps and serpents will not sting him; Wild beasts will not pounce upon him; He will not be attacked by birds of prey" (*Dao De Jing*, LV); the genuine Rectitude, De, as rectitude of Dao, means with respect to the World a total compliance with the Law (the Hindu Dharma) or Rule,[2] it means the childhood of humanity, that is,

---

[1] *Taoïsme*, p. 113.
[2] We envisage here the Rule as the Latin *norma*, meaning "principle, rule, paradigm." It seems that *norma* derived from Greek *gnomon*, related to the

the Golden Age, when everything was done with rectitude ("cor*rectly*").

The four "virtues" represent, of course, the *arcanes* of Wen Wang's formula, in the proper sense of the Arabic word *el arkân*, as the determinative attributes of the Principle, but we also have to stress the correspondence between the celestial and terrestrial virtues, in full concordance with the *Tabula Smaragdina*, and thus, we could picture a double spiral from a celestial viewpoint and a double spiral from a terrestrial point of view, in the first case the dragon being noticeable, and in the second case the mare replacing the dragon.

"How great is the initial cause of activity, Qian! It is the origin of all; it is the whole Heaven." Hence, the first "virtue" is the greatness and refers, as Zhu Xi explained, to the Great Principle, the initial cause, *yuan*,[1] the greatness being the typical characteristic of the Principle, from which the De of Heaven results. Lao Zi said: "Call it Dao. For lack of a better word, I call it great. Being great, it flows. It flows far away. Having gone far, it returns. Therefore, Dao is great" (*Dao De Jing*, XXV); and: "The great Dao flows everywhere, both to the right and to the left. The ten thousand things depend upon it; it holds nothing back. It fulfills its purpose silently and makes no claim. It nourishes the ten thousand things, and yet it is not their lord. It has no aim; it is very small. The ten thousand things return to it, yet it is not their lord. It is very great. It does not show greatness, and is therefore really great" (*Dao De Jing*, XXXIV).

---

name of the instrument used to measure the field; this instrument is directly related to Fu Xi's square.

[1] Here it is the ideogram for *yuan*.

We notice the legs and we could assume that one leg is bent to show the effort made or just it was drawn like this to gain some space. But in this ideogram the two superior horizontal traits indicate the "head," origin and principle of all ten thousand beings, so we prefer to consider the bent leg suggesting the "one-footed."

We note in Lao Zi's dictum the double spiral "extension – going away – returning," enclosed in the *principial* greatness, in perfect compliance with the *Yi Jing* and with Wen Wang's formula; we note also the appellative "the great," identical with the greatness found in the *Yi Jing*, but also with Nicolaus Cusanus' maximum (confoundable with the apparent minimum in the world). Greatness is above change, and, using Mathematical language, we can say that the maximum of a function is marked by making zero its derivative, which means lack of variation, that is, fixity and constancy. In the Hindu tradition, *Âtmâ* is greater than Heaven, greater than Atmosphere, and greater than Earth; it is the Greatest. In the Christian tradition, the Kingdom of Heaven is a tree (similar to Zhu Xi's tree) greater than any plant; in Islam, Allâh is the greatest (*akbar*). It is what the Far-Eastern tradition calls Tai Ji, "The Great Extreme," the ideogram *da* meaning "great, big." [1]

"The clouds travel, the rain increases its effects; the beings grow in the current of forms:" this is the meaning of the second

---

[1] The ideogram represents a man with his arms extended:

大 大
大

Greatness, on the other hand, is symbolized in various traditions using a crown or horns (related words) as emblems. They suggest both power and height; for this reason Fu Xi, Moses and others are described with horns. *Gua Gou* (no. 44) defines the superior continuous line as *gou qi jiao*, "to reach the high horns" (the ideogram *jiao* pictures the horns of an animal), and Zheng Zi said: "what is extremely hard, energetic and very high are the horns." Ovid transmitted the tale about the horns that grew on Cipus' head as a sign of royalty. In the Islamic tradition, the expression *Dhû-l-Qarnayn* is related to the imperial function. As a curiosity, we mention here Tomaso Campanella who considered himself as having horns, like Moses, and an "elected one." However, the emperor with the crown on his head was always called "the greatest"; the Arabs called Alexander *El-Iskandar dhûl-qarnein* and he was also "the Great."

virtue, *heng* – liberty in activity (*qian*). The clouds represent the reservoir of the celestial waters, that is, an image of the Universal Possibility, even of Shakti from the Hindu tradition, and the rain symbolizes the influences of the Heavenly Activity; "the influence of Heaven,[1] acting freely, produces all the ten thousand beings," Zhuang Zi said. Liberty, *heng*, characterizes mainly the production of manifestation with regard to the fact that the Principle's Activity is without conditions, preferences, sympathies and antipathies, that this Activity flows freely, and we can understand this when we think of how the sun shines, supplying light and heat freely, without preferences, allowing all the ten thousand beings to evolve, in conformity with their nature, in the "current of forms," that is, in the manifestation.[2]

"The end and the beginning are illuminated by a great light; the six situations appear in time. Also following time, they ride the six dragons to cross the Heaven." Zhu Xi explained: "The beginning is greatness, *yuan*; the end means perfection. The seer uses the six positivities to travel the Way traced by Heaven, Dao; these are the genuine greatness, *yuan*, and intelligence, *heng*, of the seer."[3]

---

[1] The *shu* ideogram represents the celestial influences; the three vertical lines, Wieger said (p. 29), symbolize the sun, the moon, and the stars, that is, "the three lights"; we should compare them with the Hindu three *nadis* and with the Sephirotic Tree.

[2] This liberty, as a virtue of the Principle, could be illustrated with the Gospel's words: "The wind bloweth where it listeth, and thou hearest the sound thereof, but canst not tell whence it cometh, and whither it goeth: so is every one that is born of the Spirit" (*John* 3:8).

[3] It is possible to translate *yuan* both as "initial cause" and "greatness," and *heng* as "liberty" and "intelligence." We use the term *heng* and its meanings in accordance to Matgioi and Philastre. However, we should mention the ideograms *hiang* and *hou*, which stand for this *heng* (Wieger 193, 195),

The World

"The Way of activity is modification and transformation. Each thing, obeying completely its nature and its destiny, maintains absolute harmony; these are the good and the perfection." Far-Eastern tradition insists, any time the occasion shows up, that the beings should behave in conformity with their nature, that everything must follow the natural course; this very conformity with nature is the warranty of harmony, yet the problem is not so simple. Even though, as a whole, Heavenly Activity, seconded by divine Will, guarantees to cover the current of the modifications and changes in accord with the nature and destiny of each being, there are Ages when the lack of harmony becomes conspicuous, exactly because of a rebellious disobedience regarding the law of conformity with nature; a state of disarray and disorder are created, a "local" anarchy, which, it is true, belongs to the total harmony, the total equilibrium which are the "sum" of the "local" imbalances.[1]

One of the *guas* where the law of conformity with nature is noticeable bears the name Lü (no. 10) and is built of Qian up and Dui down.

gua Lü

and represent, the first an exchange of favours between superior and inferior (see our work *Money: The Evil Eye*), the second liberality and generosity of the superior.

[1] René Guénon defined the Hindu *dharma* inspired by the Far-Eastern tradition: *dharma* is "the conformity with the essential nature of the beings, realized by the hierarchical and in order constitution of their assemble"; *dharma* represents the "law of harmony," while *adharma* is "the «non-conformity» with the nature of the beings, the unbalance, the breaking of harmony, the destruction of hierarchy" (*Introduction*, p. 187).

"When the beings are reunited, immediately the rites are born; therefore, *gua* Xiao Xu is followed by *gua* Lü, since – Zheng Zi commented – by reuniting the beings together the hierarchies and distinctions result, of great and small, of superior and inferior, of beautiful and ugly, for this reason ritual rules are established and these rules have to be observed for a cohabitation in proper conduct and decorum."

gua Xiao Xu

Gua no. 9, Xiao Xu, is built of Xun (wind) up and Qian down, and follows *gua* Bi, the "association," signifying the "gathering," the "reunion," which means that the gathering of a crowd in a society[1] is followed by the reunion of the individualistic tendencies into an assembly that functions by fixing and stopping the activity (Qian, the inferior trigram) in this assembly with the help of obedience and humbleness (Xun, the superior trigram), an obedience with respect to the Principle, of course.[2]

Even though apparently weak and soft, humbleness is in fact so strong that it defeats even the supernal activity, fastening it as

---

[1] In the Hindu tradition, this "gathering" is the work of a cosmic principle, Manu, equivalent to Wang, the Daoist emperor (as a universal function).

[2] There are two other hexagrams dealing with the *principial* humbleness: *guas* Qian and Yu (no. 15 and 16). "When a man holds a high position and is nevertheless modest, he shines with the light of wisdom; if he is in a lowly position and is modest, he cannot be passed by." "Dao of Heaven and Dao of Earth, they are the reason to be for everything; it is nothing else but the absolute submission. Heaven and Earth move with submission; therefore sun and moon do not swerve from their courses, and the four seasons do not err." But even the next *gua*, Sui (no. 17), alludes to the *principial* humbleness: "If a man would rule he must first learn to serve"; the thunderbolt descends in the middle of the marsh and the marsh follows its movement: we note here the perfect description of the *avatàra* that humble descends in the world from his infinite height.

a Shekinah (the divine presence of Judaism) in the center: it is the way Daoism developed, advising us to use weakness to defeat the force of the adversary, but especially, it is the archetypal image of an unconditioned compliance before a superior, and as Qian becomes humble, so must all the members of the new society just instituted become; yet this would mean a fixation in a paradisiacal state, which contradicts the laws of cyclical evolvement of the manifestation, and for this reason Xiao Xu signifies "the small halt," because the humbleness of the beings that constitute human society cannot but for a moment, during the "coagulation" of the society, stop the activity; immediately after this small halt, the activity will start manifesting and will take back its superior position (in *gua* Lü), promulgating the rites and hierarchies.

"Heaven is up; the marsh is what is down[1]; we see the distinction between superior and inferior, due to the eminent and the humble, a natural consequence of the existence of beings (in a normal hierarchy), the origins and fundament of the ritual rules of proper conduct and decorum." *Gua* Lü shows conformity with nature: the emblem of the active principle up; the emblem of the passive principle down; and the ten thousand beings hierarchically differentiated in accord with their nature between the two poles. "The inferior passively obeying the superior, negativity suffering the activity of positivity, this is the precise rule of all things in the universe."

---

[1] Here, Heaven represents the superior Waters and the marsh the inferior Waters, a partition found explicitly in the *Bible*, but also in other traditions. In some traditions, supreme humbleness, as a step on the initiatory path, is illustrated by the neophyte's fixation in a marsh. Sometimes, the trigram Dui is considered a "lake," but we prefer "marsh," since the marsh suggests a mixture of water and earth. The marsh implies mud, and the mud is, in some traditions, the symbol of the end of the cycle when the inferior elements govern, where initiatory death is also illustrated by a moribund hero fixed in mud. "Save me, O God; for the waters are come in unto my soul. I sink in deep mire, where there is no standing: I am come into deep waters, where the floods overflow me" (*Psalms* 69: 1-2). The marsh and mud are tokens for *materia prima*, and in some traditions man is made of mud. It is no coincidence that the French *marais*, English mire, marsh and mud, Slavic *mrak*, "darkness," and also the Sanskrit *marú*, "desert," are all words starting with the letter M.

"In the old times, starting with the high rang dignitaries and descending in a hierarchic order, each one's situation corresponded in an exact way to his virtues (tendencies, rectitude); each one had his position for all his life and in compliance with his nature and conditions. (...) The peasants, craftsmen, and merchants worked in their own domain, and their liberty of action had limits, hence their tendencies and desires were fixed and determined; the hearts, in the universe, beat as one heart."[1]

The concord is underlined in *gua* Tong Ren (no. 13), built of Qian up and Li down.

The concord is the "identity" of the hearts, fire and heaven being alike, since fire has the tendency to rise toward heaven and become similar and in accord with it.[2] "The tendencies of the universe – Zheng Zi commented – are different in thousands of ways; the essence of existence is unique. (...) The divine man[3] searches the heart of each man, in the innumerable multitude, and he sees only one heart. (...) The essence of existence is something so subtle that the divine man exclaims: 'the expression «the identity of the heart» brings into memory the perfume of the most suave flowers.'"

"In the following ages, the aspirations of all, from common men to high officials, were diverged toward ambition and glory; the every day tendencies of the peasants, craftsmen and

---

[1] This is *concordia* and the principle of castes.
[2] For this reason, fire and smoke are so important in a Hindu sacrifice; also, this is the meaning of the sacred pipe in the Amerindian traditions.
[3] The Daoist initiation implies, for each step, the realization of a new man; for example: *dedao*, the adept, *zhenren*, the realized or veritable man (where the ideogram for *zhen* alludes to "ten eyes" = "the seer"), and *shenren*, the divine or spiritual man (*shenren* has the body, *xing*, and the spirit, *shen*, united in Dao; "he has the heart identic to Heaven and the body identic to Dao").

merchants were deviated toward richness and luxury; in the innumerable multitude, each one's heart fights a general rivalry; the universe sank into disarray. In these circumstances, trying to avoid the disorder and turmoil was impossible, mainly because the aspirations of the superior and inferior ones were not limited and determined anymore. The veritable man regards *gua* Lü as the symbolic image of social order."

"There is no greater sin than desire; no greater curse than discontent (for not having enough); no greater misfortune than wanting something for oneself. Therefore, he who knows that enough is enough will always have enough" (*Dao De Jing*, XLVI). And the commentaries of the *Yi Jing* continue: "If the inferior man is content with the simplicity of his humble position and acts accordingly, he will act without errors. Yet the man (of this declined age) is incapable of being content with a poor and humble position, and therefore he advances, guided by desires, trying to escape poverty and humility, but not as a result of a desire to do something. If he succeeds in advancing, the arrogance and conceit overflow, causing mistakes."[1]

The state of humbleness and poorness[2] has the capacity to stop and master, even though for a short time, activity, as illustrated by *gua* Xiao Xu, while arrogance feeds disarray and ignorance; therefore, for Dante, one of the greatest sins was *superbia*, and for the same reason the end of the cycle is dominated by ignorance and arrogance. The order belongs to Heaven; *gua* Wu Wang (no. 25) stated it, its name being "the lack of disorder."

gua Wu Wang

---

[1] This is the "confusion of the castes." No other comments are needed, but we may take a look at our modern society and understand even better the difference between order and chaos.

[2] "Blessed are the poor in spirit, for theirs is the kingdom of heaven" (*Matthew* 5:3).

The hexagram Wu Wang is built of Qian up and Zhen (thunderbolt or lightning) down, the thunderbolt representing the movement. Here the movement is in concert with the will of Heaven and Heaven supervises and guides the thunderbolt, which suggests a *Fiat Lux*, the production of the Cosmos as Order. The hexagram indicates also a state of innocence and sincerity, of natural humbleness and lack of error and disorder, typical for the Golden Age, when the universal manifestation, Man and the Cosmos are directed by Heaven and follow the natural laws. "Movement obeying Heaven means lack of disorder, while movement caused by human appetites indicates disorder. The lack of disorder is absolute sincerity; absolute sincerity is Dao of Heaven. Within Heaven's Activity, which produces and transforms the beings, and in the indefinite series of their changes in the world, each one follows the destiny traced by its own nature[1]; this is the lack of disorder. The seer covers the way of lack of disorder, reaching great liberation. The lack of disorder is Dao, the Way of Heaven (Zheng Zi's commentary).

However, a state of disorder allows differentiation of perfection; the one who complies with his genuine nature and overcomes the adversity of the external anarchy, after firstly doing so with the internal one, will obtain perfection and the *principial* light: this is the seer, the veritable man. "The veritable man follows the four virtues, obeying the activity embodied by *gua* Qian," the *Yi Jing*'s commentary affirmed. "During the seers' sojourn in this world, though they know well that the Rule (Lat. *norma*) is in the process of disappearing, how could they impassively witness the disorder, without remedying it? They have to exercise discreetly their influences upon everything that did not reach an extreme and irremediable point of no return; they have to resist decadence, to stop evil, to gain a respite" (*gua* Dun, no. 33); these "respites" make the cycle not a linear descent, but a sinuous one.

---

[1] There is here a very important suggestion regarding what the Hindu tradition calls *swadharma*, in relation to the appellative "puppeteer" for the Principle and to the real significance of the Christian "freewill."

Modification, Zhu Xi commented, is a progressive transformation; the transformation is the perfect fulfillment of the modifications. The beings receive their nature; Heaven confers them their destiny.[1] The transformation is the limit of the modifications, it is the passing through as a result of a sudden break, and it is a jump, beyond form, beyond the "current of forms." "The transformation is the process of absorbing the beings: it is the good and the perfection (*li* and *cheng*)."

The second branch of the double spiral means the initiatory way of surpassing the modifications by a transformation that constitutes a perfect and absolute accomplishment, but also means the path covered by the manifestation, under the guidance of Heaven's Activity, in order to be absorbed into the Principle; it is the phase of "complication," which follows the phase of "explication" (marked by *heng*, the liberty). "The form," Matgioi said, "is the direct means of modification; the transformation is the final and definitive goal, that is, the reintegration beyond forms. Following this way and reaching its apex, the Will of Heaven is fulfilled and the tetragram's fourth term is realized. (...) Dao of Heaven comprises both the productions into forms and the return beyond forms. (...) There is the production of the beings by modification of the Being. (...) The transformation indicates the return of the beings that are modified into the unmodified Being" (in conformity with Lao Zi's path: greatness – extension – going away – returning).

The fact that the last term of Wen Wang's formula is perfection (*cheng*), and that the Principle is Perfection, plainly demonstrates why in the "current of forms," in a world dominated by modifications and changes, it is impossible for perfection to exist, and it does not matter how hard somebody

---

[1] As we said, each being builds its destiny forced by its own nature (*swadharma*) and in conformity with the plan of divine Providence; in other words, even the state of anarchy that appears as a consequence of lack of compliance with their nature is part of this celestial plan.

strives to obtain perfection in the realm of manifestation, this endeavour is doomed to failure.

Actually, divine Providence plays with us, therefore the Hindu tradition names the manifested world *lila*, a game; Providence implanted in the very nature of all beings the desire for perfection, and celestial Activity imposes on each being a natural tendency toward perfection and completion; but, at the same time, it placed the being in the world, where perfection is unattainable as a worldly realization. There are three situations: the infernal, *tamasic* situation, when the beings are so strongly degraded that they have not the least desire for perfection, and they are, on the contrary, attracted toward chaos and disorder; the human, *rajasic* situation, when the beings search for perfection in the world of change, desiring to be always happy and well and forgetting that, in conformity with the duality of manifestation, where good is, also bad is, where joy is, also sadness is, that there can never be something everlasting in the world, perfect and immutable; and eventually, the *sattwic*, divine situation, when the beings realize perfection as Perfection and they are liberated from the world of changes, they escape the indefinite chain of modifications, finding salvation in the Axis of the World.

These three situations compose the three-dimensional cross, which Lao Zi illustrated with this apothegm: "Scholars of the highest class, when they hear about the Dao, earnestly carry it into practice. Scholars of the middle class, when they have heard about it, seem now to keep it and now to lose it. Scholars of the lowest class, when they have heard about it, laugh greatly at it. If it were not (thus) laughed at, it would not be fit to be the Dao" (*Dao De Jing* XLI). Matgioi commented on the *Dao De Jing*: "When humanity is united with Heaven, it loves It; when it is separated from Heaven, humankind fears It; when humanity opposes Heaven, it curses It." It seems that each being has the freedom to choose one of the three situations, yet, in fact, the beings obey Heaven's Activity and, as Matgioi said, "total liberty does not exist but in Infinity, and a being becoming in the current of forms cannot be the beneficiary of total liberty, since otherwise this being would immediately be God"; "what has originated in Heaven ascends; what has originated on earth descends, in this way each being follows its nature," the *Yi Jing*'s commentary stated.

The Activity of Heaven, Qian, reigns upon the double spiral. This journey, following the Will of Heaven, Matgioi affirmed, signifies a voyage without and a return within, through the current of forms, a river with its spring and mouth confoundable; and after the perfect accomplishment of the transformation, with the absorption of the modifications completed, there always is a return to the beginning of Wen Wang's formula, just ahead of the initial cause. Since all ten thousand beings return to active Perfection, Qian, essentially identical with Heaven's Activity, Matgioi underlined, Dao, the Way that imposed the journey through the terms of the tetragram, exists and will exist forever; therefore, another cycle will start, and this one will also obey the rule of Shi bing wen: "Modification is the process that produces all ten thousand beings; the transformation is the process that absorbs them."

The Universe, Matgioi said, passes, until reaches its final transformation, through all the modifications of the "current of forms," in conformity with the principles of activity, good and harmony.

Each of these modifications is unique; each cycle has its own characteristics and there is no "repetition" in the "current of forms," since the Universal Possibility is infinite and excludes "monotony." Ibn 'Arabî explained: "Because It's infinity, there is nothing within the divine Presence, absolutely nothing that could repeat itself – and this is a fundamental truth." Moreover, universal manifestation is characterized by change and modification, and so, there is no place for immutability and constancy, each being differing from all others. Matgioi affirmed: "In the name of the principle of activity, nothing passes twice through the same 'current of forms.' (...) After one form is exhausted, another modification occurs, with the certitude that there is no return to the old one."[1]

Matgioi illustrated the principles that compose Wen Wang's formula using a symbolic geometric figure: "An indefinite line (the principle of causality) that passes only once through the same points (the principle of activity); established curves as intersections of spatial surfaces, which wind one above the other (the principle of good); and all the points of one element are equally distanced from the analogue points of the superior element and of the inferior element (the principle of harmony). There is no other spatial surface to satisfy these requirements but the cylindrical helicoid." In other words, Matgioi considered, to symbolize the "current of forms," a geometric figure representing an infinite cylinder with a helix composed of an indefinite number of spires wound on the cylindrical surface; each spire is different from the others, even though analogous, which also suggests that the study of past modification could give a hint about the secret of future modifications. Lie Zi said: "The sage, *zhen-ren*, knows what will go in by seeing what came out, knows the future by observing the past. This is the principle by which he knows in advance" (*Lie-zi, Explaining Conjuctions*, 1).

We could consider a spire of the three-dimensional helix symbolizing Humanity and a point of the spire as representing the present terrestrial humankind – a modality of Humanity. And let us note Matgioi's remark: "the human form will always be the human form [since the spires do not intersect each other]; it is impossible for a man to give birth to an ox and for an ox to give birth to a man, or for a plant to give birth to a piece of metal; (…) it is therefore impossible for a monkey to give birth to a man." The seeds of the formal manifestation are in an indefinite variety and it is out of the question to have a form substituted by another or, even if two forms appear as neighbours, as very closed, between them could exist

---

[1] For this reason, the reincarnationist theories are ridiculous, likewise the "eternal return" of Nietzsche. Not to say that the "transformation" of a form in another one, stipulated by the perverse concept of evolution, is impossible.

innumerable forms, differing in an infinitesimal way, which means – Matgioi concluded – that "the anthropoids will always be anthropoids, monkeys, monkeys, and men, men, as long as the current of forms will flow in the universe."

We should add other two important ideas expressed by Matgioi. Heaven's Activity, reflected on the plane of beings, appears as Personality, which is the immortal Axis that sustains the law of "rebirths," in each cycle an individuality being born due to the activity of personality upon a composition (corporeal and psychical, for example). Personality is the source of all the successive individuals (for the formal world, but Personality activates also in the informal domain), and it is unaffected by the death or birth of the individual, being independent and at the same time identical with itself, while the individual is completely attached to the composition, changing with it. The human individual, a result of the corporeal and psychical composition, appears, develops and disappears, together with the composition, while the personality remains unchanged and therefore it is the expression of Heaven's Activity.

Consequently, the cycles of "rebirths" depict a three-dimensional helix belonging to a personality, each spire representing an individual, and the passing point from one spire to another means the individual's death at the same time as the birth of a new individual, in different conditions, but with regard to the same personality. Personality is the river bed, always unchanged, whereas the "current of forms" is the river with its waters always changing, the river's spring and mouth symbolizing the Principle. The passing from an individual to another, from one form to another, is in the nature of the "current of forms," since the river wouldn't be a river if it didn't flow, modifying continuously its waters.

When the individual dies, being born on another spire, his constitutive composition is dissolved, disintegrating, and the corporeal and subtle elements become available to be used, if such be the case, to coagulate other compositions, in various modes; hence, when a man dies, his constitutive elements will disintegrate and will never again form what was called that specific man, and, consequently, his memory and sentiments will disappear and the rebirth on a new spire will not be a "recollection" of the previous existence, because the new composition doesn't contain the memory that belonged to a bygone world. Even if the psychical elements, which the Far-Eastern tradition called "errant forces," were again integrated in an individual, their combination will be a different one, the possible arrangements being an indefinite number.[1]

The second important idea refers to the conditions that determine the birth of a specific individual as a result of the personality's activity. On the one hand, Matgioi said, the acts of an individual are transmitted as "vibrations" along his personality and, in conformity with the law of concordant actions and reactions, they will influence the constitutive elements of a future existence. On the other hand, the laws of Wen Wang's formula must be observed. The passing from one spire to another occurs in an imperceptible way, without shocks or sudden changes, aiming at infinity; and, indeed, the cylinder's generatrices, vertical parallels, will meet only at infinity, when the cylinder becomes a cone and the moment of the Transformation, of the Reintegration into Perfection, takes place; we may note that by projecting this three-dimensional figure on a horizontal plane one of the branches of the double spiral is obtained.[2]

---

[1] The modern theories regarding reincarnation or the spirits ("the Spiritist doctrine") have stupid and absurd pretensions by advocating the idea that the new individual could keep elements from a previous existence, or that the human physical-psychic aggregate, after death, will remain unmodified. The reincarnationist theory downgrades the personality's activity to one spire only, that is, to one individual only, which leads to the ridiculous conclusion that the individual is identical with personality.

[2] Another two-dimensional symbol of the cylindrical helix is Yin-Yang, where the dark zone represents the inferior (and anterior) spires, and the luminous zone the superior (and posterior) spires, while the S-like curve that divides the circle into halves suggests the very helix projected on the plane. Disregarding this S-like curve, many modern minds dream of an "eternal return" and a "repetition of history," which would imply an indefinite rotation in the same circle, contradicting the law of activity and illustrating in fact an impossible stagnation, the Principle being degraded to something trivial.

The celestial double spiral, associated with Qian, is explicated in the *Yi Jing* as the Dragon's Way,[1] a way composed of the six traits belonging to the first perfect *qua*, Qian.

The first line, the inferior or interior one, represents the initial cause, the source of the current of forms, it is "the hidden dragon; wu-wei." The Dragon is the Intelligence, Zheng Zi affirmed, with unlimited modifications; it is the Personality, the symbol of Dao's modifications and transformations, of the Activity, of Perfection; it is "the stem sustaining all the ten thousand beings," the perfection, which – Zhu Xi said – corresponds to the winter solstice and to man's intelligence.

The second trait represents "the visible dragon in the field," illustrating the liberty to produce the manifestation and the beginning of arts and crafts, "the time when Shuen was cultivating the land and was fishing," it is the time when the dragon's virtue spreads, reaching the ten thousand beings.

The third trait designates the danger encountered by those capable of breaking the chains of changes and of the world, of those who, even if they are in an inferior situation, have to surpass their incertitude and decide: will they follow the complicative branch of the double spiral, climbing to Heaven, or, with resignation, they will sink into the inferior waters – this is the meaning of the fourth trait; the dragon could or could not ascend. The initiate has decided: he will follow the Dao of Heaven, toward perfection, in accordance with goodness, and this is "the fifth line; the dragon flying in the sky," and "the

---

[1] The ideogram of the dragon (*long*) is:

emperor accomplishes on earth the plan of Providence; he represents the Heaven and guards the link between men."[1]

Finally, the upper trait of the hexagram Qian means "the Dragon ascended, there are regrets," because, after reaching Perfection, another cycle follows, a new birth, and the situation is not permanent for the current of forms. But the Perfection is the sage's residence and the dragon's virtue is a state of the veritable man: "the dragon's virtue – the virtue of the perfect sage"; the one who has the dragon's virtue, will be situated in the "just center," with "justice and righteousness," the way of the dragon being an imperial way, the microcosmic thread knitting with the macrocosmic thread, the dragon's ascension corresponding to the perfect sage's ascension: "what has a celestial origin will ascend."

The way of the dragon, associated with the first hexagram, Qian, of the *Yi Jing*, could be related not only to the symbolism of the double spiral, but also to that of the ladder, considering the six continuous lines. We should imagine a reverse ladder having the shape of V,[2] with three descending steps and three ascending ones, the ladder's legs touching Heaven, where the initial cause and perfection, the two extremes of the ladder's legs, melt together. The V shaped reverse ladder suggests a cone with an infinite opening (the maximum), while the vertex (the lowest point) is the Center of the World, the minimum. "The end and the beginning are illuminated by a great light, the six situations are revealed in time" (the *Yi Jing*'s commentary).

The terrestrial double spiral is associated to Kun, the second perfect *gua* of the *Yi Jing*, this hexagram teaching "the way of the mare."

---

[1] The fifth trait is the emperor's place.
[2] See the Kadosh Ladder (René Guénon, *L'ésotérisme de Dante*, Gallimard, 1981, p. 13).

"Kun – Zheng Zi commented – is the antithesis of Qian; the four virtues are the same, but perfection's nature is different; in the case of Kun, perfection exists by flexible mildness and passivity. The mare is meek and obedient; therefore she was used as a symbol." In fairy-tales, the mare plays an important role and she is always an emblem of the inferior, feminine pole,[1] in contrast to the stallion, which, nourished with fire and being able to fly, is the equivalent of the luminous dragon.

Qian is the supreme Principle as Infinity; Kun is the supreme Principle as Universal Possibility, the former – the active aspect, the latter – the passive aspect of Perfection. Therefore, "the way of the mare," like "the way of the dragon," elucidates, as much as our individual means permit, the absolute Principle, with the remark that we should accept in our human mind a hierarchy, Qian outshining Kun and being "closer" to the absolute Principle.[2]

We find in the *Yi Jing*: "Preceding – blindness, following – possibility to guide in accordance with goodness," and Zheng Zi commented on this dictum: "If the negativity (*kun*) precedes the positivity (*qian*), that means blindness and error, if it stays behind, it will be in order, reaching perfection." The blindness signifies ignorance and disarray, and a symbolic matriarchate depicts such a state of ignorance, an unnatural state, one of decadence typical for the end of a cycle. In some fairy-tales, this situation is described by saying that not the rooster but the hen governs and sings in the house. "The way of negativity means not to give the tone, but to be in accord"; "even though negativity has beautiful qualities, she hides them,[3] in order to focus on serving the emperor[4]; she does not dare to have

---

[1] Often, the mare's residence is a marsh or the bottom of an abyss.

[2] In the Hindu tradition, the *principial* and fundamental dyad of manifestation is the pair Purusha – Prakriti, yet Purusha is also a name for the non-dual Principle.

[3] For this reason the bride hides her face under a veil. In different traditions, the woman's head should be covered.

[4] The emperor, as the groom, is a symbol of the Lord of the World.

exclusively the command. This is Dao of Earth, of the wife, of the vassal."

The hexagram Kun is built of six horizontal discontinuous lines,[1] and it symbolizes the apex of passivity, the pure substance, the Earth; as Universal Possibility, it is equivalent to the Hindu Shakti, it is the Mother of the ten thousand beings. "The productive faculty of passivity is maximum, the birth of all ten thousand beings occurred because of it, due to a passive submission to Heaven's Activity and obeying the Heaven's influence; this is Dao of Earth." The apex of the productive faculty corresponds to the first term, *yuan*, of Wen Wang's tetragram. The universal manifestation, the Cosmos, is produced by "cooperation" among the analogue virtues of activity and passivity. "All ten thousand beings – Zheng Zi commented – owe their beginning to activity and their birth to passivity; here it is the logical way of paternity and maternity." The manifestation, Zhu Xi said, has as fundament the positive-negative duality, without which it cannot exist.

"The ampleness of passivity contains all the ten thousand beings"; this is the second virtue: the capacity to encompass, the infinite ampleness of the Universal Possibility induces the liberty (*heng*) of expansion under the influence of Heaven's Activity. "Passive obedience before Heaven's influence, for accomplishing the work – Zheng Zi stated –, this is the ampleness of the virtue of Kun's passivity, which extends to all the ten thousand beings, supporting them and being in accord with the lack of limits for Qian's activity." The function of the feminine pole is to "support" the Cosmos; the function of the masculine pole is to "cover" the Cosmos[2]. Heaven's ideogram

---

[1] The broken line, called the duality, Zhu Xi said, is negativity's number, is passivity.

[2] "The ten thousand beings carry on their back the *yin* and embrace in their arms the *yang*" (*Dao De Jing*, XLII). This statement seems mysterious, but here the ten thousand beings represent the mediator, Ren – Man, who combines Heaven and Earth. As Guénon explained, the "interiority" belongs to Heaven and "exteriority" to Earth; Earth appears with its dorsal side and Heaven with its ventral side, and therefore *yin* is "outside" and *yang* "inside" (*La Grand Triade*, pp. 38, 41).

(Tian) shows the superior pole covering the ten thousand beings (represented as a man):

天 天

"Dao of submission necessarily implies one's duty to be silent and hide his talents and merits; if he does a good thing, the vassal attributes it to the emperor, maintaining the straight way, rectitude. To be silent and to hide merits, this is the possibility for perfection. Thanks to the greatness and brightness of his knowledge only, the vassal can hide in obscurity. The ignorant and superficial man, when he has done a good thing, fears only one thing – the world will not find out what he did. If the vassal hides and dissimulates his knowledge, the way somebody would tie the mouth of a sack, without letting it manifest outside, he will be without culpability and without applause."

This commentary of the *Yi Jing*, related to the hexagram Kun, deserves attention, because the way of submission and humbleness is an initiatory way beyond its religious significance. In the Christian tradition, Christ affirmed: "Even as the Son of man came not to be served but to serve" (*Matthew* 20:28); and when Jesus healed a leper he told him: "And saith unto him, See thou say nothing to any man" (*Mark* 1:44); and when he healed a blind man: "And he sent him away to his house, saying, Neither go into the town, nor tell it to any in the town" (*Mark* 8:26); eventually, at Capernaum, Christ "sat down, and called the twelve, and saith unto them, If any man desire to be first, the same shall be last of all, and servant of all. (*Mark* 9:35).

The *Yi Jing*'s commentaries highlight more than one important aspect, among which a special one is the position of the sage with respect to the Principle: the sage, with regard to Qian and the supreme Principle, is a humble servant, a vassal, exactly as a vassal is with respect to the emperor,[1] and he has to

---

[1] To become a perfect sage one has to listen to the heavenly Mouth (the *Shrutis* were heard):

follow the way of humbleness with the help of which he empties the Self of ephemeral elements, of the ego's arrogance, of the individuality's *superbia*; he performs good, aiming at perfection, but in secret, rejects the praises that bear the chains and the fruits of deeds; on the other hand, with regard to Kun, the sage is the master, the emperor, armed with the intellectual pride of the Self.

Secondly, from an initiatory point of view, the smallest on earth is the greatest in heaven and Zhu Xi said: "The positivity is the greatness; the negativity is the littleness," namely, what is submission and passivity in Kun's domain, becomes supremacy and activity in Qian's domain, in this way the double spiral of Earth is fulfilled, with the way of humbleness as the complicative branch. "The way of passivity, Kun, is not submission? It obeys Heaven," the *Yi Jing* affirmed.

The Perfection's duplication in Qian and Kun allows, as a consequence of the union between the positive and negative, the production of universal manifestation, and this is the meaning of the third perfect *gua*, Zhun, generated when the activity of Heaven penetrates the hexagram Kun, the first trait (the inferior one) and the fifth line (the emperor's position) becoming continuous lines, and hence Zhun is built of Zhen (thunderbolt) down and Kan (water) up.[1]

gua Zhun

---

[1] Kan means water, but also cloud and rain.

"When Heaven and Earth exist, immediately all the ten thousand beings are produced; what fills up the space between Heaven and Earth is nothing other than all the beings. For this reason *gua* Zhun follows Qian and Kun. Zhun means 'to fill up.' Zhun means the beginning (Qian) and the birth (Kun) of the beings." "The activity Qian – Zhu Xi commented on it – presides over the beginning of the beings and the passivity Kun produces and accomplishes them. (…) The positivity precedes; the negativity follows; the positivity provokes by its activity; the negativity supports and receives."

Gua Zhun is usually regarded illustrating "difficulty at the beginning." The commentaries stress how difficult is to pass from chaos to order and, as the human birth implies effort and difficulties,[1] so the birth of light from darkness is difficult[2]; any beginning is difficult and requires an effort, and, from an initiatory perspective, the initiate has to overcome difficulties by his own efforts.

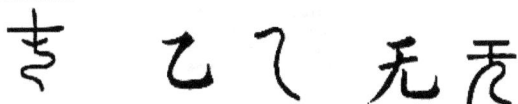

The Zhun ideogram describes the seed of a plant making efforts to escape the underground darkness and reach the light outside; the second ideogram represents the germination, illustrating the seed's effort to sprout (Wieger 34), and the third ideogram, *wu*, which is a symbol for non-manifestation and suggests the "one-footed," is commonly regarded as an image of man's effort against an obstacle (Wieger 160). This "effort," which is repeatedly emphasized, symbolizes from a metaphysical viewpoint Heaven's invisible activity that is indispensable for Cosmos, Year, and Man to exist and fulfill their destiny.

From a symbolic perspective, Zheng Zi stated, Zhun illustrates the generation of the cloud and thunderbolt. Such a symbolism can be found in different traditions: *zhen*, the

[1] "I will greatly multiply thy sorrow and thy conception; in sorrow thou shalt bring forth children" (*Genesis* 3:16).
[2] The clouded sky and the thunderbolt are the image announcing the chaos changing into order.

thunderbolt, has a very rich meaning in the Hindu tradition (as *vajra*)[1]; in Greek mythology, it is Zeus' perfect weapon, and Thor's hammer, in German mythology, is an equivalent of the thunderbolt; it is also the main attribute of Saint Elijah, and it represents the luminous emblem of the masculine, active principle.

The cloud is the reservoir of celestial waters (*kan*), symbolizing the Universal Possibility (at the highest level) and the passive feminine principle. The thunderbolt liberates the cloud's waters, and the waters – celestial influences – fecundate the Earth, producing the ten thousand beings; we must observe that here the Mother of ten thousand beings is presented as the divine Maiden (the Hindu Shakti), not as the terrestrial Widow (the Hindu Prakriti).[2]

In the *Yi Jing*, the terrestrial widow is shown, next to the thunderbolt, in *gua* no. 16, Yu, built of Zhen up and Kun down.

gua Yu

---

[1] The ideogram, showing the thunderbolt and the cloud, is:

[2] *Guas* no. 3, 4 and 5 (Zhun, Meng, and Xu) compose a series illustrating the production of the ten thousand beings caused by Heaven's activity and the celestial influences, in relation with the Being sprouting from the Non-Being. The Xu ideogram stresses the rain and the thunderbolt as heavenly influences. The universal manifestation is a "new plant" (neophyte), first as a seed (Zhun), then as a young plant (Meng), which grows under the rain's influence (Xu):

The *principial* activity (and it is important to keep this in mind) operates both on the celestial plane (the Maiden who produces the rain) and the terrestrial plane (the Mother who produces the substantial manifestation). "The thunderbolt is engulfed by the earth; then, it comes out from the earth, and it bursts out brightly, causing quakes. First hidden and gathered in complication, then bursting with noise, as sound; it is the symbolic image of music" (Zheng Zi).

In the Hindu tradition, the production of the universal manifestation is symbolized by *Parashabda*, the primordial Sound. The paradisaical state, of the beginning, is characterized by musical harmony, and this music, in the Far-Eastern tradition, was associated with the thunderbolt bursting out from the earth.[1]

Gua no. 25, Wu Wang, is built of Qian up and Zhen down

gua Wu Wang

Zheng Zi said: "The thunderbolt's quake is propagated in the whole Cosmos; the negativity and positivity become united in a harmonious way; they crash into each other and produce the sound; in that moment, they wake up the dormant and resting larva, they give the initial impulse to the vegetal germ, and give life to beings." The thunderbolt, as the Principle's scepter, orders the chaos and produces the Cosmos (Greek "order"), and for this reason *gua* Wu Wang means "the lack of disorder" and the lack of disorder is Dao of Heaven; "Dao, the Way of Heaven, gives life to all ten thousand beings, and each one complies to its own nature and destiny, without any disorder."

---

[1] The music is related to the traditional theory of rhythm. Any traditional art is an application of the rhythm science.

The ten thousand beings, just born, are in a pseudo-germinative state, their possibilities being yet dormant (see *gua* no. 4, Meng, which follows Zhun),[1] and activity is required of the Hero, of the *avatâra*, who, risen in Heaven, (*gua* no. 5, Xu, following Meng), will descend into the world (*gua* no. 6, Song)[2] to organize the crowd into a civilized society (*gua* no. 7, Shi, and *gua* no. 8, Bi), establishing its ritual rules (*gua* no. 9, Xiao Xu, and *gua* no. 10, Lü); thus, the manifestation is completely produced and developed, and we should observe that Yin-Yang acts like a paradigmatic seal, the white could not exist without the black, and the black without the white – worldly reflex of the *principial* Unity.

---

[1] We see the mountain and the abyss, suggesting youthful folly, because when things have just been born, they are always wrapped at birth in obtuseness and obscurity. There is though another meaning related to the subterranean center, symbolizing the non-manifestation and the supernal darkness; see Meng's ideogram with the boar sheltered underground (in this case, the childish folly is Lao Zi's wisdom and Zhuang Zi's rejection of erudition):

[2] An ancient ideogram shows the ancestor descending in the temple and a hand offering an oblation (Wieger 372). But we can consider it as an illustration of the *avatâra* coming down through the "gate of gods"; similarly, the newborn comes in the world with his head downwards (see the ideogram *qi*, chapter 5).

gua Meng   *gua* Xu   *gua* Song   *gua* Shi

gua Bi   *gua* Xiao Xu   *gua* Lü   *gua* Tai

The next *gua*, no. 11, Tai, underlines this very Unity: "it is built of simple *gua* Kun of negativity up, and of simple *gua* Qian down, *gua* of activity. The celestial and terrestrial influences, positive and negative, become united in harmony, and consequently the ten thousand beings are born and normally evolve toward perfection. (…) The celestial influence descends, the terrestrial influence ascends." We witness the initiatory wedding of Heaven and Earth, by which the current of forms reaches perfection; it is the ascendant phase; it is the union that makes Fu Xi take over the feminine attributes and his wife and sister, Niu Wa, the masculine attributes. If we represent the hexagram on a circle (a well-known representation), we note that Qian is inside and Kun outside, and Zheng Zi said: "positivity is the sage, the superior man, negativity is the inferior man; the superior man will take the inner place [the kernel]; the inferior man will take the outer place [the skin]. (…) Qian's active force is within; Kun's passive submission is without, which means inner activity and exterior submission; it is Dao of the veritable man."

The perfect seer is identical to "the feathered serpent," mentioned in the Gospel[1]; the veritable man is wise inside and harmless and meek outside. *Gua* no. 15, Qian, built of Kun up and Gen (mountain) down, illustrates this state; Zheng Zi commented on it: "the earth means inferiority and smallness; the mountain is tall and big, and is placed in the middle of the earth: it is the symbolic image of exterior humbleness and smallness, and of interior greatness and highness, hidden within"; it is the androgynous way of perfection and accomplishment.

gua Qian

The attainment of the summit, when the Wedding takes place and the state of veritable man is realized, will be followed, inexorably, by a fall, and the *principial* wedding will continue, inevitably, with a cosmic divorce, with a separation of the active from the passive, to make possible the current of forms to flow and observe its destiny; therefore, *gua* Tai is followed by *gua* no. 12, Pi, named "decadence" (Qian up, Kun down), and concentrating in an emblematic way the whole cyclical decadence.

gua Pi

---

[1] "Behold, I send you forth as sheep in the midst of wolves: be ye therefore wise as serpents, and harmless as doves" (*Matthew* 10:16).

The World

Zhen Zi explained: "Heaven and Earth united, the negativity and positivity develop in harmony, bringing prosperity; Heaven situated up, Earth situated down, that means Heaven and Earth absolutely separated, which brings decadence.[1] Decreasing and increasing, expanding and contracting are cause and effect both ways, and this succession has no end; the prosperity reaching its extreme limit, a reaction must exist; when declining is at maximum, prosperity follows." We note here the double spiral with an ascendant phase and a descendant one, reflected in the cosmic cycles, the succession of the seasons, man's ages, the moon's phases and the tides, with the remark that what appears as prosperity from one point of view, is decadence from another viewpoint, since in manifestation the ascendant and descendant phases coexist simultaneously; also, with regard to the cosmic cycles, we should add that their evolvement starts with the situation when Heaven is united with Earth, continues in a descending direction, while at the same time there is an increasing divorce between Heaven and Earth, and ends when Heaven and Earth are completely separated; after that follows the ascending phase of Heaven's and Earth's reunification outside manifestation.

---

[1] Decadence occurs at all levels. The correlation between the superior and inferior guarantees the peace of the empire, the emperor promulgates the rules and the vassals "bear him on their heads," following the rules; when decadence occurs, the superior and inferior don't have any relation anymore, and Dao of the country does not exist anymore. Also, "the way of the inferior man increases and that of the superior man decreases," it is the reverse of what the Christian tradition expresses in these words: "He [Christ] must increase, but I [John the Baptist] must decrease" (*John* 3:30).

FOUR

THE COSMOGONY

gua Pi *gua* Sui *gua* Gui Mei *gua* Tai

The four hexagrams presented here symbolize a synthesis of cosmogony. Yet, to properly understand their significance we have to implicate the symbols found in different traditions and which, in fact, belong to the primordial Tradition.[1]

In the Hindu tradition, Brahma produced the Cosmos "simply by way of sport," as a pastime (*Brahma Samhitâ* XVII). Playfully, the Principle unveils one of its many facets and manifests the Cosmos; playfully, the Principle unveils another facet and "falls" as Dragon, together with the World; and, revealing another face, the Principle comes down as the solar

---

[1] The traditional Chinese cosmogony has the theory of the five "elements" as its fundament. The five "elements" (symbolically called water, fire, wood, metal, earth) are rather "agents" and they cannot be compared to Hindu *bhûtas*. However, the present chapter strives to describe the cosmogony from another perspective, even though we fully understand the importance of the five "agents."

Hero to save the decaying Cosmos and behead the Dragon. At the same time, the Principle remains immutable, infinite, without parts, unchanged in itself. Brahma is, therefore, the Creator, the Savior and the Devil all-together, the same as his Shakti is the one-and-only, yet has many faces. The Principle is the supernal Sun, super-luminous, absolute and unmovable; yet it "comes down" as *Oriens* (*Sol Invictus*, the Savior) and also "falls" as a lamed, "mortal" sun to produce and maintain the Existence.

The Principle is a Master Puppeteer.

It is useless to try to discover the terrestrial origins of the puppet theater, but there is a general opinion that China was the place where puppetry started as an art; in fact, due to its symbolism, puppetry has no historical origins. It is said that the legendary king Mu, on his way home from Kunlun Mountain (a symbol of *Axis Mundi*), noticed a carpenter performing a dance with wooden dolls he had made.[1] The puppet theater is one of the most explicit illustrations of the divine Play (Hindu *Lîlâ*), since the ten thousand beings are "the puppets," which the Master Puppeteer, Principle and spiritual Sun, rules with its strings, each string representing an integral and total being, a "personality"; the string is the absolute "thread of life," an immortal thread, which constitutes the axis of what René Guénon called "the multiple states of the being," but, as long as this thread, this personality, appears as different from the Great Person, Mahâ Purusha, it will continue to feed the whirl of the multiple existences, and only the breaking of the string will cause the liberation from the whirl, from the chain (*pâsha*), and will transform the being from "pure animal" (*pashu*) into Man, when the string is absorbed into the Golden String, Dao's Activity, and the being is bound forever to this Chain.

Striving to break the chain only to be chained again would appear to be a dim-witted endeavour. The *Rig-Vêda* transmitted

---

[1] Puppetry is related to the Chinese shadow theater (the shadow puppets were made of animal skin), and to the ancient mask theater. In the Middle Ages, the Christian tradition used puppetry to transmit its sacred tales; the name "marionette" (puppet controlled by strings) means "little Mary."

the prayer: "Liberate me from the curse of Varuna, from the claudication of Yama," where "claudication," from the Latin *claudicare*, "to limp," refers to having the legs tied up, like Saturn, and has, similar to "Varuna's bonds," two facets: the limping, with regard to the world, means imperfection, ephemeral, evil; the limping, with regard to the Principle, means One without the second, the Golden Chain, the Dragon; we could reformulate the *Vedic* prayer: "Liberate me from the Varuna's bonds, to be bound to Varuna, and save me from limping to become lame as Varuna." It is the upside down thinking (*pratyakcêtanâ*), used in all the traditions, but considered today a characteristic of Zen.

In the Hindu tradition, *Axis Mundi* is also called *ashwattha*, "the horse's station," the horse being another emblem of Dao's Activity, of the spiritual Sun, of Prâna, Brahma's Breath. The horse is, consequently, identified with Prajâpati, the Lord of all ten thousand beings, and *ashwamedha*, "the horse sacrifice," symbolizes the spiritual "binding and unbinding."

The *Brhadâranyaka Upanishad* commences with the words: "Om. The head of the sacrificial horse is the dawn, its eye the sun, its prâna the air, its open mouth the fire called Vaishwânara, and the body of the sacrificial horse is the Year. Its back is the heaven, its belly the atmosphere, its hoof the earth, its sides the four cardinal points, its members the seasons, its joints the months and fortnights, its feet the days and nights, its bones the stars and its flesh the clouds. (...) Its forepart is the ascending sun, its hind part the descending sun, its yawning is lightning, its body shaking is thundering."

As we have already seen, in the previous chapters, even though we did not explicitly draw attention upon it, the *Yi Jing* hides a triple significance related to the triad Cosmos – Year – Man. The *Brhadâranyaka Upanishad* suggests the same triad; in fact, any traditional doctrine has to shelter this triple symbolism.

"Inside the Year, the Man (Purusha, Prajâpati) felt the desire to talk. 'Bhûr!' he exclaimed; and there was the Earth. 'Bhuvar!' he exclaimed; and there was the Atmosphere (the intermediary space). 'Svar!' he exclaimed; and there was the Sky" (*Satapatha Brâhmana* XI.1.6.3-4).

"The Three Mothers in *the World* are Aleph, Mem and Shin: the Heavens were produced from Fire; the Earth from the Water; and the Air from the Spirit is as a reconciler between the Fire and the Water. The Three Mothers, Aleph, Mem and Shin, Fire, Water and Air, are shown in *the Year*: from the fire came heat, from the waters came cold, and from the air was produced the temperate state, again a mediator between them. The Three Mothers, Aleph, Mem and Shin, Fire, Water and Air, are found in *Man*: from the fire was formed the head; from the water the belly; and from the air was formed the chest, again placed as a mediator between the others. These Three Mothers did He produce and design, and combine; and He sealed them as the three mothers in *the Universe, in the Year and in Man* – both male and female" (*Sepher Yetsirah*, III, 3-5). Paul Vulliaud said: "Sepher Yetsirah considers the Universe from the viewpoint of harmony. Hence, this symbolism results, of the 'signs' or 'witnesses,' called the World, the Year and the Man. (...) The Cosmos, Year and Man were the 'witnesses' because everything refered to them, since they were images of each other."[1]

Indeed, any "sign" has a triple meaning and purpose: a cosmogonic one (the production of the World), a cyclic one (the rotation of the World) and an initiatory one (the Liberation), and from this perspective the horse contains all three "witnesses," since the horse is The Three Worlds, and the Year, and the Universal Man as a synthesis of the initiatory realization. Yet, even though each "sign" hides the triple meaning, always there is a fourth one, beyond all the symbols, corresponding to the Principle,[2] and for this reason the horse is essentially the supreme Sun, and primarily his head is the Sun.

In the *Satapatha Brâhmana* (XIV, I), there is a tale about the sage (*rshi*) Dadhyac threatened by Indra with beheading if he unveils the secret initiatory lore (*madhu-vidya*); hence, the

---

[1] Paul Vulliaud, *La Kabbale Juive*, Émile Nourry, 1923.
[2] Therefore, *Âtmâ* has four conditions, and the *Yi Jing* is the Book of Changes, but contains, beyond the triad Cosmos – Year – Man, the mystery of Dao.

Ashwins, twin brothers, having the Sun as father and the mare as mother,[1] will replace brahmana's head with a horse's head, and this very horse's head will transmit the esoteric teaching. Indra will behead Dadhyac, and the horse riders Ashwins will bring back the initial head. The sacrificial and ritual act of beheading is a special step of the initiatory journey, and here it connects the symbolism of the horse with Man, the third term of the triad. In the *Brhadâranyaka Upanishad* (II, 5.16), the silent meditation is highlighted, associated with the sun, and transmitted by a horse's head, and also the secret meditation (on the Self), the spiritual realization being inseparable from the cosmogonic act.

The head of *Yajna* (the Sacrifice), for example, after the sacred act of beheading, became the Sun; the rite *Pravargya* will operate the restoration.[2] As in the case of the horse's head, so the sun at the beginning of the cycle and of the world leaves the World Tree (the beheading) and comes back at the end of times: from this angle should be understood the association of the sacred horse with the Year. René Guénon affirmed that, in different traditions, the sun represents the fruit of the World Tree, the tree being indeed the "sun's station,"[3] and the Chinese character signifying the sunset depicts the sun resting in the tree at the end of the day.[4]

---

[1] It is the same mare of the *Yi Jing*. On the other hand, the trigram Qian, Heaven, has the horse as an emblem, the dragon being attributed to Zhen, the thunderbolt.

[2] For more about the symbolism of beheading see the third volume of the triptych "René Guénon and the Traditional Spirit," *The Quest for the Center.*

[3] This is the meaning of "solstice"; we note the equivalence with *ashwattha*, "the horse's station." The ideogram for a tree's fruit shows the sun as fruit (Wieger 280):

[4] The ideogram for sunrise (Wieger 282) shows the sun in a tree (we should notice the tree's symbol, with three roots and three branches):

The Cosmogony

In the Far-Eastern tradition, as we saw, the horse is replaced by the dragon; and the *Sepher Yetsirah* stated: "The Celestial Dragon, Tali, is placed over the Universe like a king upon the throne; the revolution of the Year is as a king over his dominion; the heart of Man is as a king in warfare" (VI, 2).

All the traditions safeguard rich data about the Dragon, either with respect to cosmogony or regarding the initiatory process. Let us remember some famous dragons: Ananta ("the infinity") – the dragon of the primordial abyss, on which Vishnu reposed; Pangu, the Universal Man of the Chinese tradition, the one who split in two the World Egg; the emperor Fu Xi; Cadmos (radical *qdm*, "primordial"), the founder of Thebes. The Dragon is associated in these examples with infinity and primordiality and so, as stated in the *Yi Jing*, it is an equivalent of the Principle.[1] All the more the dragon should be present as a symbol for the terms of the triad Cosmos – Year – Man. There is the well-known picture of the World Tree and the dragon wound around it, where the dragon's coils represent the cosmic helix, the degrees of the universal Existence, and the cosmic cycles, while the tree is Dao's Activity; in the Hindu tradition, the *Axis Mundi* is Mount Meru and the dragon Ananta is wound around it. In Orphism, the god Phanes is born from the World Egg as Universal Man, the Egg being the Zodiac; the superior half of the World Egg, which is Phanes' hood, represents Tian, the Heaven that covers, and the inferior half is Di, the Earth, supporting the god, who symbolizes Ren, the Mediator and the Grand Triad's middle term.[2]

In the Chinese tradition, Pangu, the dragon, is described very similarly, the primordial god sustaining Heaven with his

---

[1] The "claudication" in the case of the dragon is extreme, since it has no legs.
[2] We refer here, of course, to the Far-Eastern triad Tian – Di – Ren (or Jen).

head and pushing the Earth with his tail ("feet").[1] Pangu is pictured as a dragon, which in this case is not the serpent wound around the Tree or Mountain, but the Universal Man as Kernel and, at the same time, as Axis linking the two hemispheres, Heaven and Earth. On the other hand, in the case of Phanes, the symbolism is more explicit, since he is encircled by a serpent, coiled around his body, and with the head resting on the superior hemisphere of the Egg, marking Hindu *Brahmarandhra* or *Kether*, the crown of the Judaic Kabbalah; so, Phanes is the dragon as *Axis Mundi*, as the Pivot of the Rule (the dragon's head indicating this aspect),[2] and, at the same time, he is the serpent as helix of the universal manifestation, and the Zodiac that describes the contour of the Egg represents the frame of the Cosmos.[3] There are statues of Mithras too, where the god has a lion's head, and a serpent is coiled around Mithras' body with the head resting on the lion's head; moreover, on the god's body the signs of the Zodiac are

---

[1] Pangu breaks the World Egg with an axe, a symbol of the thunderbolt, producing a terrible bang (the primeval sound). About the Chinese mythical history see Jacques Lionnet, *Remarques sur la tradition chinoise*, Études Traditionnelles, no. 299, 1952. We should also mention the twofolded symbolism of the axe: the ideogram of *gua* Xian (no. 31) shows a halberd, but in this case the weapon is used to unite the Egg's two halves.

[2] There is a "polar" symbolism and a "solar" one, both legitimate. The Principle is the spiritual Sun, the Universal Man is the Sun (see the description of the sacrificial horse), but we must not forget that the Principle is also the Pole around which rotate all the ten thousand beings; the Pole is the Pivot of the Rule and its sign is the *swastika*. "This point is called the Pivot of the Rule, the Pivot of Dao. As soon as one finds this pivot, he stands in the centre of the ring, where he sees infinity, which is not the changing views, not the affirmations, nor the negations. (...) The Principle operating as Pole, as Axis of the World, can be named only the Pole and the Axis of the universal evolvement" (*Zhuang zi*, 2, 3/C; 25, J). The Axis of universal evolvement is illustrated by a tale of the Far-Eastern tradition: the emperor Yao, the son of celestial emperor Diku and of his third wife Qingdu, had in his palace a tree called mingjia, which daily produced a pod; but, in the middle of the month, the pods started to fall, on the last day of the month just one was still in the tree; and every month this cycle was repeated.

[3] "One aspect Dragon [the Axis], one aspect serpent [the helix]," Zhuang Zi said (Granet, *La pensée chinoise*, p. 116, Zhuang-zi, 20, 1/A).

printed, and we saw already that Fu Xi's dragon had the trigrams printed on his back (in this case, the dragon is the Universal Man, and the Zodiacal signs or the trigrams are the elements of the Cosmos).

In some traditional tales, the World Tree produces three or twelve golden fruits, which a dragon guards or robs. The Latvians transmitted a tale about the Sun Tree situated in the middle of the ocean, having the sun as its golden fruit, and the sun, at the end of the day, always returned to the Tree. In the Hindu tradition, there are twelve aspects of the sun, each one governing an age; at the end of the cycle all twelve come back simultaneously to the Axis of the World, reentering the primordial and essential Unity of their common nature. The twelve suns are equivalent to the twelve gods of the Greek mythology, to the twelve Adityas of the Hindu tradition.

The supreme Sun has Aditi as Shakti, and Vivaswat the sun, is Aditi's son. Manu, the Lord of the World, is Vivaswat's son and the ancestor of Ikshvâku, the founder of the solar dynasty: "I explained this everlasting yoga to Vivaswat, Vivaswat has transmitted it to Manu, and Manu to Ikshvâku" (Bhagavad-Gîtâ IV, 1).

Aditi could be described as an absolute and super-luminous Sun, source of light, milk and honey, "the infinite Light," as Shri Aurobindo said, a Light so blinding, so powerful, that it appears as superior Darkness and "seventy veils" are needed to filter it, to colour it, to lame its power (shakti), in order to become manifested (Fiat Lux). Aditi is the Mother as Universal Possibility, but she is also the Widow (Indra had killed his father and Aditi became a widow) as the pole of the universal manifestation. She is pure, undivided and infinite, full of order and without duality (advaya), Conscience, Shri Aurobindo affirmed, while her sister, Diti, is ignorance, separation, finite, duality. Aditi is mother of avatâras and dêvas; Diti is mother of pitris and pitaro manushyâh, but, as the Being is encompassed by the Non-Being, so Diti is contained by Aditi, and, in fact, Aditi (understood as Aditi-Diti) governs both immortality and mortality.

Mircea A Tamas

Aditi has either twelve suns as offspring ("Who are Adityas? They are the twelve months of the Year" – *Brhadâranyaka Up.*, III.9.5), or eight (see *Maitrâyanî Samhitâ*, 1.6). We must note that Aditi's children are pairs of twins, because, as usually happens in the case of all sacred tales, the hidden symbolism is manyfold and a synthesis of innumerable meanings and aspects.[1] The last pair of twins is special: one became Indra and just born he launched himself upwards; the other one fell down, a "dead egg." This "dead egg" is Mârttânda, to whom the sons of men belong; he became Aditya Vivaswat, the ancestor of Manu and Yama Vaivaswata; Mârttânda was born "unformed" (not "deformed") and his brothers gave him shape.

"Let us with tuneful skill proclaim the birth of gods. (…) The Being, in an earlier age of gods, from the Non-Being sprang. Thereafter, from the Being were the celestial quarters born. (…) Earth sprang from the Productive Power (the Being), and the celestial quarters from the earth were born. Daksha was born of Aditi, and Aditi was Daksha's child. (…) When the gods, like sages, caused the swelling of the worlds (like the milk that swells a breast), then you brought Sûrya, the Sun, forward who was lying hidden in the ocean. Eight are the sons of Aditi who from her body sprang to life. With seven she went to meet the gods: she cast Mârttânda far away. So with her seven sons Aditi went forth to meet the earlier age. She brought Mârttânda thitherward to spring to life and die again" (*Rig-Vêda*, 10.72).

As any *avatâra* unites the divine and the human natures, so Mârttânda, born in accordance to a "reversed thinking," from the main oblation (and not from the remains, as happened with his brothers), is the synthesis Aditi – Diti, and therefore he is indeed superior to the other Adityas; he is the midnight Sun, the Sun of initiatory realization, he is the real golden embryo, the integral seed, the primordial Avatâra and man's prototype.[2]

[1] The *Yi Jing's* hexagrams perfectly illustrate the twins' doctrine; this doctrine is not just a theory, but it is fully and actually realized during the initiatory process.
[2] The name Mârttânda meant initially "born from an egg," and we could advance the supposition that he has a bird's form, and so he is "the sun-bird"

100

The Cosmogony

Shri Aurobindo retold the story of Mârttânda: "We are told that there are eight sons of the cosmic Aditi who are born from her body; by seven she moves to the gods, but the eighth son is Mârttânda, of the mortal creation whom she casts away from her; with the seven she moves to the supreme life, the original age of gods, but Mârttânda is brought back out of the Inconscient into which he had been cast to preside over mortal birth and death. This Mârttânda of the eighth Sûrya is the black or dark, the lost, the hidden sun. The Titans (*asuras*) have taken and concealed him in their cavern of darkness and thence he must be released into splendour and freedom by the gods and seers through the power of the sacrifice.[1] (...) Sûrya the divine Knowledge lies concealed and unattainable in the night and darkness, is enveloped and contained in the ignorance and error of the ordinary human existence. (...) This is the first aspect of the Sûrya that he is the supreme Light of the truth attained by the human being after his liberation from the Ignorance."[2]

We are told that Mârttânda (Vivaswat) was born unformed, without hands, without legs, equally long and wide,[3] and his older brothers mutilated and crippled him, carving a form similar to their own. Mârttânda is the *principial* and non-dual Dragon, the perfect sphere without any specifications, beyond forms. The production of the Cosmos means "to form" it, to give birth to all the forms, and Mârttânda illustrates this cosmogony, his non-form being carved into forms; but he also passes from unformed to deformed, since he suffers a

---

or "the fire-bird" (that is, the phoenix), or that he has a serpent's form (both the bird and the serpent are born of eggs, which consolidates the idea of a feathered serpent), all this having precise equivalences in the Far-Eastern tradition.

[1] It is the objective of the initiatory process.

[2] Sri Aurobindo, *The Secret of the Veda*, Sri Aurobindo Ashram, 1971, p. 426.

[3] He was a sphere, like Plato's androgynous primordial form, in accordance with Guénon's spherical universal vortex. There are fairy-tales where one of the heroes is called the Bird-Long-Wide.

mutilation, his power being crippled (the older brothers cut and remove pieces of his flesh).[1]

The apparent increase of the limitative conditions of *Âtmâ* represents such a crippling, from its non-conditioned state, the Fourth (*Turîya*), to the corporeal state, passing through the informal and the subtle states. Ibn 'Arabî said: "The Essence of God, overflowing, manifests the universe of *jabarût*, and this one, overflowing, manifests *malakût*; *malakût*, overflowing, will manifest *mulk*."

Yet, the Hindu tradition describes the cosmogony and the production of the Three Worlds in an ascending order: the corporeal world (*Bhûr*), the subtle world (*Bhuvar*), and the informal world (*Swar*), in accordance with the order followed by the three *gunas* when they became differentiated (*tamas – rajas – sattwa*). This cosmogony is from the point of view of Prakriti, and it evolves from inferior to superior; it is what we call the *prakritian* cosmogony. On the contrary, to limit or restrict *Âtmâ* with more and more conditions means a true "darkening" from *yang* to *yin*, and represents the cosmogony from the viewpoint of Purusha; it is what we call the *purushan* cosmogony.

This is the mystery of *Fiat Lux*: from a *prakritian* point of view, the light rises from darkness (Vivaswat), the cosmos (order) from chaos, *yang* comes after *yin*, *sattwa* after *tamas*, *Swar* after *Bûr*; from a *purushan* point of view, the pure and blinding light is mutilated and crippled, it is veiled and coloured, disabled and diluted, conditioned and limited, and so the states of manifestations are produced as its "conditions."

It is well-known that all the genuine traditions transmit the same essential lore. René Guénon had no respite in stressing in his works this fundamental truth. Even if, sometimes, the garments are different, the methods are different, and the words or signs are different, the sacred kernel of the primordial Tradition is one and the same and recognizable in all various

---

[1] There is another dragon, called the Omniform, Vishvarûpa, the son of Twashtri. Agni is also the "omniform light" (*jyotir asi vishvarûpam*), and so is the Sun. The omniform light, like Mârttânda, is crippled in order to produce the *Fiat Lux*.

secondary traditions. With this in mind, we should admit that the Far-Eastern tradition transmits no different knowledge, even though its appearance is so dissimilar to others (the hexagrams, for example, seem to be very unusual in comparison to other traditional scriptures).

The Chinese tradition, transmitted over the ages, describes the legendary emperor Dijun one-footed, with a bird head, and wearing horns. From what we said above, Dijun's look perfectly matches the symbolism discussed here. The one-footed Dijun was considered to be *Manu*, the Lord of the cycle, the founder of various countries and nations; his descendants have taught mankind all the crafts, music and dance, a typical gesture at the beginning of a cycle. Concerning the symbolism of the "one-footed" we will elaborate in the next chapter, but we understand that Dijun is depicted as a dragon and axis of the cycle. Dijun had three wives: one gave birth to the people characterized by one head and three bodies (an allusion to the one Being and the Three Worlds)[1]; the second one, the solar goddess, with the Sweet Waters as residence, gave birth to ten boys – ten suns; the third wife, the moon goddess, gave birth to twelve girls – twelve months (moons).

Evidently, the ten suns are equivalent to the Adityas of the Hindu tradition. In one version, Diku's second wife, an extraordinary woman who did not walk but float, riding the clouds, had a dream where she was swallowing the sun and each time she gave birth to a son, in total eight sons – eight suns. Diku is another name for Dijun, and we see, as in the Hindu tale, the number of suns varies, depending on the viewpoint with respect to the cyclic data.

The ten (or eight) suns had as residence the "Sun Valley," in fact an ocean (symbolizing the Abyss),[2] where the suns often took a bath and where, in the middle, the huge tree *fusang* (*Axis Mundi*) grew up, nine suns finding rest on its lower branches, the tenth having its retreat on a top branch; the tree is the

---

[1] The triad has many applications in the Chinese tradition, starting with the *Yi Jing* and with the ancient ideograms.

[2] We note the equivalence valley – ocean.

supreme solstice. The suns followed a well established order: when one was coming back to the tree, another sun would leave, crossing the sky and covering a defined path, and so humankind saw always only one sun.[1] In the time of Yao's reign, the ten suns broke the natural order and decided to cross the sky together, following various paths, and overflowing the world with a blinding light and burning the earth with their power, causing fires and turmoil.[2]

The Chinese tradition describes here the Dragon with ten heads as supreme Principle, as the Light of the superior Darkness, a light that cannot exist in manifestation, because the manifestation cannot exist under such an omnipotent and pure light. This light has to be crippled, to become a mutilated and a lame light, which means that the dragon has to be beheaded, and the last head will become the sun, the one sun to shine on the sky. The divine emperor Dijun sent to the dying earth an *avatâra*, having the appearance of a master archer, called Yi; the hero will kill with his arrows nine suns, leaving in the sky just one, much less powerful; with each sun's death, a golden *lame* crow will fall to the earth. The *purushan* cosmogony is expressed here in a very precise manner.[3]

---

[1] This sun was for them Mârttânda. The sunrise was announced by three dawns: *chenming*, "the coming of the dawns," when the sun takes a bath and then climbs the tree; *feiming*, "the early aurora," when the sun is on the top of the tree and starts its journey; *danming*, "the full aurora."

[2] The Lithuanian traditional data contain a poem about the morning star (the sun's daughter), ready to get married, but the thunderbolt struck down the holm oak and the tree's blood soiled the maiden's dress; she had to purify her dress at a lake with *nine* rivers, in a garden with *nine* roses, and she will wear the white purified dress on "this day of rejoicing when nine suns will be shining" (Hugo de Larish, *La tradition lithuanienne dans les chansons populaires*, Études Traditionnelles, no. 236-237-238, 1939, pp. 336-337). The holm oak symbolizes *Axis Mundi* and the thunderbolt is the Principle's Activity at the end of times (it is comparable to the sixteenth card of the Tarot, "the Lightning-struck Tower"); we note the Wedding and the nine suns shining together in non-manifestation.

[3] Zhuang Zi interpreted the legend of the ten suns, considering the supreme Light above the light of the suns. "Dao that is displayed is not Dao. Words that are argumentative do not reach the point. (…) Therefore the knowledge that stops at what it does not know is the greatest. Who knows the argument

The Cosmogony

Some traditional data, dressed in Christian garments of the Orthodox Church, present Saint Elijah with his fiery chariot as the Lord of thunders.[1] Saint Elijah is described either lame or with a paralized hand, or blind of one eye; he was crippled on purpose, because he was too powerful and his thunders and lightnings were destroying the world. Saint Elijah's mutilation makes possible the existence of the world.[2]

This crippling is the "corporealization" of the cosmogonic act, symbolizing limitation, definition, and measurement, Saint Elijah being confined in order to tame his power and blinding light.[3] But the crippling is also an allusion to the primordial non-duality, Saint Elijah representing the supreme and *principial* Dragon, without legs, without hands, even without eyes.[4]

Hephaestus was another famous cripple. He is related to Saint Elijah, since he is the craftsman who manufactured Zeus' thunderbolts. Hephaestus, like Mârttânda, is an aspect of the eternal Avatâra; he is the son of the Virgin, Hesiod stressing

---

that needs no words, and the Way that is not to be trodden? He who is able to know this has what is called 'The Heavenly Treasure-house.' He may pour into it without its being filled; he may pour from it without its being exhausted; and all the while he does not know whence (the supply) comes. This is what is called 'The Store of Light.' The sage possesses the comprehensive enlightenment, which illuminates the whole without differentiating the details. It is this Light, superior to the ten suns, which in the past Shun praised to old Yao" (*Zhuang-zi*, 2, 7/E).

[1] The Apostles John and James are the sons of Thunder; John governs the esoteric path of knowledge, and James the initiatory path of crafts.

[2] Ananda K. Coomaraswamy described a similar scenario, in the Hindu tradition: at the beginning, Prajâpati was alone and he wanted to become multiple. He breathed out Agni from his mouth, like a dragon blowing fire; but it was a devastating fire, like Saint Elijah's, and the earth was "bald," without vegetation. The fire needed to be tamed and its power diminished, and *soma* was poured into the fire, a sacrifice that permitted the plants to grow and the sun to rise.

[3] In the Greek mythology, when Zeus displayed all his power of light, fire and thunders, Semele died, transformed into ashes; Semele, a common human, could not stand the *principial* light, and neither could the world exist, but by crippling this light.

[4] Even the sacrificial cutting in pieces of the Universal Man is nothing else but a mutilation, a *purushan* cosmogony.

that Hera conceived him "without love embracement."[1] Hephaestus is thrown from heaven and the fall makes him a cripple; or, because he was born disabled (in both legs), he was thrown down from the gods' residence. He found shelter in a submarine cave, where he hid for nine years; he appears to be a hidden sun, like Mârttânda.[2] As Mârttânda is thrown down into the world, so Hephaestus is crippled and thrown into the world; his coming into sight after hiding constitutes an act equivalent to the birth of the thunderbolt within the earth (as the *Yi Jing* stated it), and represents *Fiat Lux*, the cosmogonic, but also *avatâric*, act.[3]

There is here a knot we must untie. The older brothers have mutilated Mârttânda, but they also "formed" him, endowing him with legs. What takes place is a "converse crippling," a *Fiat Lux*; the dragon without feet (*apâd*) is mutilated and deformed

---

[1] Hera is, like Aditi, the divine cow (Homer called her "with cow-like eyes," βοωπιζ). Hera, the queen of the gods, had only two children, two boys: Ares (the god of war) and Hephaestus. By comparing them with Shiva's sons, Ganesha and Skanda, Hephaestus seems to correspond to Ganesha (Ganesha is often represented as a deformed figure, or even unformed, like Mârttânda before mutilation).

[2] This is a good example to show that the *purushan* and *prakritian* cosmogonies are, in fact, one and the same. In some traditional tales, the dragon steals the sun, the moon and the stars, and hides them; their liberation means *Fiat Lux*.

[3] The thunderbolt hidden within the earth, a symbolic image found in the *Yi Jing*, brings us to another symbol, from Greek mythology. The Cyclopes, Hesiod affirmed, were the children of the *principial* dyad, Uranus and Gaea (Heaven and Earth); they were: Βροντηζ, "the thunder," Στεροπηζ, "the lightning," and Αργηζ, "the brightness," suggesting the lights of the Three Worlds, their central eye (the Cyclopes were one-eyed) referring to spiritual vision, but also to *principial* mutilation. Uranus chained his sons in a subterranean cave: it is the descending of the *principial* light into the Center of the World as hidden sun, from which the *Fiat Lux* will burst out as light and sound. As Guénon showed, there is a strong relation between sound and light described, for example, by the words *Verbum*, *Lux* and *Vita*, found in St. John's Gospel, and it is not difficult to notice a correspondence with the three Cyclopes (*Verbum* is the thunder, *Lux* is the lightning, and *Vita* is the brightness). The Cyclopes became Hephaestus' helpers, manufacturing Zeus' thunderbolts. We add that Saturnus, another son of Uranus, was described with chained legs or even one-footed.

The Cosmogony

in order to be provided with feet, and undoubtedly Hephaestus
and Saint Elijah's limping, in itself, alludes to the Non-Being as
source of light and manifestation, because "to be lame,"
Coomaraswamy affirmed, is an euphemism for "to be without
feet," and without feet or without hands is only the primordial
and everlasting Dragon – the supreme Principle.

"The Yin and Yang reflected light on each other, covered
each other, and regulated each the other" (*Zhuang-zi*, 25, 11/J).
There is no partisan thinking with respect to Reality. There is
no biased cosmogony. There is no *Fiat Lux* only, but at the
same time *Fiat Lux* and *Fiat Umbra*. And even if, theoretically,
we understand or think that we grasped the meaning of
simultaneity, there is still a long, long way to the realization of
it.[1]

Being bestowed with feet signifies passing from non-
manifestation to manifestation, from non-action (*wu-wei*) to
action, from darkness to light, from potentiality to act; it means
to make actual the possibilities of manifestation, to "measure"
them; and this is precisely what Vishnu is doing when he
produces the Three Worlds by "measuring" them with his foot,
which marks three gigantic paces; and this is what the Sun is
doing by "measuring" the possibilities of manifestation with its
rays, which are its innumerable feet. It is, of course, *Fiat Lux*,
the *prakritian* cosmogony that occurs simultaneously with the
purushan cosmogony when the feet are crippled.[2]

---

[1] There is, today, a general opinion, influenced by the modern mentality, that
treating such topics as the cosmogony is obsolete and the energy should be
directed to tackling subjects of actuality, more positive and less abstract or
philosophical. We must stress that, from a traditional viewpoint, *cognosco* is
nasco, and no knowledge is knowledge without a conscious realization.

[2] René Guénon wrote: "The idea of measure is intimately related to that of
'order' (Sanskrit *rita*), regarding the production of the universal manifestation,
since, in accordance with the etymological significance of the Greek word
χοσμος, it is a production of 'order' from 'chaos'; the latter is undefined in a
Platonician sense, and the former is defined. This production is also
assimilated by all the traditions with an illumination (*Fiat Lux* of *Genesis*),
'chaos' being symbolically identified with *tenebras*, 'darkness': it is the
potentiality from which the manifestation is made actual, and here the
substantial face of the world, described as the tenebrous pole of existence, is

Dionysius the Areopagite described the non-manifestation as "super-luminous darkness" and Thomas Aquinas said that it is called "darkness" (*tenebras*) due to its "extreme luminosity," that is, "blinding luminosity"; "Cosi mi circonfulse *luce viva*;/ E lasciommi fasciato di tal *velo*/ Del suo fulgor, che nulla m'*appariva*."[1] *Fiat Lux* alludes to the inferior *tenebras*, to the infernal chaos (*post tenebras lux*), not to the supernal night, to the blinding light that has to be crippled. Consequently, the naissance of the feet as a symbol of the world's genesis means starting the World Wheel, making actual Prakriti's possibilities, in this case "the footless" being the *asura*, the Titan, the infernal dragon.

Ananda K. Coomaraswamy treated the *prakritian* cosmogony *in extenso*, stressing that *asuras* and *dêvas*, the Titans and the Angels, are *ab intra* identical, in accordance with the Supreme Identity (*tad êkam, sadasat*), expressed as *Sarpyâ vâ âdityâh*, "the serpents are the suns"; *ab extra* the serpents represent the anterior states (the former gods, parents of the present gods), the dark, tenebrous states, while the suns are the superior, luminous states (the gods). The passing from darkness to light occurs due to a sacrifice consumed in different ritual modes, either by beheading the serpent, or by throwing away the serpent skin, or by endowing the "dragon" with feet, in essence, *Fiat Lux*, the genesis of the world, signifying the passing from the anterior dark cycle to the new luminous one; the former emperor, who became at the end a dragon, was sacrificed and transformed into the new emperor – the sun rising from the

---

taken into consideration, while the essence is the luminous pole, because it is its influence that actually illuminates 'chaos' and extracts the 'cosmos'; and, on the other hand, all this is in accord with the various meanings implied by the Sanskrit word *srishti*, which designates the production of manifestation and which also contains the ideas of 'expression,' 'conception,' and 'luminous radiation.' The solar rays make the things appear by illumination, they make them visible, and we can say symbolically that they manifest them."

[1] Dante, *Paradiso*, XXX. 49. "Even as a sudden lightning that disperses/ The visual spirits, so that it deprives/ The eye of impress from the strongest objects,/ Thus round about me flashed a living light,/ And left me swathed around with such a veil/ Of its effulgence, that I nothing saw."

cave where the dragon concealed it (*ab intra* the sun being the dragon), similar with the rising of the Cyclopes. The Titan is a potential Angel, the Angel a Titan made actual, since the darkness *in actu* is light, and the cycle that dies contains *in potentia* the seed of the new cycle.

Often, making the new cycle actual is realized by beheading the dragon, and its head becomes the new sun. Coomaraswamy listed the heads of Namuci, Vritra and Makha, dragons beheaded by Indra, their heads being forced to rotate around heaven and earth (*dyâvâprithivî anuprâvartata*) – this is the sacrifice called *pravargya*. Vishnu, like Makha, is beheaded by his own bow and the head became our sun, while the rest of his body remained lying down on earth (*pravrij*). In the *Taittirîya Br.*, *pravargya* derives from *prâvartata*, ("to advance rotating"), but Coomaraswamy considered it more plausible, as in the *Satapatha Br.*, to derive it from *pravrij*, a word referring to the position of the body after the beheading and associated with the expression "to permit the blind to see and the lame to walk," which signifies "the completion of the sun's procession" (the sun being at the beginning *apad*, footless, and hiding in the darkness as a serpent, similar to Soma, who "because he was without feet, he was Ahi the dragon"[1]).

The dragon's body is used in a ritual Eucharist, the gods sharing and eating it, but this "mutilation" is without question, as in Mârttânda's case, a double cosmogony, a power diminishing and a foot-providing act. "From Purusha's head Heaven was extracted, from his feet the Earth" (*Purushasûkta*), and from Ymir's skull Heaven was crafted and from his flesh

---

[1] The ideogram for the newborn (*zi*) shows this one without feet; this ideogram means also a spiritual master (Wieger 233):

We see that, in fact, there is one foot or a dragon's tail; the three hairs are also significant (see our work *The Everlasting Sacred Kernel*, Rose-Cross Books, 2002, p. 38).

the Earth.[1] It represents, in other words, the mutilation of omniformity and the birth of feet, here Purusha and Ymir being the dragon "without feet and hands" (*apâd ahastah*). *Rig-Vêda* describes Agni as a dragon "without feet, without head, hiding his both ends," which illustrates precisely the definition "without beginning and without end" regarding the infinite Principle (Ananta, Ain Soph); when duality was named and the Dragon became Tian and Di, Heaven and Earth, the dragon's two extremities were made actual: this is the primordial mutilation, an equivalent of "anti-crippling" the one-footed into two-footed.

We have to be careful though. Truly infinite is only Infinity, that is, the supreme Principle as Aditi – Diti, as Brahma nirguna – Brahma saguna together; all the others are only substitutes for Infinity. Uroboros, the serpent biting its tail, is a well known symbol of the Hermetic tradition; but this one symbolizes only a limited cycle, since the reflection of infinity is the helix of manifestation with spires that have no beginning and no end, the end of one spire being the beginning of the next one. The reflection of infinity is perpetual change, the game without end of generation and corruption, of production and dissolution, or weaving and unweaving, so perfectly described in the *Yi Jing*. "The Year is in Sâman. (...) Year is endless (*ananta*), its ends (*antau*) are winter and spring; after this, the extremities of the string become united; the serpent remains coiled; like the necklace, so is the Song without end" (*Jaiminîya Up. Br.*); night and day's paths are "without end," Heaven and Earth's movements follow "endless ways" (*Rig-Vêda*).

There is a very subtle difference between non-duality and unity, and for this reason René Guénon sometimes made no visible distinction between non-manifestation and the informal manifestation. Similarly, there is a subtle difference between "without head, without feet" and "one-footed" or "with one head," which brings us to stress that only the immutable and

---

[1] Ymir was a primordial giant in the Norse mythology.

truly endless Head, the only one genuinely without ends,[1] has reality, the game played in the world being an illusion; the Sun "in fact never rises and never sets," but "rotates around itself."

Genesis (*jâtavidyâ*, *bhâvavritta*) represents the Dragon's slaying, making visible the two ends or "heads" (the head through beheading and the feet through their explication). Yet, simultaneously, the "reconstruction" of the "endless" (without "ends") Dragon takes place, by reuniting the parts of the chopped dragon, reuniting Heaven and Earth, Sun and Moon.[2] The sacrifice of Genesis is not complete unless "what was scattered is reunited,"[3] which implies a spiritual realization aiming at the resurrection of the dragon as the new emperor of the next cycle and Universal Man: it is the hidden meaning of Osiris' tale, of Zagreus' tale; it is what happened to *Dadhyanc Atharvan* when he regained his head; and it is Hephaestus and Mârttânda's return to heaven.

The double cosmogony, together with the double spiral of the Cosmos, Year, and Man, occur simultaneously and are reflected in a whirling succession, but in fact do not occur at all: it is incomprehensible.[4] To permit the human mind to grasp somehow what is impossible to understand in a rational, discursive way, in the Hindu tradition the Principle (even if unchangeable and immutable, without duality and immovable) is considered to act through his "energy" (*shakti*), which is feminine compared to him. Shakti is the divine Maiden, the lunar Virgin, Sophia, Helen of Troy, *Madonna Intelligenza*, Dante's Beatrice, target of the spiritual realization. Shakti is the

---

[1] To be "without beginning and without end" means to have the beginning and the end in non-manifestation. Though, the ideogram of Dao is composed of the two "ends," one-foot with three footprints on the left side, and a head with three hairs on the right side.

[2] In the Chinese tradition, Shen and Shang are Diku / Dijun's sons. Because they always fought each other, their father separated them, one becoming the morning star, Shang-xing, and the other the evening star, Shen-xing, and they never met again. *Gua* no. 12, Pi, illustrates this situation.

[3] This expression is well known in Masonry.

[4] A 15th Century Greek-Orthodox hermit, who lived nearby Constantinople, said that the coming of Antichrist started with the beginning of Christianity.

"dark cloud" of the Judaic tradition, the Black Virgin as celestial Queen who, due to the Principle's "non-active activity" (*wei wu-wei* of the Far-Eastern tradition), generates the spiritual influences. These influences descend upon Prakriti, representing the divine Activity of Purusha, and in consequence, Prakriti emerges from her indifference and produces the universal manifestation. Prakriti is Shakti's projection and the Black Virgin is, at the same time, Shakti and Prakriti.[1]

Guénon's statement requires a clarification, indispensable for the economy of the present work. René Guénon later wrote more thoroughly about an important subject, after Coomaraswamy published some articles regarding the symbolism of "the two nights." The article *Les deux nuits* was published in 1939 and, compared to what he wrote in 1937-1938, brought deeper teachings; here Guénon unveiled the symbolic correspondence between the three initiatory deaths (and the three rebirths) and the "three nights," related to the three levels: corporeal, psychical, and spiritual. Considering that "the night" was the phase of darkness needed to pass from one initiatory degree to another, or from a degree of the universal manifestation to another, Guénon underlined the essential significance of the two extreme "nights": one, understood as infernal darkness, as chaos; the other one, understood as supernal darkness (the super-luminous darkness of the non-manifestation), this second meaning being usually ignored. The night of chaos referred to the "material" indifference, as an inverted reflex of the *principial* indifference of the non-manifestation, of the supernal night. This night with its chaotic

---

[1] "Shakti is the maternal 'power,' 'the divine Activity.' Therefore, she is inherent to Brahma or to the supreme Principle; she is incomparable higher than Prakriti; Prakriti is, in fact, only a reflection of Shakti in the 'cosmologic' order. We note the inverted analogy: the supreme Activity is reflected in the pure passivity and the 'almightiness' of the Principle is reflected in the potentiality of materia prima. Shakti, as the divine 'art' abiding in the Principle, is identical to the 'Wisdom,' Sophia, and, in this case, she is the mother of Avatâra. Using the Western terminology, Shakti is *Natura naturans*, and Prakriti – *Natura naturata*, even though both are named Natura" (René Guénon, *Études sur l'hindouisme*, Éditions Traditionnelles, 1979, p. 102).

indifference, applied to the whole universal manifestation, is precisely that of Prakriti, the maternal pole identical to *materia prima* of the ancient cosmological doctrines of the Occident, signifying the state of pure potentiality, the reflected inverted image of the *principial* state of the non-manifested possibilities. Guénon presents the fundamental specification that the production of manifestation has to be seen in an ascending sense (from the maternal chaos towards cosmos and light, the *prakritian* cosmogony), as well as in a descending sense (from the super-luminous, paternal darkness, the *purushan* cosmogony).

René Guénon wrote: "The inferior sense of the darkness regards the cosmologic order [*prakritian*], while its superior sense refers to the truly metaphysical order; their relation – we may note – helps us to understand that the universal manifestation's origin and development have to be seen both in an ascendant and descendent sense. If this is the case, it means that the manifestation does not proceed only from Prakriti, when its whole development is a gradual transition from potentiality to act, which could be described as an ascendant process; but it proceeds in fact from both complementary poles of the Being, that is, from Purusha and Prakriti, and, with respect to Purusha, its development is a gradual separation, away from the Principle, which is a true fall. This consideration contains implicitly the answer to many apparent contradictions, especially with regard to the cosmic cycles, their evolvement being regulated by a combination of tendencies that correspond to two opposite or rather complementary 'movements.' (...) Hence, we could easily understand that there is no contradiction in considering the universal manifestation's point of departure or origin as the inferior darkness (*tenebra*) – on the one hand, and, on the other hand, in considering the traditional lore regarding the spirituality of the 'primordial state,' since the two things don't refer to the same viewpoint. (...) We have regarded the inferior sense of the darkness as a reflection of its superior sense, which is true from a point of view; but, at the same time, from another point of view, it is somehow the 'converse,' if we consider the word illustrating how the reverse and the obverse oppose each other like the two faces of the same thing; and this requires more explanations. The former viewpoint, which takes into account the reflection, refers, of course, to the manifestation and to any being situated in the domain of manifestation; but, with respect to the Principle, where the origin and the end of all things meet and are unified, we cannot talk anymore about reflection, because there truly is only one and the same thing, the manifestation's point of departure necessarily being also the point of arrival, in non-manifestation. From the viewpoint of the Principle, regarded in itself (if we are allowed to use such language), we cannot differentiate anymore the two aspects of this unique thing, because such a distinction is valid only with respect to the manifestation."[1]

This is a fundamental text. It clarifies why we have to present *Fiat Lux* as a "fall," without banishing though the *prakritian* perspective.

We are ready now to return to the four *guas* presented at the beginning of this chapter. In the Chinese tradition, the double cosmogony is announced already by the hierogamic exchange of attributes between Fu Xi and Niu Wa. The emperor carries the square, a symbol of Earth, and the empress the compass, a symbol of Heaven.

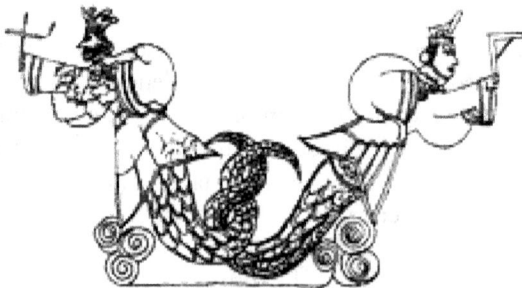

---

[1] René Guénon, *Initiation et réalisation spirituelle*, Éditions Traditionnelles, 1980, p. 241, *Les deux nuits.*

The Cosmogony

In the Far-Eastern tradition, the eight trigrams constitute a family.

☰	☷	☳	☵
Qian	Kun	Zhen	Kan

☶	☴	☲	☱
Gen	Xun	Li	Dui

Qian is the father, Kun the mother; Zhen is the eldest son, Kan the second son and Gen the youngest son; Xun is the eldest daughter, Li the second daughter and Dui the youngest daughter. As we have already affirmed, the trigrams have countless meanings, but one is most interesting for our topic. This family has to be associated with the data from the Hindu tradition, where Purusha is the father, Prakriti the mother, and the children are the three lights and the three *gunas*. The ideogram of Dao suggests, among many other meanings, this family: the one-foot is Prakriti, the three footprints are the three *gunas*, the head is Purusha, and the three hairs are the three lights.[1]

In a Wallachian fairy tale, the cosmogonic symbolism of the family is unveiled. The father, Purusha, is not perceptible, since in fairy tales and other initiatory and sacred tales the Principle is invisible and its activity is not a substantial one, but an "activity of presence." The mother is usually a virgin or a widow to stress the invisibility of the father. In this case, there is a mother-in-law (that is also the title of the fairy-tale), who represents Prakriti, and her three sons are the three *gunas* (Sanskrit *guna* is a masculine word); on the other hand, the three daughters-in-law symbolize the three lights of Purusha. The fairy-tale deserves

---

[1] In various traditions, the hair was the residence of *shakti*, the divine power; Samson's story is well known.

long commentaries, but for now we should confine ouselves in pointing out the similarity between this family and the family of the trigrams. There are some apparent differences, but in the traditional symbolism the wife is also a sister (see Fu Xi and Niu Wa, who are brother and sister, husband and wife), which makes the daughters-in-law also daughters, and mainly daughters of Purusha, of Heaven (Qian). We notice a *yin-yang* balance, the *purushan* influences being *yin* with reference to Purusha, and the *prakritian* influences being *yang* with respect to Prakriti. In other words, the hierogamic exchange, illustrated by the primordial pair Fu Xi and Niu Wa, is present in this fairy-tale as well.

Without any doubt, the cosmogony implies a separation of One in *yang* and *yin*, followed by a reunification based on a hierogamic exchange; however, this reunification is not the absolute wedding of non-duality, which occurs only in non-manifestation, but a reflection in manifestation characterized by the union of the masculine and feminine influences, while the two poles are separated in a cosmic divorce and placed at the two "ends" of *Axis Mundi*.[1]

Gua Pi, no. 12, illustrates this cosmic divorce, but we can consider this hexagram describing the primordial separation of One in Heaven and Earth.

This hexagram means "stagnation," the *Yi Jing* affirmed, and there is no union between Heaven and Earth, which produces the decline. What is above has no relation to what is below, and on earth confusion and disorder prevail. The division of One into two does not automatically bring the "order" (the Cosmos). When Heaven and Earth are disunited, life in nature stagnates

---

[1] It is the situation when the Sun is cursed to be forever separated from the Moon, and the morning star, Shang-xing, from the evening star, Shen-xing.

and there is no production of the ten thousand beings, since Dao of Man and the Great Triad are absent.

However, "chaos hides the seed of order" and this standstill does not last forever, but also it does not cease of its own accord and the right man (the elder son) is needed to end it. *Gua* Sui, no. 17, shows the simultaneous commencement of the *purushan* and *prakritian* cosmogonies, when the influences of the two poles start the hierogamic exchange, when the light of Purusha is born into the world (*avatarana*) and when the *guna* of Prakriti rises to cripple and shadow the celestial light.[1]

If we want to confine ourselves to a synthesis of the cosmogony, we have to consider not all the three sons and three daughters, but only the two "ends," that is, the eldest son and the youngest daughter.[2] *Gua* Sui is built of Dui (marsh) up and Zhen (thunderbolt) down, that is, of the youngest daughter up and the eldest son down.[3] The thunderbolt, Dao's Activity, comes down in the middle of the marsh – it is the first indication of cosmogony; it is the descending of the *avatâra* at Prakriti's bosom, inside the subterranean cave; it is Hephaestus and Mârttânda's forced fall. Heaven's influence comes down and Earth's influence goes up, unveiling the hierogamic exchange between the eldest son and the youngest daughter. The superior line accepting to take the inferior place describes

---

[1] In the Hindu tradition, an apparently surprising thing is the birth of Buddhi, the Intellect, the Great, and the Celestial Ray, as a production of Prakriti. Only considering this double movement and two-folded cosmogony as presented in the hexagrams do we fully understand why it is possible to have Buddhi as Prakriti's son.

[2] In the Chinese traditional society, the eldest son played a major role, as a substitute of the father.

[3] As Philastre explained, "the transformation of *gua* is a permutation of the traits." In the present case, *gua* Sui is obtained from *gua* Pi by substituting the first with the last trait.

the humbleness of the superior, consciously displayed, in front of the inferior; the noble, though *yang*, behaves as *yin* with respect to the common people, which generates satisfaction. The example given by Heaven is happily followed by Earth, and so, the differentiation of light is followed by the differentiation of *gunas*, the descending of the continuous line is followed by the ascending of the discontinuous line, and the *purushan* cosmogony is a role model for the *prakritian* cosmogony.

Let us also note the ideogram of *gua* Sui.

It includes a wall (three vertical bricks on the left side), a hand over a square (on the right side), and one foot tracing three prints (in the middle). If we regard the ideogram in comparison to the Hindu tradition, the three bricks, as well as the three footprints, allude to the cosmogony of The Three Worlds, the bricks suggesting the three lights; the one-foot is the symbol of Dao in manifestation.[1]

Gua Gui Mei (no. 54) is built, like *gua* Sui, of the eldest son and the youngest daughter's trigrams, but in this case the eldest son (Zhen, the thunderbolt) is up, and the youngest daughter (Dui, the marsh) is down.

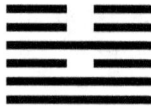

Now, the hierogamic exchange has developed, since two continuous lines are at the bottom, replacing two broken lines, which took the top positions, all these suggesting the differentiation of two lights and two *gunas* during the

---

[1] In Siam and Cambodia, there was a tradition regarding the king, who had to stand on one foot, near a tree (Granet, *La pensée chinoise*, p. 487).

cosmogonic process, compared to one light and one *guna* in *gua* Sui. The hexagram is usually deciphered as a symbol of marriage between the eldest son and the youngest daughter, who is not the main wife but a concubine, that is, not the feminine pole, but its influence.[1] The marriage of the young maiden depicts the great meaning of Heaven and Earth: "if heaven and earth don't unite, all the beings fail to come into existence," so the young maiden is "the beginning and the end of humanity." This affirmation in the *Yi Jing* alludes to the two ends of the dragon and the cosmogony (the Cosmos); it also suggests the indefinite helix of the cosmic cycles and of all the secondary cycles (the Year). The double cosmogony is a *hierogamos*, a sacred marriage, which is also the symbol of Man's spiritual realization (the thunderbolt moving above the marsh, like the Holy Spirit above the Waters).

The hexagram Gui Mei includes also a reference to the one-footed and one-eyed symbolism, the commentaries considering the youngest daughter as one-footed or lame and with weak eyes or one-eyed; yet, though lame, the young girl can still walk, though almost blind, she can still see. If, on the one hand, the young bride is a concubine, an influence of Prakriti, on the other hand (and this is her mysterious function), she is an image of the Principle, one-footed and one-eyed, which includes the idea of a *purushan* cosmogony (mutilating the light).

Zhu Xi, in his commentary called "the primitive sense," affirmed that *gua* Tai derives from *gua* Gui Mei, the third trait changing place with the fourth one. *Gua* Tai, no. 11, is the accomplishment of this very subtle and complicated cosmogony. We can see the completion of the hierogamic exchange: Earth up and Heaven down, with Niu Wa holding the compass and Fu Xi the square. The median or "nuclear" trigrams are Zhen, the thunderbolt and eldest son, and Dui, the marsh and youngest daughter. They are in the middle and

---

[1] The commentary said: "The moon that is nearly full." The old Chinese ritual requires the union between king and queen to take place in a night with full moon (Marcel Granet, *La religion des chinois*, Payot, 1980, p. 40). The 21st degree of the Scottish Rite is connected to the full moon.

mingled together, which underlines the perfect union and harmony, and the lack of any sectarianism.

The ten thousand beings are now able to be born. The hexagram means Peace (the symbol of the Center of the World), when heaven seems to be present on earth, and everything follows the laws of harmony and order. The points of the compass mark the cosmogony, and we see the light (the three continuous lines) in an inferior position, indicating *Fiat Lux*, and the darkness (the three broken lines) in a superior position, indicating *Fiat Umbra*.

FIVE

THE PRINCIPLE'S TRACES

THE STUDY OF various Chinese pictograms on the bones of horned cattle and turtle shells concluded that Dao, the Principle (which has different names and is the father of the suns), is depicted lame, with a bird's head and horns. "Jun is identical to Dao"; "Kui is the same as Jun"; "Kui is one-footed"; "Kui has horns." We already know that Fu Xi was described as having a dragon's tail and horns, and the legendary emperor Dijun was one-footed, with a bird's head, and wearing horns.

The symbolism of the one-footed dragon has,[1] as all the fundamental symbols, indefinite meanings and complicated significances.[2]

The ideogram for lameness is (Wieger 160, 812):

---

[1] Gilis said in a note: "In the Hindu tradition, *aja-ekapâda*, "the unborn one-footed," with both a polar and solar symbolism, is assimilated by some hymns to a "dragon coming from the abyss," which has to be viewed as standing vertically on his tail. As Pierre Grison affirmed, a similar assimilation exists in China, where the one-footed is 'like a dragon.'" (Charles-André Gilis, *Le Maître de l'Or*, Vers la Tradition, no. 86, 2001-2002, p. 15). Pierre Grison stated: "The trigram Zhen ('quake, shock'), which corresponds to a thunderbolt, has also the meaning of cosmic fecundity, and corresponds to the dragon" (*Notes sur le jade*, Études Traditionnelles, no. 382, 1964, p. 66).

[2] See also J. Lavier, *Les Secrets du Yi king*, Sand, 1984, p. 19.

Even though the bent leg is thought to suggest an effort, we must consider the metaphysical meaning of the "one-footed." Moreover, the non-manifestation *wu* has an ideogram where we observe the same lameness:

There is one *gua*, no. 39, which helps us to understand the double meaning of the "one-footed."

Gua Jian is called "obstruction" or "difficulty"; "Obstruction means difficulty," the commentary said. The Jian ideogram illustrates "lameness:" a man with a wounded foot rests in a shelter.

From a worldly viewpoint, the one-footed man represents difficulty; he needs to make an effort to advance and overcome the obstruction. From a metaphysical perspective, the difficulty requires effort and the effort is an image of heavenly pure activity. Moreover, the effort required from the one-footed man is an inner effort, a spiritual one. Therefore, the commentaries on *gua* Jian affirmed that, "in difficult times, sages and saints are needed; only then the difficulties of the universe are overcome." "A great man is needed, and then the situation is remedied." "The difficulties of the universe are not easily surmounted; without being a sage or a saint it is impossible." "The veritable man returns from outwards to inwards and works to improve his virtues." This great man is the "one-footed."

As we affirmed previously, even though *Âtmâ* is said to have four "conditions," four "states," *Âtmâ* in itself is non-conditioned, and so are Purusha and Prakriti. The Dragon is not different: it stays immutable and unchanged,[1] and its mutilation (signifying the Genesis of the World) is only relative and apparent, since the Dragon was and will be forever the One-Footed, Saint Elijah's disablement and Hephaestus' crippling unveiling what was already there *ab initio*.

Sarpyâ vâ âdityâh, "the serpents are the suns" (*Pancavimsha Brâhmana*, XXV, 15, 4), and even though *Fiat Lux* means the rising of the sun from the dark serpent's skin and the birth of many feet, in the Hindu tradition, the Sun is especially called *êkapad*, "one-footed," and that is how the pure Being, the primordial and eternal One has to be. The visible foot, *Axis Mundi*, explains the invisible Foot, and then, the ten thousand feet (*sahashrapâdam*) explain the visible one-foot. It is the way of the Tradition into the World and therefore of the *Yi Jing*. At the beginning, the *guas* did not need any explanations; then, with the decadence of the cycle, the commentaries were required.

In Sanskrit, *ekapâda* means "one-footed" and represents the *Axis Mundi* as celestial Ray (or as the "seventh Ray") of the spiritual Sun. Before manifesting itself, the supreme Principle (Hindu *Brahma nirguna*, Brahma without qualifications and attributes) is a Dragon without eyes or feet, without traces, a turtle retreated inside its shell, the peacock with its tail folded. Producing the universal manifestation (the whole Existence), the Principle opens its eyes and forms one foot, the axis of the universe, with this foot it jumps (like Vishnu) three steps, manifesting The Three Worlds (corporeal, subtle and angelic), and so producing (and unveiling) Its "traces." The *Axis Mundi* – the solar Ray, the unique foot – producing the Existence,

---

[1] The serpent, the frog, and the turtle have the ability to remain immovable for a long time, which makes them perfect symbols for the Principle.

multiplies itself into "one thousand feet" (Sanskrit *sahashrapâda*), i. e., a multiplicity of solar rays, reflecting the unique Ray.[1]

Ekapâda, like Brahma, is neutral. *Ekapâda* is father and mother, and son and daughter, and friend and fiend, and dragon and hero, and brother and sister, and husband and wife, and alive and dead, and one and multiple. That is why the "feet," the things existing in the Cosmos, are explanations of *ekapâda* and symbolic assistants in the quest for the supreme Truth.

However, we must not forget for a moment the "ten thousand feet" of any genuine symbol. To be lame could be a reference to the *principial* and non-dual Dragon, could symbolize the birth of the world – an imperfect and lame world, could represent the contemplative knowledge (*wu-wei*), and could signal the descent of the *avatâra*.[2]

Between *ekapâda* and *sahashrapâda* there is a "broker," archetype of the multiplicity, the "two-footed" (*dwapâda*), by definition the World being the domain of duality (in the Cosmos, all the couples coexist: good-bad, warm-cold, etc.). The primordial duality represents the two fundamental principles called Heaven and Earth, but the "two feet" could express, from a spiritual point of view, the immortal and the mortal "soul," the sacred kernel and the profane skin, light and shadow. Therefore, in some initiatory rituals the neophyte has one foot uncovered (the axis of the universe, the naked truth)

---

[1] See Ananda K. Coomaraswamy, *La doctrine du sacrifice*, Dervy-Livres, 1978, p. 47. See also Coom., *Metaphysics*, p. 391.

[2] Some initiatory organizations expressly specified the impossibility of a lame or blind candidate being initiated, since such an individual could not perform properly the required rites. "And David said on that day, Whosoever getteth up to the gutter, and smiteth the Jebusites, and the lame and the blind that are hated of David's soul, he shall be chief and captain. Wherefore they said, The blind and the lame shall not come into the house" (*2 Kings*, 5:8). It is said that Confucius' father had a lame son and he remarried (against the custom) and so Confucius was born and became the head of the family's rites, since a lame individual could not perform the required operations of the ritual. In the Chinese family, the eldest son had to be "without lesions, mutilations or cuts" (Granet, *La religion*, pp. 76, 86). On the other hand, from a spiritual perspective, "when you have the legs smashed, God offers you wings" (as Djalâl al-Dîn Rûmî said).

and the other one covered (the world): it is another way to represent the limping, since in fact, there is only One Foot, immutable in non-manifestation, but generating footprints and traces in manifestation (Sanskr. *padavî*, Lat. *vestigium pedis*).[1]

Aditi is the nude Perfection, Diti is the veiled one; they are the twin mothers of Agni: "one is tenebrous (*krishnam*), the other one shines"; the sisters are equivalent to the pair Night and Day, the two Dawns, "the black day and the white day," *ahash ca krishnam ahar arjunam ca* (*Rig-Vêda*). From a *prakritian* perspective, the elder sister, the Night, is the inferior darkness; the night is "the maiden without feet born before the beings with feet," and the day is the maiden who escaped the tenebrous garment and changed from barren into fertile woman.

In the *Mahâbhârata*, the Sun is described as one-footed, and the foot appears alternately tenebrous and bright. Varuna crosses the canopy of heaven with one foot, and this foot is gold-like in the morning and copper-like in the evening (*Rig-Vêda*, V, 62), that is, bright and tenebrous; from a *prakritian* viewpoint, the golden foot is the finite domain (*ditim*), while the copper foot is the infinite domain (*aditim*). The primordial Purusha is described in the *Rig-Vêda* as having one thousand heads, one thousand eyes and one thousand feet[2]; Coomaraswamy explained that we have to understand this multiplicity rather *in potentia*, in a latent state, since the dragon is omniform.

---

[1] An ancient ideogram shows the veneration of one footprint in a temple (Wieger 375):

[2] Hecatoncheires, Cyclopes' brothers, had "one hundred arms" and "fifty heads."

In the Far-Eastern tradition, Dao is the One-Footed. The spirit of the sun is a lame golden crow; Huangdi's chariot driver was the fabulous one-footed bird *bifang*.[1] Dijun is described as one-footed, with a bird's head and horns[2]; he corresponds to Manu of the cycle. The mythical emperors Diku and Shun are identical to Dijun, but we have to consider them rather as projections of the same regulating principle for different ages or cycles. Their sacred biographies are rich in symbolic data. Dijun's friends, for example, were three types of birds: imperial birds, phoenixes *luan* and phoenixes,[3] these birds ensuring the peace and harmony of the world. Diku had four wives, each one giving birth to an *avatâra*, a future emperor. The first wife, Jiangyuan, stepped into a gigantic footprint (a trace of the One-Footed Principle in manifestation[4]) and therefore she gave birth to Qi,[5] called "the abandoned one," "the thrown away one,"[6] because he was thrown away three times, like Mârttânda or Hephaestus; in the end Qi was rescued on birds' wings and become a founder of humankind, teaching men how to work the land.[7] Jiandi, Diku's second wife, had a younger sister,

---

[1] *Bifang* was similar to a crane. The crane, like a heron or stork, was an equivalent for the feathered serpent, and was also, in Daoism, the vehicle of the immortal sages. In the Norse mythology, Thor, the god of thunderbolts, had his fiery chariot drawn by goats, and one of the goats was one-footed or lame.

[2] We should keep always in mind the double sense of a symbol. It is said that the devil is horned and lame (as a consequence of falling from heaven).

[3] The three types of birds are related to the three lights.

[4] Maspero mentioned the manifestation of the "Lord of Dark Heaven," who appeared in front of Emperor Huizong as an enormous foot (Henri Maspero, *Le Taoisme et les religions chinoises*, Gallimard, 1971, p. 177).

[5] In another version, a maiden called Huaxushi stepped on the gigantic footprint, near the Thunder Marsh, and gave birth to Fu Xi; Fu Xi's father was considered in this case to be the God of the Thunderbolt.

[6] The ideogram *qi* represents two hands rejecting a newborn child (Wieger 235):

[7] When he died, Qi was buried at the bottom of *Axis Mundi* (the tree Jianmu).

Jianci, and their father had locked them in a jade tower, where only a nightingale could enter, leaving two eggs there; Jiandi swallowed the eggs and gave birth to Qi (we note the same name). Shun, who is often confused with Diku, was born miraculously from a blind father and a phoenix, without a mother. Shun's eyes had two pupils each, like Yao's phoenix; Shun, after an initiatory process, married Yao's two daughters.[1] These various data could be multiplied indefinitely, but each one should require a meditation, which is beyond our present purpose.

There is though, in Shun's story, a special aspect, on which we would like to elaborate. Diku had four wives, Dijun three and Shun two. The number of wives varies from one tale to another, but, besides the historical fact regarding the Chinese custom of having more than one wife (the so-called concubines),[2] there is also a much more important symbolic meaning. The wives reflect the one-and-only feminine principle with respect to different levels of reality. In the Hindu tradition, as René Guénon explained, Mâyâ-Shakti and Mâyâ-Prakriti are the two wives of the Principle; they are also the two mothers of the *avatâra* and of the universal manifestation. This duality is in accordance with Yin-Yang, with the two poles Heaven and Earth; yet this special symbolism is not about masculine and feminine principles, but about two sisters, a heavenly and a terrestrial one, the former being *yang* and "masculine" with respect to the latter. Shun's tale is in concert with this perspective, since Shun had two mothers, two sisters as wives, and two daughters. If we accept Shun as the equivalent of an *avatâra*, his two mothers should correspond to Shakti and Prakriti. His mother, who died after he was born, was

---

[1] Shun corresponds to Garuda, Indra's bird, and his brother, Xiang ("the elephant"), to Indra's elephant, Airâvata.

[2] "A nobleman marries two sisters. (...) A grand lord is allowed to have three and a king four groups of wives" (Granet, *La religion*, p. 36). There is a Chinese saying: "Heaven is one and Earth multiple."

considered almost a goddess, living in heaven,[1] while his step-mother was an infernal creature[2]; Shun's father was blind, a suggestion that he was the king-dragon of the old cycle. This duality is fundamental. Regardless of whether it is symbolized by twin brothers (like Shen and Shang, Diku's sons), by brother and sister (like Fu Xi and Niu Wa), or by twin sisters, the duality always aims at *yin* and *yang*, at heaven and earth, at immortality and mortality, at the two hemispheres of the World Egg.

The One-Foot is both golden (light) and copper-like (dark), naked and covered. When the hexagrams were traced, one continuous was drawn first, the One-Foot, the super-luminous Ray.[3] To express the universal manifestation, this one trait had to be duplicated, and two twin traits were born, but no twins are identical: one is a boy, the other one a girl, or one is immortal, the other one mortal, or one is luminous and the other one tenebrous, one *yang* and the other one *yin*; also, to produce the manifestation, it is necessary to mutilate the super-luminous light, to cripple the continuous line, and so, the second trait is a broken one. The continuous trait is equivalent to Shakti and the broken trait to Prakriti; the first trait is Shun's celestial mother, the second one – his wicked stepmother.

Twashtri, "the carpenter," was in the Hindu tradition the Great Architect of the Universe. He decided to marry off his celestial daughter Sharanyû or Sanjnâna,[4] and he gave her Mârttânda (or Vivaswat) for a husband: it was the sacred

---

[1] Therefore, in some versions, Shun's mother was considered to be a phoenix.
[2] There are many fairy-tales, belonging to different traditions, where the superior and inferior mothers are present.
[3] In the traditional art of painting, the empty paper symbolizes the primordial Void; the drawing of the first trait represents a cosmogony. Moreover, the Chinese traditional artist understood the Unique Trait of his brush as Dao.
[4] For this story, we follow Rig-Vêda, Vishnu-Purâna and Mârkandeya-Purâna.

wedding of the Sun and the Dawn. "Sanjnâ, Twashtri's daughter, was the Sun's wife. She gave him children, called Manu, Yama and Yamî"; "Twashtri's noble daughter, named Sanjnâ, was Mârttânda's wife, and she gave birth to Manu, who, as Vivaswat's son, was called Vaivaswata. Sanjnâ used to close her eyes when the Sun was looking at her. Her husband cursed her and she gave birth to Yama, a son, and to the changeable river Yamunâ, a daughter." In Sanskrit *yama* means "twin," and Yama – Yamî, the primordial pair, are literally The Twins. It seems reasonable to see the reflection of the One-Foot (*êkapad*) in the world, first the dyad (*dwâpada*), then the multiplicity (*sahashrapâdam*), as a production of twins. Yama and Yamî are twins, but also husband and wife, like Fu Xi and Niu Wa, but in the *principial* order. On the other hand, Manu and Yama are also twin brothers, the first representing the cosmic Intelligence that reflects the pure spiritual Light and promulgates the Law, the second being Dharma-râja, the King of Justice.

But Sanjnâ also has a twin sister, a mortal and finite being,[1] who generates the Platonic shadows, who weaves the veils that will filter the blinding light and will cripple it, and Mârttânda, the Sun, will become less powerful in order to permit the universal manifestation to become.[2] "Because she could not stand the Sun's burning fire (*tejas*), Sanjnâ hired Chhâyâ (Sanskr. *chhâyâ* means "shadow, copy") to replace her and she retreated into the forest to follow an ascetic life (*tapas*). The Sun confused Chhâyâ with Sanjnâ and the shadow-wife gave birth to three more children: Shanaishchara, another Manu, and a girl, Tapatî."

Sanjnâ is the continuous trait, and Chhâyâ the broken trait. The former is *yang*, the celestial mother; the latter is *yin*, the terrestrial mother. Similarly, Buddha had two mothers and

---

[1] We find the eternal pair Aditi – Diti.

[2] We should mention that, as reflections in our social life of the supernal laws, many punishments, inscribed in the codes of laws, implied mutilations, which deprived the criminals of their powers. It is known that any capital punishment is a reflection of a *principial* and initiatory death.

Moses had two mothers too[1]; Abraham had two wives, Sarah and Agar, and the twelve Jewish tribes had two double mothers.

In a way, Chhâyâ, or the "illusory Sanjnâ," is similar to Shun's step-mother, since she does not care about Sanjnâ's children[2]; as a result of her altercation with Yama, Chhâyâ curses him to lose a foot, and Yama, like Saturn, becomes the one-footed! Yet this mutilation makes Yama and Manu complain to their father, unveiling the truth that Chhâyâ is not the real wife, the real mother. The Sun forces the shadow-wife to confess, and then, through meditation (*samâdhi*), he discovers the place where Sanjnâ was hiding in the form of a mare: "Fearing the Sun's burning heat (*tâpa*) and his fire (*tejas*), she took the form of a mare (*vadavâ*) and started to practice austerities (*tapas*)." The Sun, changed in a horse, finds Sanjnâ, and from their union the Ashwins and a girl Revantâ will be born.[3]

Qian Shi Bao made the following comment: "Among those that cross the heaven, nothing could be compared to the dragon; among those that cross the earth, the horse has no equal. Therefore, *gua* Kun has the mare as symbol"; "the mare means what is passive, obedient, and what walks with an equivalent energy." In the Hindu tradition, the horse is the symbol for the Universal Man and "the horse sacrifice" is a *Fiat Lux*. In the *Rig-Vêda*, book I, hymn no. 163 is called "The Horse;" it is said: "O Vasus, from out of the Sun you fashioned forth the Horse. Yama are you, O, Horse, you are Aditya. They say you have three bonds in Heaven that hold you.[4] Three bonds, they say, you have in heaven that bind you, three in the waters, three within the ocean."[5]

---

[1] He had actually three "mothers."
[2] Snow-White's stepmother hides the same symbolism. There are other fairy-tales, where a wicked servant, who will persecute the children, replaces the genuine wife.
[3] We already know the significance of the mare as Passive Perfection and of the horse as Active Perfection; also, we may remember *ashwamedha* mentioned in the previous chapter.
[4] The three bonds are the three continuous traits of the *Yi Jing*.
[5] The three bonds in the water are the discontinuous traits.

Heaven is the horse, Earth is the mare, but to have the Great Triad completed, Man is needed. In this case, Man is the Twins, the Ashwins. Man is necessarily implicated in the spiritual process; hence the Ashwins are presented as pupils of the sage Dadhyanc (the one with a horse head), who taught them the esoteric doctrine (*ashnâpinaddham madhu*). The Ashwins could be compared to Christ's two natures and, of course, to the *Yi Jing*'s two traits, the continuous and the broken one. They have a redeeming and illuminating function, and like Christ, they heal the blind (Rjrâsva) and the lame (Vispalâ); they also resurrected Rebha, who was lying torn into pieces. This last deed, associated with the fact that "they change the world into a shining form, like the bright sky" (*Rig-Vêda*, IV, 45) is an equivalent to the Chinese initiatory motto: "Destroy the darkness (*jing*) and restore the light (*ming*)," and to the Masonic task of spreading the light and gathering what was scattered.[1]

The birth of the Ashwins did not solve Sanjnâ's problem, since she still "feared the Sun's burning heat and fire"; "to diminish the Sun's ardent blaze, Twashtri forced him under his mill wheel (*chakra*) and disabled him, shadowing a part of his brightness, until there remained only one eight of his brightness, because more than that was not bearable. (...) Celebrated by gods and divine sages, this mass of incorruptible light himself gave up his brightness. Earth was produced from that part of his brightness called *rik*, Atmosphere from that one identical to *yajur*, and Heaven from that identical to *saman*.[2] (...) From now on the Sun displays only the sixteenth part of his brightness."

Gua no. 36, Ming Yi, illustrates what the Hindu tradition narrated with regard to Vivaswat.

---

[1] Restoring Rebha, Osiris, Prajâpati or Purusha means gathering what was scattered. About the Chinese motto and Masonic formula ("répandre la lumière et rassembler ce qui est épars"), see René Guénon, *La Grande Triade*, Gallimard, 1980, p. 140, and René Guénon, *Symboles fondamentaux de la Science sacrée*, Gallimard, 1980, p. 301.

[2] We observe here the *purushan* cosmogony: the three lights (considered the mutilated parts of the Sun) have produced The Three Worlds.

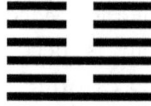

The hexagram Ming Yi is called "Darkening of the Light," or "Wounded bird," both appellations clearly suggesting the mutilation of the Sun.

The ideogram of this *gua* shows the moon lighting a window (Ming),[1] and an archer (Yi). Of course, the archer is Yi, the hero who killed nine of the ten suns, saving the world and disabling the blinding and burning super-luminous Light, which explains the name of the *gua*: "Darkening the Light"; also, each time Yi shot a sun, a crippled golden crow fell to earth, and the other name "Wounded bird" refers to this fact. The hexagram is built of Kun (earth) up and Li (fire) down, describing another well-known symbolic aspect – the hiding of Hephaestus and Mârttânda in the subterranean cave, or, what many fairy-tales transmit, the abduction of the sun and moon by the infernal

---

[1] The association sun – moon represents the modern ideogram for light (*ming*), but this association occurs only in non-manifestation, where the sun and moon can meet again, hence this ideogram should refer to the super-luminous Light. The ancient ideogram for *ming* represented precisely this association sun – moon, which was, in a more recent epoch, replaced with the pair window – moon (see Jacques Lionnet, *Notes sur le caractère "Ming"*, Études Traditionnelles, no. 374, 1962, p. 255); in this still old ideogram of *gua* Ming Yi, the light is crippled, since only the moon is present, and the moon is a shadow (*yin*) in comparison to the sun (*yang*). We should note that, as it was normal to compare the sun and the moon with eyes, so it was to compare them with windows (there is a well-known proverb saying that "the eye is the soul's window").

132

dragon (Titan, *asura*). The commentary of this *gua* also mentions "darkening of the light injures him in the left thigh," which indicates a crippling and a lame man.[1] However, from a "familial" point of view, Ming Yi is built of Mother up and the middle (second) daughter down; we should see here an equivalent to the pair Sanjnâ – Chhâyâ,[2] the relation mother-daughter being secondary.[3]

Nevertheless, we must not overlook that, even though crippled and his light used to produce The Three Worlds, the Sun remains in reality immutable and super-luminous. Even though Mârttânda was thrown down as a common mortal, he is the same as the immortal Sun of the supernal darkness. "At the beginning, the Sun was down here; the gods took him into the celestial world" (*Maitrâneya Samhitâ*); "arrived in this world, the Sun feared death, since this world is associated with death; He sang hymns, praising Agni, and Agni took him back into the celestial world" (*Taittirîya Samhitâ*). The Sun returns to Heaven, albeit he never left Heaven, and, only from a finite perspective, the Sun is duplicated and replaced with a pair of twins, immortal and mortal,[4] because the individual mind does not grasp easily the full significance of the endless continuous trait, and even less the essential and abyssal meaning of the void surrounding the trait, which forced the birth of a second line,

---

[1] "And Jacob was left alone; and there wrestled a man with him until the breaking of the day. And when he saw that he prevailed not against him, he touched the hollow of his thigh; and the hollow of Jacob's thigh was out of joint, as he wrestled with him. (...) And Jacob called the name of the place Penuel: for I have seen God face to face, and my life is preserved. And as he passed over Penuel the sun rose upon him, and he halted upon his thigh" (*Genesis* 32:24-31).

[2] We may assume that the central daughter (Li, the light) is Sanjnâ, and then the Mother hides her, having as result the shadow Chhâyâ.

[3] Dante said in *Convivio*, III, 12.14: "Oh nobilissimo ed eccellentissimo cuore che ne la sposa de lo Imperadore del cielo s'intende, e non solamente sposa, ma suora e figlia dilettissima!," praising "the celestial emperor's wife, and not only wife, but also sister and much beloved daughter."

[4] "The Immortal born, the brother of the mortal" (*Rig-Vêda*, I, 164, 38).

the shadow, the broken trait, and then of the trigrams, and, eventually, of the hexagrams.[1]

Consequently, the duplication of the *Yi Jing*'s fundamental trait is equivalent not only to doubling the mother or wife, but also to the Sun's duplication, which is explicitly told in the *Mahâbhârata*.[2] The maiden Kuntî, using Shiva's gift (a ritual prayer), asked the Sun to descend to her, and this one is forced to obey, appearing in front of the virgin, beautiful and miraculous, "honey-yellow"; but his brightness was reduced to half,[3] since "by his wizardry he had split himself in two, and thus came there and went on shining in the sky." The half-sun that came down was the mortal Mârttânda, the broken trait; the half-sun that remained in heaven was the immortal Mârttânda, the continuous trait.[4]

---

[1] As René Guénon explained, the trigram is a symbol of the Great Triad: "the superior trait represents Heaven, the median trait represents Man, and the inferior trait Earth"; with regard to the hexagrams, "the two trigrams superimposed correspond entirely to Heaven and Earth; the median term is not visible, but it is the hexagram itself that, uniting the celestial and terrestrial influences, expresses the 'mediator' function [of Man]" (*La Grande Triade*, p. 123). Even if *gua* Pi illustrates the divorce between Heaven and Earth (from the viewpoint of the universal manifestation), it describes what Guénon said; we also could consider the upper *digram* as representing Heaven, the inferior *digram* as representing Earth and the nuclear *digram* symbolizing Man (who unites the celestial and terrestrial influences).

[2] *Vanaparvan*, The Book of the Forest, The Robbing of the Earrings.
[3] Kuntî could not survive in front of a "full-size" Sun, only a crippled one, a half-sun, was accessible to her.
[4] From the union with the half-sun that came down, Kuntî the virgin gave birth to the solar Karna, whom she cast away in a basket set afloat on the river Ashwa (Sanskr. horse); the divine child is found by a *second mother* (he is now born on earth, the river being a ladder from heaven). We find this gesture in fairy-tales, indicating the birth of an *avatâra*. Similarly, Moses and Sargon were thrown into a river, packed in a basket.

The Book of Changes exists only because human beings cannot directly grasp Dao, the Principle or the Void. The 64 hexagrams were generated only because human beings could not grasp the dyad Yin – Yang and the triad Cosmos – Year – Man, by considering just the two halves of the Sun, the continuous trait and the broken trait.

In the Islamic tradition, a famous *hadît qudsî* states: "Allâh has 70 veils of light and darkness. If these veils were taken away, the splendour of His Face would burn everything that His eyes meet." The veil of light is an equivalent to the continuous trait, and the tenebrous veil to the broken trait. A combination of light and shadow is needed for the World to exist; and even the light is a veil of light. Yet, the *hadît* underlines that there is not one or two, but 70 veils of light and darkness. Similarly, the *Yi Jing* uses six traits, combining the continuous and the discontinuous traits in *ba guas* (the trigrams), and the trigrams in hexagrams. The last two hexagrams of the total of 64 describe, somehow emphasizing and crowning the Book of Changes, the wedding and indispensable cohabitation of light and darkness, of light and shadow, of the immortal and mortal, of the two halves of the One-and-only Sun.[1]

The last *gua*, no. 64, is Wei Ji, built of Li (fire) up and Kan (water) down.[2]

---

[1] The Sun is here a symbol of the Principle and not the sun as an emblem of the alternating phases, as described by Zhuang Zi: "decay and growth, fullness and emptiness, darkness and light, the phases of the sun and of the moon – the one-and-only cause produces all these" (chap. 21). This Sun is illustrated by the only sun left after the Great Archer killed the other nine suns, the sun that governs light and shadow; the two halves of the Sun are represented in the Chinese tradition by the rising sun (lord of Heaven) and the descending sun (lord of Earth) (Granet, *La pensée chinoise*, p. 239).

[2] The ideogram is:

We notice immediately the pair fire – water, used in many traditional doctrines to express the opposition, the conciliation of contraries, and the duality.[1] On the other hand, the upper simple *gua* represents the second daughter and the lower one the second son. The second daughter is also the middle daughter, as the second son is the middle one, both indicating the center, the invariable and balanced middle; moreover, the trigram of the middle daughter is soft inside (in the center), suggesting the valley, the emptiness, and the trigram of the middle son is hard inside (in the middle), suggesting the mountain, the plenitude. The second daughter up and the second son down do not reflect a hierogamic exchange, but separation, since they are the influences of Heaven and Earth and so, the hexagram is a replica of *gua* no. 12, Pi.

There was an old Chinese rite regarding rainmaking. In many traditions to make rain was a major rite, because beyond its obvious significance of giving life, of bringing the burnt and dry earth to life, it symbolizes the descent of the spiritual influences at the beginning of a new cycle.[2] The Chinese ritual was based on the idea that crossing a river will bring the rain. The river-crossing symbolism was developed by René Guénon and

---

[1] In the Christian tradition, for example, baptism is with water and fire.

[2] When the ten suns come together, the earth is burnt and the world dies in flames. To start a new cycle and a new world, the rain, that is, the divine presence of Heaven, is needed. About thunderbolt (the Hindu *vajra*) and rainmaking see Guénon, *La Grande Triade*, pp. 63-64, 121. The ideogram for rain is:

雨 雨

The superior horizontal line symbolizes Heaven; it is also suggested that Heaven covers (the cloud) and we notice the central axis, which is a symbol for the descending celestial influence.

Ananda K. Coomaraswamy,[1] who explained its main significance: crossing a river means to pass from one world to another, and especially to pass from Earth to Heaven, from mortal to immortal.[2] In the Chinese ritual, a group of boys competed with a group of girls, in the river, since rainmaking was a result of the confrontation of a dragon *yang* and a dragon *yin*.[3]

Gua Wei Ji describes precisely this situation. It is called "before crossing the river" or "before completion" and we note that, even though the light and the shadow of the "70 veils" alternate, they are not in their proper places. It is a time of transition from disorder to order, the transition from stagnation and separation (*gua* no. 12, Pi) to peace and union (*gua* Tai, no. 11), as the commentary said.[4] The hexagram commences with describing a little fox crossing a river and getting its tail wet in the middle of the river, and ends by warning against one wetting his head. There is here again an allusion to the center (the

---

[1] See Guénon, *Symboles fondamentaux*, p. 343.

[2] The ideogram *heng* presents the heart crossing a river and is translated as "constancy, perseverance" (Wieger 28) (this *heng* is different from what Matgioi calls *heng* and which is the ideogram *hiang*, Wieger 193).

This ideogram is also attributed to *gua* Heng (no. 32), an illustration of constancy and liberty (with application to marital union).

[3] Granet, *La religion*, pp. 28-29. We may note another Chinese custom regarding rainmaking: the dance that uses only one foot. As Granet stated, "the dance with one foot (*yi ju*) is the chief's great duty" (*La pensée chinoise*, p. 66). And related to the ritual dance, we mention here a famous Daoist dance called "the pace of Yu," illustrating Yu's *limping* and following a labyrinthine route (Max Kaltenmark, *Lao tseu et le taoïsme*, Seuil, 1965, p. 165). Similarly, Theseus and his companions executed a dance called "the Crane," in Delos, consisting of a series of serpentine figures and representing the Cretan labyrinth. (Plutarch, *The Lives of the Noble Grecians and Romans*, Encyclopaedia Britannica, 1952, p. 7). Note that the crane is an image of the "Feathered Serpent," and also represents the bird of the immortal Daoists.

[4] The disorder implies the counter-initiatory forces, and the commentary of this *gua* indicates the importance of destroying them (the demons, *gui fang*).

middle), but also to the two "ends." The fire (Li) going upwards and the water (Kan) downwards illustrate the disorder and the separation. On the other hand, the central or nuclear trigrams are also Li and Kan, but in the center Li should be above Kan to reflect the normal hierarchy; the commentary affirms that Kan and Li, because of their middle traits (continuous and broken), are the representatives of Qian and Kun, and in *gua* Tai, we saw, Kun is up and Qian down. In other words, the second son should be down, and the second daughter up, but this situation has to take place in the center, with respect to the middle trigrams, since we refer here to the influences of Heaven and Earth.[1]

The order and the right position of the traits, of the second son and daughter, of fire and water occur in *gua* no. 63, Ji Ji.[2]

We see here the continuous and luminous traits in the first, third and fifth positions, that is, in the celestial places, and the discontinuous and darkened traits in the second, fourth and sixth positions, that is, in the terrestrial places.[3] Their alternation is now in accordance to proper order. The middle

---

[1] For the same reason, in this hexagram, specifically the *middle* son and the *middle* daughter are present. At the same time with the hierarchy, the hierogamy should be obeyed as well: the middle traits of the nuclear trigrams should be a broken trait up and a continuous trait down, but all this occurs in *gua* Ji Ji.

[2] The ideogram is:

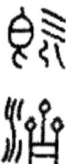

[3] 1, 3 and 5 are celestial numbers, and 2, 4 and 6 are terrestrial numbers.

son is up and the middle daughter down,[1] the fire is down and the water up, illustrating the hierogamic exchange (the Alchemical liquid fire) and the sacred wedding; the joint influences of Heaven and Earth occur in the Center.

The hexagram is called "after completion" or "after crossing the river," which openly indicates, on the one hand, the completion of cosmogony (of "order"), the passing from chaos to light, and on the other hand, the spiritual realization as a sacred wedding in the Center, where *coincidentia oppositorum* occurs. *Gua* Ji Ji is the only hexagram in which all the traits are in their proper places.[2]

The commentaries on this hexagram also warned about the danger of wetting the two "ends," the tail and the head, which alludes to the initiatory process of crossing the river without looking back and without procrastinating, but suggesting too the Year with its indefinite helix of changes. For this reason *gua* Ji Ji is placed before *gua* Wei Ji, stressing the endless flow of the "current of forms," since after the completion, what was before completion starts all over again.

---

[1] In the center, on the contrary, the nuclear trigram representing the second son is down and the second daughter up.

[2] Coomaraswamy, presenting the bridge's symbolism, mentioned that at one end is chaos, darkness (the world of *asuras*), and at the other end is light and order (the world of *dêvas*) (Ananda K. Coomaraswamy, *The RG Veda as Land-Nama-Bok*, Luzac & Co., 1935, pp. 12, 32).

SIX

THE YEAR

FU XI AND Niu Wa exchanged their attributes to make the World Wheel turn. Yang and Yin united their influences in harmony and peace. *Guas* Ji Ji (no. 63) and Tai (no. 11) describe this ideal situation when the compass and square are interlaced and take each other's place.[1]

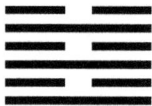   

Gua Ji Ji   *Gua* Tai

On the other hand, when the compass and square are separated, disharmony and disorder reign, as illustrated by *guas* Wei Ji (no. 64) and Pi (no. 12).

---

[1] In Masonry, this interlacing is connected to the initiatory process. It is not without reason that René Guénon often referred to Masonic symbolism when he studied the Far-Eastern tradition in his *La Grande Triade.*

Gua Wei Ji   *Gua* Pi

Yet, there is an additional situation, which characterizes the evolvement of the Year, that is, of the cosmic cycle: when the compass changes gradually into a square. Guénon called this situation "the solidification of the world" – the change "from sphere to cube," and in the *Yi Jing* it represents the progressive modification of Qian into Kun.[1]

Gua Qian   *Gua* Kun[2]

Qian and Kun are the first two hexagrams of the 64 *guas'* cycle,[3] but they symbolize a synthesis of the whole series of

---

[1] The degradation from compass to square or from sphere to cube designates the expansive branch of the double spiral. The compressive branch is "from square to compass" – a well-known Masonic initiatory formula.

[2] *Gua* no. 47 is also called Kun; it represents "exhaustion" and also the misery at the end of the cycle, suggested by drought and an imprisoned desiccated and altered tree:

Gua no. 47 is built of marsh up and water down. The traditional commentary of Zheng Zi explains that, since the water is under the marsh, the symbolic image is a desiccated and altered tree, without water, which represents the misery.

[3] Even if the circular arrangement of the 64 hexagrams is not the most ancient recorded one, we have to consider it as traditional, since the *ba guas* present

changes; yet ultimately, *gua* Qian alone is a synthesis of the double spiral and of the whole helix of changes. We have already said, the Book of Changes has an indefinite number of meanings and we can find them as "explication" in the 64 *guas'* vortex, with the traditional commentaries, or as "complication" in one hexagram or one trigram, or even in one trait. Thus, even if Qian and Kun are the *guas* no. 1 and 2, they represent the sphere and the cube, Heaven and Earth, the compass and square, and many changes could be inserted between them; but, of course, if we consider the *Yi Jing's* standpoint, 64 hexagrams are enough to symbolize all changes. However, from the solidification of the world perspective, the hexagrams will flow like this: Qian, Dun (no. 33), Guan (no. 20), Kun.

Gua Qian   *Gua* Dun   *Gua* Guan   *Gua* Kun

The commentary on hexagram Kun says: "When the tenebrous power (negative, broken traits) begins to grow rigid (to coagulate) and continues in this way, things reach the point of solid ice." Even though some modern translations erroneously consider this statement to be alluding only to the winter season (*gua* Kun marks the winter solstice), we should understand its symbolic meaning without any difficulty: the coagulation of ice illustrates the solidification of the world.

Moreover, the commentaries point out to the three-dimensional cross, stressing the dragon's vertical activity in *gua* Qian and the mare's horizontal movement, covering the surface of the earth, in *gua* Kun. Since the hexagram Qian describes the

---

such a figure (there are two dispositions: of Fu Xi and of Wen Wang, Granet, *La pensée chinoise*, pp. 155-156); the square ("terrestrial") form of the eight trigrams is the equivalent of the circular ("celestial") form (Guénon, *La Grande Triade*, p. 136). Moreover, Matgioi translated the name *Yi Jing* as "The changes in a circular revolution" (*La Voie métaphysique*, p. 19).

dragon's six positions in time, we may consider this *gua*, from a *principial* perspective, connected to time,[1] and *gua* Kun related to space, time being somehow more qualitative than space.[2] In fact, Qian describes in a *principial* manner the dragon's flight, its pure activity being a symbolic time-space combination. With the solidification of the world, time changes into space, and we may see the conversion of Qian into Kun as an illustration of such a change; but, even better, we should consider the concerted influences of time and space,[3] similar to the concerted influences of Yang and Yin.[4]

The change of time into space, as Guénon said, explains the expression "the end of time" (the end of the world is never described as "the end of space"). The end of time depicts the exhaustion of the cycle, and in different traditions the cycle is called Year or even Time.[5]

The *Maitrâyanîya Upanishad* explained the concept of Time and Year in the Hindu tradition: "The Sun is the cause of Time. The

---

[1] "The six situations emerge in time," the *Yi Jing*'s commentary specifies, even if "in time" does not mean our common time.

[2] As Granet said, time is "round" and space "square," which, from this standpoint, relates time with the heavenly sphere and space with the earthly cube; Earth, which is square, is divided into squares, and therefore the kingdom is square and the city is square (Granet, *La pensée chinoise*, pp. 77, 80-81). René Guénon said too that time corresponds to Heaven (the cycles are essentially astronomic) and space to Earth (the terrestrial surface is the measurable space) (*La Grande Triade*, p. 77).

[3] Time and space are two of the five "conditions of existence," as Guénon explained. Only symbolically can we talk about time and space when we refer to the universal manifestation.

[4] *Guas* Wei Ji and Ji Ji illustrate the combined influences. Yet even *gua* Qian, built exclusively of continuous traits, hides the double influence; only the supreme Perfection, Dao, or the Void, is beyond the duality Heaven – Earth.

[5] In the Far-Eastern tradition, Time has a cyclic nature (Granet, *La pensée chinoise*, p. 85). It is interesting that, as Granet stressed, the exhausted cycle doesn't disappear into nothingness, but it is conserved into the "outside darkness." Similarly, the new cycle "measures" the new square space, and the emperor banishes the "barbarians," the malefic and decayed forces of the previous cycle, beyond the sides of the square, into the darkness, at the margin of the world (Granet, *La pensée chinoise*, pp. 82, 84, 87, 88-89). Guénon already explained how the exhausted possibilities of a cycle are conserved in non-manifestation.

(visible) form of Time is the Year (...). Of the Year one half (when the sun moves northward) belongs to Agni, the other to Varuna (when the sun moves southward). (...) And then there (are the months) one by one, belonging to Year, each consisting of nine-fourths of the asterisms,[1] each determined by the sun moving together with the asterisms. Because Time is imperceptible by sense,[2] therefore this is its evidence, and by it alone is time proved to exist. (...) As many portions of Time as there are, through them the Sun proceeds: he who worships Time as Brahma, from him Time moves away very far. And thus it is said: From Time all beings flow, from Time they grow[3]; in Time they obtain rest; Time is visible and invisible. There are two forms of Brahma, Time and non-Time.[4] That which was before the (existence of the) Sun is non-Time and has no parts. That which had its beginning from the Sun is Time and has parts. Of that which has parts, Year is the form, and from the Year (the Cycle) are born all creatures; when produced by Year they grow, and go again to rest in Year. Therefore Year is Prajâpati, is Time, is Food, is the nest of Brahma, is Self. Thus it is said: Time ripens and dissolves all beings in the great Self, but he who knows into what time itself is dissolved, he is the knower of the Veda" (VI, 14-15). "This (Garhapatya) Fire with five bricks is the Year. (...) This Earth (the Garhapatya-fire) here is the first sacrificial step for Prajâpati. (...) This Atmosphere (the Dakshinagni-fire) here is the second sacrificial step for Prajâpati. (...) This Heaven (Ahavaniya-fire) is the third sacrificial step for Prajâpati" (VI, 33).

The three steps are depicted as three vertical bricks in the ideograms of Yang and Yin. The Yang ideogram shows the sun with its rays lighting the wall of three bricks; the Yin ideogram

---

[1] Two constellations and a quarter are the twelfth part of the passage of the sun through the twenty-seven Nakshatras.
[2] The time is observed considering the movement in space.
[3] It is the "current of forms."
[4] Symbolically, Time is the manifestation and non-Time the non-manifestation.

shows the sky covered by clouds (suggesting a veiled sun) and obscuring the wall.

In the Hindu tradition, the Year as cosmic cycle is called Manvantara. It is divided in four ages, with decreasing durations, proportional to 4, 3, 2 and 1. We note that $4 + 3 + 2 + 1 = 10$,[1] ten symbolizing the whole Year; but this descendent order (from a temporal point of view) becomes reversed from a "spatial" perspective, if we consider the production of manifestation as a spatial or geometrical genesis: $1 - 2 - 3 - 4$. The Decade is a token for perfection, the complete development of One, and the Chinese ideogram for sage identifies the seer with the interval between one and ten (Wieger 69):[2]

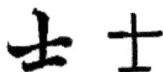

土 土

René Guénon described in *La Grande Triade*, using the numbers of the Pythagorean Tetraktys,[3] two triads: $1 - 2 - 3$ a first genre, and $2 - 3 - 4$ a second genre. The first triad, in accord with Far-Eastern tradition, is composed of the Great Extreme (Tai Ji) – 1,[4] Heaven (Tian) – 3, and Earth (Di) – 2; the second triad is composed of Heaven (Tian), Earth (Di), and Man (Ren) – 4, representing the famous Great Triad. "The Dao produced One; One produced Two; Two produced Three; Three

---

[1] The Pythagorean Tetraktys signifies precisely the sum $1 + 2 + 3 + 4 = 10$.

[2] In the Far-Eastern tradition, the Year or the cycle was mainly considered from the viewpoint of the two phases (ascendant-descendant), in which case $10 = 3 + 2 + 2 + 3$. For man, $100 = 30 + 20 + 20 + 30$ years, and we note the four ages; a king will leave temporal power at the age of 70 (Granet, *La pensée chinoise*, pp. 86-87).

[3] In the Far-Eastern tradition too, the numbers are not just quantities, but they have a qualified nature and for this reason they are in correspondence with the cycles and time (Granet, *La pensée chinoise*, pp. 132, 492).

[4] The Great Extreme is identical to the Great Unity (Tai Yi). As the Being is the affirmed Non-Being, so Tai Ji is the affirmed Wu Ji.

produced All things" (*Dao De Jing*, XLII); Lao Zi's adage finds its reflection in the Pythagorean Tetraktys.[1]

The *Yi Jing*'s various commentaries allude, inevitably, to the doctrine of sacred numbers, and we give a few examples: "Heaven is 1, Earth is 2, Heaven is 3, Earth is 4; Heaven is 5, Earth is 6; Heaven is 7, Earth is 8; Heaven is 9, Earth is 10." "There are five celestial numbers and five terrestrial numbers.[2] In each of the five situations, two numbers are in accord; the sum of the celestial numbers is 25 and the sum of the terrestrial numbers is 30. Together, the sum is 55. Thus, the modification and transformation are accomplished." "1 modifies and gives birth to water, while 6 transforms and produces it; 2 transforms and gives birth to fire, and 7 modifies and brings it to perfection; 3 modifies and gives birth to wood, and 8 transforms and brings it to perfection; 4 transforms and gives birth to gold, and 9 modifies and brings it to perfection; 5 modifies and gives birth to earth, and 10 transforms and brings it to perfection." "The blades of spiritual grass for *gua* Qian are 216[3]; the blades for *gua* Kun are 144[4], in total 360." "Unity is circular surrounded by 3; duality is squarely surrounded by 4." "The sage triples the heaven, doubles the earth and finds support in numbers. Heaven is round and Earth is square; what is round is 1, and what surrounds it is 3."[5]

---

[1] "Man [4] imitates the Earth [2]. Earth [2] follows Heaven [3]. Heaven imitates Dao [1]. Dao follows what is natural [having no other model than itself] [Zero]" (*Dao De Jing*, XXV).

[2] As we said, 10 is the number of perfection, of completion. For this reason, *ten* thousand beings mean all the beings. Ten is the Sun's number (in the Far-Eastern tradition there are ten suns) and since Man is controlled by the Sun, there are ten months of gravidity (and not nine) (Granet, *La pensée chinoise*, p. 127). The ideogram for "ten" is a cross, marking the four cardinal points and the center:

$$+ \quad +$$

[3] 216 = 2 x 108.
[4] 144 = 12^2.
[5] Man has a round head and square feet, in accordance with Heaven and Earth (Granet, *La pensée chinoise*, p. 297). In modern times, the round becomes

The number 55, mentioned above, is also important as the product of 5 x 11. 11 is the number of hierogamy, 5 + 6, where 5, due to a hierogamic exchange, belongs to Earth and 6 to Heaven.[1] "5 and 6, this is the union of Heaven and Earth"; 5 is the center of the odd numbers (1, 3, 5, 7, 9) and 6 of the even numbers (2, 4, 6, 8, 10).[2] The number 5 plays a fundamental and central role in the magic square,[3] but 5 is also 4 + 1, the center and the four cardinal points.[4] Guénon explained, in a full chapter, the symbol of Ming-Tang and its equivalence to the magic square and to the well-known diagram of the eight *guas* circling the Yin-Yang[5]; we may add Wieger's comments regarding the ancient custom of having eight squares of land

---

square, suggesting the solidification of the world and the change "from sphere to cube"; therefore the ideogram for "skull" changed from round to square (Wieger 110):

We note the center and the four corners.

[1] Heaven and Earth are not measurable as such; 5 and 6 are their "measures," that is, the celestial and terrestrial influences, *yang* and *yin* (Guénon, *La Grande Triade*, p. 79).

[2] Granet, *La pensée chinoise*, pp. 165-166. In the Far-Eastern tradition there are two cycles, a solar one based on number 10, and a lunar one based on number 12; Chinese mythology admits ten suns and twelve moons. We note that 5 x 12 = 60 and 6 x 10 = 60. Due to the hierogamic exchange, the cycle of 12, related to 6, refers to Heaven and Time, and the cycle of 10, related to 5, refers to Earth and Space; but we must not consider rigidly such a classification, since Heaven and Earth, Time and Space are strongly interconnected (Granet, *La pensée chinoise*, pp. 130-131, 493). About 10 and 12 see also Guénon, *La Grande Triade*, p. 80.

[3] The number 5 is the center of the first nine numbers, and therefore symbolizes the Center. The eight trigrams correspond to the eight numbers (1, 2, 3, 4, 6, 7, 8, 9) and to the "magic square," and they can be arranged to form the *swastika* (Granet, *La pensée chinoise*, pp. 156, 163, 168, 498, Jean-Louis Grison, *Notes sur les Trigrammes*, Études Traditionnelles, no. 384-385, 1964, p. 221).

[4] This symbolism can be found in many traditions, to mark the center (in the Christian tradition: Jesus Christ and the four Apostles; in the Islamic tradition: the Prophet and the four Caliphs; in Egypt: Horus and the four animals, etc.).

[5] *La Grande Triade*, pp. 135, 136, 140.

(belonging to eight families) around a central square containing the well.[1]

In the Hindu tradition, Mount Mêru indicates the center, symbolizing the polar Axis or the World Axis, the top (North) of it being the residence of *dêvas* (gods), and the bottom (South) the location of *asuras* (dragons). In accord with the *Surya-siddhanta*, Mount Mêru is the axis of the Earth, four continents being placed around it, with their four geodesic centers (four cities) situated equidistant on the equator: Bharatavarsha with the city of Lanka, then, to the West, Ketumalavarsha with the city of Romaka, Kuruvarsha with Siddhapura, and Bhadrarsvavarsha with Yamakoti.

The four cities are placed towards the four cardinal points, the peak of Mount Mêru being the North for each of them. The four cities symbolize four spiritual centers that successively governed the terrestrial world, and they correspond to the four Ages (*katuryugas*). If we consider the lunar four phases as reflections of the four *yugas* and we multiply 4 by the number of Nakshatras asterisms,[2] we will have: 4 x 27 = 108, a fundamental cyclic number. If we multiply the number of Nakshatras asterisms by 16 (the parts of the lunar disc), we obtain: 27 x 16 = 432 (108 x 4 = 432), another fundamental cyclic number.

---

[1] Wieger 269. The ideogram illustrating this arrangement is:

井

The number 8 and the squares are, of course, in relation with the symbolism of the game of chess (64 squares correspond to 64 hexagrams); in *Parzival*, the queen Belacane's city of Patelamunt has 16 gates: eight gates face west toward black Moorish army and the other 8 gates face east toward the army of white Christians fighters (Wolfram von Eschenbach, *Parzival*, Vintage Books, 1961, p. 19).

[2] With respect to the Vedic astronomical science (*jyotishavedanga*), there were 27 Nakshatras asterisms (half of the fundamental number 54), which made it possible to observe the variable positions of the sun, moon and planets, and to correlate the movements of the sun and moon.

The Year

Symbolically, the four *yugas* last 4000, 3000, 2000 and 1000 years (we note the proportion 4 – 3 – 2 – 1). Each *yuga* is preceded and followed by a dawn and a dusk, which link the cycles together; therefore, the Golden Age, *Krita-yuga*, is valued at 4800 years (4000 + 400 + 400), *Treta-yuga* at 3600 years, *Dwapara-yuga* at 2400 years, and *Kali-yuga* at 1200 years. Consequently, a Manvantara or a Mahâyuga will be valued at 12,000 years. Because each divine Year lasts 360 terrestrial years, a Manu Age will last 4,320,000 years.[1]

These numbers, together with others from different texts, expressing the duration of the cosmic cycles, cannot be taken *ad litteram*, and they do not represent a "chronology"; their "astronomical" values constitute a protective shield against profane indiscretion, since the knowledge of the real values for the cosmic cycles could lead to various prophecies with regard to the end of time, and such types of prophecies no genuine tradition has encouraged.

However, as René Guénon explained,[2] what we have to consider for a Manvantara is the number 4320, without other zeros.[3] "The great Yu said: Within the six directions…" (*Lie-zi*, *The Questions of Tang*, 5); the six directions describe the three-dimensional cross and the universal manifestation, corresponding to the 6 "days" of "creation." If 4320 is multiplied by 6, the cyclic number 25,920 is obtained; this number is the astronomic duration of the precession of the equinoxes, and defines the main basis of the cyclic periods in

---

[1] The cyclic numbers 10,800 and 432,000 are to be found also in other traditions. Censorin mentioned Heraclitus' *Great Year* of 10,800 years and the Babylonian Berossos pointed out a cosmic period of 432,000 years. Often, the ancient Greeks and Persians evaluated the *Great Year* as having 12,000 or 13,000 years (see René Guénon, *Formes traditionnelles et cycles cosmique*, Gallimard, 1980, p. 23). The *Satapatha Brahmana* stated that Prajâpati (the Principle of universal manifestation) is the Year, his Word, which produces the World, being collected by the *Vêda*, which is divided into 10,800 moments of the Year, as the *Rig-Vêda* contains 10,800 units of 40 syllables each, that is 432,000 syllables in total.

[2] *Formes traditionnelles*, p. 21.

[3] We note that 432 is the double of 216, the *gua* Qian's number, mentioned in the *Yi Jing*.

149

the cosmic order. Half of this duration, 12,960 years, represents a Great Year, and a Manvantara, as Guénon stated, contains five such Years.[1] Lie Zi alluded to a similar Great Year, when he declared: "The great Yu said: Within the six directions, inside the four seas, everything is lit by the sun and moon; the time is determined by the stars, ordered by the four seasons, presided over by the Great Year"; this Great Year is considered to be the Year Star, with a duration of 12 terrestrial years, referring to the planet Jupiter.[2]

Leonard Woolley's investigations produced a list of the antediluvian Chaldean kings, which specified the traditional duration of king A-lu-lim's reign – 28,000 years, of king A-lal-gar's reign – 36,800 years, and of king En-me-en-lu-an-na's reign – 43,200 years.[3] 28,000 + 36,800 = 64,800 years and this value René Guénon considered being the duration of a Manvantara, composed of five Great Years (5 x 12,960).

The first Great Year, in relation to the primordial race (in the Hindu tradition, Hamsa), could be considered the Center, while the other four represent the four cardinal points; René Guénon suggested a correlation between the five successive Great Years and the five bhûtas,[4] which associates the first Great Year with the quintessential element, the Ether, and here again we touch on the symbolism of $1 + 4 = 5$.

René Guénon described the five elements using two different representations: a ladder-like and a cross-like one. The ladder-like representation presents the elements from a cosmogonic perspective, as given in the Upanishads, in the progression: ether – air – fire – water – earth. The cross-like representation places air as a neutral element along the horizontal diameter of a circle, fire as the upwards element

---

[1] We remark again the importance of the number 5 (Guénon, Formes traditionnelles, p. 23). The emperor, during his good government, was the warrantor of "Five relations" (human relations), "Five rites" (regarding the society and its relation with gods), and "Five penalties."

[2] Nevertheless, five such Great Years make a Cycle of 60 years.

[3] C. W. Ceram, Gods, Graves, & Scholars, Alfred A. Knoph, 1968.

[4] Formes traditionnelles, p. 23.

along the vertical diameter, and water as the downwards element along the vertical diameter. Ether is on the top and earth at the bottom.[1] A similar picture could be drawn for the castes. In fact, René Guénon presents such a diagram for the castes, similar to the one for the elements, in which Brâhmana is the upwards half-diameter, Kshatriya the horizontal diameter and Vaishya the downwards half-diameter; Hamsa (the primordial people beyond the castes) is on the top and Shûdra is at the bottom.[2]

From a cosmogonic perspective, the castes are in the following progression: Brâhmana – Kshatriya – Vaishya – Shûdra, and in the Hindu tradition the four castes are in correspondence to the cardinal points North – East – South – West.[3] In a letter to Gaston Georgel, Guénon suggested these associations: North – white race – water; East – yellow race – air; South – black race – fire; West – red race – earth.[4]

René Guénon built the cross-like diagrams for elements and for castes based on the traditional theory of the three *gunas*. We find in *Vishnu Purana*: "When Brahmâ, with respect to his goal, wanted to produce the world, the beings in whom sattwa prevailed were generated from his mouth; others in whom rajas prevailed were produced from his bosom; others in whom rajas and tamas were strong were produced from his thighs; eventually, others were born from his feet, having tamas as their main characteristic. From these beings the four castes (varnas) were composed: Brâhmana, Kshatriya, Vaishya and Shûdra, which were born from his mouth, bosom, thighs and feet."[5]

Guénon said: "... the hierarchisation of the four varnas, imposed by the gunas that predominate in each caste, is

---

[1] See the figure in René Guénon, *Études sur l'Hindouisme*, Éditions Traditionnelles, 1979, p. 59.
[2] See the figure in Guénon, *Études sur l'Hindouisme*, p. 79.
[3] See A. M. Hocart, *Caste*, Methuen & Co., 1950, p. 27, and Guénon, *Symboles fondamentaux*, pp. 120-121.
[4] Gaston Georgel, *Les Quatre Âges de l'Humanité*, Archè, 1976, p. 17.
[5] *The Laws of Manu* says the same thing: "But for the sake of the prosperity of the worlds he caused the Brâhmana, the Kshatriya, the Vaishya, and the Shûdra to proceed from his mouth, his arms, his thighs, and his feet."

identical with that of the elements (*bhûtas*)." If we consider that the production of the castes and races follows a cosmogonic succession, like in the case of the elements, we should assume the associations: Ether – Hamsa – primordial race; Air – Brâhmana – yellow race; Fire – Kshatriya – black race; Water – Vaishya – red race; Earth – Shûdra – white race. On the other hand, with respect to the cardinal points, the associations should be: North – Brâhmana – white race – water; East – Kshatriya – yellow race – air; South – Vaishya – black race – fire; West – Shûdra – red race – earth.

From the point of view of the doctrine of three *gunas*, as we have already mentioned, *sattwa* (and the white colour) predominates in Brâhmana, *rajas* (the red colour) predominates in Kshatriya, *rajas* mixed with *tamas* (the yellow colour) predominate in Vaishya, and *tamas* (the black colour) predominates in Shûdra, revealing an obvious correspondence with the "degrees of subtlety" of the elements.

However, in a traditional society, the organization of the city required the four castes to be placed in the four cardinal points, in connection with the four *yugas*. Following a solar circumambulation (*pradakshinâ*), starting with the Northern point, the successive four castes are obtained, in a natural descendent order. Guénon remarked that Brâhmana is placed at the North, being linked to the polar tradition, and Kshatriya is placed at the East, belonging to the solar tradition.

The same ambiguity is found in the case of the five Great Years. When we consider the solar circumambulation, the four cardinal points correspond to the four *yugas*, but if we have to consider the five Great Years, the first one, which is the "center," has to be placed at the Pole, that is, at the Northern point. In fact, we should use a spatial figure, in which the primordial race, the Ether, and the first Great Year are at the North Pole, while the other four races, Great Years and *bhûtas* are equidistantly situated on the equatorial circle.[1] Returning to

---

[1] The *swastika* is a well-known symbol of the Pole, and, as René Guénon explained, the four branches represent the four tangents to a circle having the

the two-dimensional plane, the equatorial circle is replaced by a meridian circle containing the cardinal points, and the World Axis, which is perpendicular to the plane comprising the solstitial and equinoxial axes,[1] and has the Nadir and Zenith as its two ends, becomes distinct (with respect to the terrestrial axis of rotation – the polar axis) and identical to the Solar Ray (Buddhi) that passes through the vertical axis of man.[2]

One of the reasons we encounter this apparent ambiguity is the difference between the "polar" and "solar" symbolism. The "polar" representation uses the poles' axis and the equator, while the "solar" representation considers the movement around the sun. René Guénon scrutinized the two symbolisms more than once. In *Le symbolisme de la croix*, he illustrated the three-dimensional cross using an astronomic symbolism: "what we have to consider is, on the one hand, the equatorial plane and the axis, which, connecting the poles, is normal to this plane; on the other hand, there are the two lines uniting respectively the two solstitial points and the two equinoxial points; we have, what we could call, in the first case, the vertical cross, and, in the second case, the horizontal cross. The assembly of the two crosses, with the same center, constitutes the three-dimensional cross, with the branches oriented along the six directions of space."[3] "The vertical axis is the polar axis (...); it is the principal axis, while the other two horizontal axes are only secondary and relative. Of these two horizontal axes, one, the North-South axis, could be called the solstitial axis, and the other, the East-West axis, could be called the equinoxial

---

pole as center; if the pole is considered the terrestrial pole, then the circle is the equator.

[1] This plane is the ecliptic plane.

[2] We see the ambiguity: if, symbolically, the World Axis is identical to the terrestrial polar axis, then the races should develop along the equator (as the four continents are presented in *Surya-siddhanta*); if the races and the four *yugas* are situated in the cardinal points, the World Axis becomes insignificant for terrestrial humanity (even though it is identical, somehow, with the axis of each human being).

[3] René Guénon, *Le symbolisme de la croix*, Guy Trédaniel, 1984, p. 30. The six directions correspond to Nadir, Zenith, North, South, East, and West.

axis."[1] "If we regard the two axes as solstitial and equinoxial ... we could say that the solstitial axis is relatively vertical with respect to the equinoxial axis, and so, in the horizontal plane, it analogically plays the role of a polar axis (the North-South axis), with the equinoxial axis playing, in this case, the role of the equatorial axis (the East-West axis)."[2]

In an article about the "solstitial gates," René Guénon also affirmed: "The vertical axis, because it unites the two poles, is of course the North-South axis; when passing from the polar symbolism to the solar one, this axis should be in a way projected onto the Zodiacal plane [the ecliptic plane], but in such a mode that it should keep a correspondence, even an equivalence as precise as possible, with the initial polar axis. In the annual cycle, the winter and summer solstices [situated on the ecliptic] are the two points corresponding to North and South in the spatial order, as the spring and fall equinoxes correspond to East and West; thus, the axis that would observe this condition is the one which unites the two solstitial points, and we could say that the solstitial axis plays the role of vertical axis, with regard to the equinoxial axis. The solstices are indeed the poles of the Year; and these poles of the temporal world become, due to a real and not at all arbitrary correspondence, the substitutes of the spatial world's poles."[3] "In accord to the correspondence between the temporal and spatial symbolisms of the cardinal points, the winter solstice is somehow the North pole of the Year, and the summer solstice the South pole, while the spring and fall equinoxes refer to East and West."[4]

In conformity to the coherence of the symbols regarding the doctrine of cosmic cycles, at the beginning of the Manvantara the polar and solar symbolisms should have coincided, and such a situation could only occur when the axis of the earth is straight, which means that the equatorial plane superposes the ecliptic plane, and the polar axis becomes perpendicular to the

---

[1] *Le symbolisme de la croix*, p. 36.
[2] *Le symbolisme de la croix*, p. 45.
[3] *Symboles fondamentaux*, p. 237.
[4] *Symboles fondamentaux*, p. 240.

plane formed by the solstitial and equinoxial axes. In such a case, the poles' axis symbolizes the World Axis, and the equator – the circle of universal manifestation, where the rotation of the worlds takes place (suggested by the *swastika*'s branches), the equator being identical to the ecliptic; the solstices and equinoxes are now totally identical to the cardinal points, and the primordial man, situated in the upper pole, sees the north in front of him, on the equator, and the south behind him, with the Nadir and Zenith congruent to the two poles. Noon will coincide perfectly with the South, midnight with the North, and the four continents will be indeed on the equator at the four cardinal points. Only in this very case, can the three-dimensional cross Guénon illustrated with an astronomic symbolism (the poles' axis and the ecliptic) be properly represented.

The discrepancy between the polar and solar symbolisms started to appear when the terrestrial axis began to tilt. "In ancient times, Niu Wa smelted stones of all the five colours to patch up the flaws, and cut off the feet of the turtle to support the four corners. Afterwards, when Gong-gong[1] was fighting Zhuan Xu for the Empire, he knocked against Mount Bu-zhou in his rage, breaking one of the pillars of heaven, snapping one of the threads which support the earth.[2] For this reason heaven leans North-West and the sun, moon and stars move in that direction" (*Lie-zi, The Questions of Tang*, 1); "But there was a giant from the kingdom of the dragon, who came to the place of the five mountains in no more than a few strides. In one throw he hooked six of the turtles in a bunch. (...) Therefore two of the mountains drifted to the far North and sank in the great sea" (*Lie-zi, The Questions of Tang*, 2).

---

[1] Gong-gong is described as a dragon with a human face and horns.

[2] In the Far-Eastern tradition, the Cosmos was similar to a carriage. The squared bottom (*dayu*) corresponds to Earth, the circular awning (*gai*) to Heaven, and the four pillars are the pillars of Earth, situated in the four corners and supporting Heaven (see also Granet, *La pensée chinoise*, pp. 218, 284).

The tilting of the axis symbolizes also the loss of primeval equilibrium and harmony, which ended with the replacement of one polar gate with two solar gates, distinguishing the divine and the human, and requiring the initiatory process to be introduced. In the same article about the "solstitial gates," René Guénon referred to the division of the annual cycle into two halves, one "ascendant" and other "descendant:" the former is the sun's path from the winter solstice to the summer solstice, the latter is the sun's path from the summer solstice to the winter solstice.[1]

If the hexagrams are organized with regard to the months of the Year, an interesting picture is revealed, illustrating the two phases, ascendant and descendant, the importance of the solstices and equinoxes, and the alternate activity of Yang and Yin.

The calendar, as an expression of the cosmic cycles, had, like in the case of other traditional societies, a particular importance; the Ming Tang was called "the Calendar House" and the emperor was the regulator of the calendar.[2] We don't intend to develop here all the complicated details and variants related to the Chinese astrology and astronomy, but to highlight the circular partition in 12 stations, correlated with 12 hexagrams. The two poles of the 64 hexagrams, Qian and Kun, contain 12 traits, suggesting a logical circular arrangement of 12 hexagrams, related to 12 stations of the Year. Even if the 12 months as we know them today are not specifically Chinese, we can use them for our illustration, since the Ming Tang, though composed of nine squares, had 12 openings (three on each side) that corresponded to the 12 months of the year, to the Zodiac and to the 12 gates of the Heavenly Jerusalem.[3]

The human cycle starts, as expected, with the summer solstice, the one the Hindu tradition calls *pitri-yâna*, "the ancestors' gate" or "the gate of men." The summer solstice is also a balance and a critical point of the cycle, which explains

---

[1] *Symboles fondamentaux*, p. 239.
[2] Granet, *La pensée chinoise*, p. 90.
[3] Guénon, *La Grande Triade*, p. 141, Granet, *La pensée chinoise*, p. 150.

why the hexagram preceding this solar station is in a converse analogy with the hexagram following it.

Gua no. 43, Guai, representing the month of May, has only one broken line, the sixth, while *gua* no. 44, Gou, representing the month of July, has only one broken line too, the first. The hexagram for the month of June is *gua* Qian, with six continuous traits, and as we know the superior and heavenly meaning of Qian, we easily understand Guénon's comments about the solstice being the pole of the Year; Qian plays, indeed, the role of a Pivot.

gua Guai   *gua* Qian   *gua* Gou

Gua no. 1, Qian, symbolizes Heaven, the Celestial Activity, the Active Perfection from which the ten thousand beings draw their reality, but it also represents the Golden Age, the paradisiacal state, the origin of the human cycle. When the World Wheel commenced to turn, inevitably the cycle's development followed a descendant way, from essence to substance, from order to disorder, from unity to disunion, until it exhausted all its possibilities; after that, an initiatory straightening – the ascendant phase – will renew the world and a new cycle will start.

Therefore, the hexagram following the summer solstice is *gua* Gou, where the birth of a broken line can be noticed at its base, this bottom trait symbolizing the seed of decadence and disarray, the germ of substantiality, passivity and quantity, and this one trait blooms and grows to spirituality's detriment (the continuous lines); the continuous traits will gradually diminish, and if, from an intellectual viewpoint, a descendant phase can be noticed, then from a substantial perspective, an ascendant phase arises.

In the Christian tradition, the summer solstice is when John the Baptist was born; he is the crying Saint John, who will diminish, while, in accord with the converse analogy, Christ (and Saint John the Evangelist), who is born at the winter solstice and represents the laughing Saint John, will increase. Christ and John the Baptist are the ascendant and descendant halves of the cycle. The fairy-tales present an emperor with a crying eye and a laughing eye, and in the Far-Eastern tradition the sun is the celestial eye, and we could consider the emperor's eyes the sun at the two solstices.

Gua Gou is built of Qian up and Xun (wind) down, expressing, undoubtedly, the preeminence of spirituality, of the Holy Spirit (in Christian terms): "the wind crosses the universe" as a messenger of Heavenly Activity. Zheng Zi commented on this *gua*: "the wind gallops under the sky, covering everything. It is the symbolic image of the emperor contemplating the enveloping whirl, the rotational circular motion that carries his orders to the four cardinal points." In the Hindu tradition, the Lord of the World, the Emperor of a new cycle of manifestation, transmits the initial impulse to the Wheel of Law (*Dharma-Chakra*), and so the world starts to function.

At the same time, "a negativity is born; from this moment, it will grow gradually, the positivity starting its decline. (...) The negativity advances, opposing the positivity. It is the warning of this *gua*. (...) This negativity means little girl.[1] One who marries a young girl wants the union to last for a long time, but here the negativity will grow and gradually develop, and it will soon suppress the positivity, defeating it, so such a marriage will not last long. When the inferior men's (feminine aspects') inherent force increases gradually, how could a durable alliance be possible?" (Zheng Zi). In *gua* Gou "the way of the inferior man increases."

However, from a human perspective, this *gua* marks a very important moment for humankind, expressing the début of the cyclic evolvement, of the double spiral's explicative branch, the

---

[1] Xun means the eldest daughter.

moment when the world starts to function, and the *Yi Jing* underlines this moment with the following words: "Great are the meaning and the moment stated by *gua* Gou!" And Zheng Zi said: "Heaven encountering Earth, all the ten thousand beings are born," which means that the broken trait is indispensable for the production and development of the universal manifestation; positivity encountering negativity causes the birth of the universal Existence.

The hexagram for the month of August is called Dun (no. 33) and is built of Qian up and Gen (mountain) down, four continuous and two discontinuous lines.

Gua Dun

Zheng Zi made this commentary: "Heaven is above, it advances rising and going farther and farther; what is inferior (the mountain) follows, rising,[1] but the superior goes away, and contradiction and opposition appear, on the one hand, and retreat, on the other hand, such that *gua* Dun means 'to retreat watching out.' Two negativities are born below; negativity grows and has the opportunity to develop completely; positivity diminishes and retreats; the inferior man seizes step by step the preponderance, the superior man retreats and watches out."[2]

Contradiction and opposition are characteristics of universal manifestation in full development, enhancing the decadence.

---

[1] The mountain is a symbol of the World Axis and, from an initiatory viewpoint, climbing a mountain means to rise to heaven as result to a spiritual realization, or, more often, it means to accomplish the Lesser Mysteries. At the beginning of the cycle, when men were in direct communication with gods, initiation was not necessary; afterwards, the example of the mountain trying to follow heaven was needed. In *gua* Dun, the mountain symbolizes "substantiality."

[2] The Dun ideogram shows the boar dissimulating its walk under the moonlight (the light also retreats).

Various traditions described the Golden Age as the age when Heaven and Earth were very close, but later Heaven, upset by humankind's misbehavior, retreated far away.

The next hexagram expresses even clearer the cyclic decadence. *Gua* no. 12, Pi, is called "decline," and marks the fall equinox (the month of September), when Heaven (Qian up) and Earth (Kun down) are in divorce. It seems the three continuous traits and three broken traits are in equilibrium, but Qian rises and Kun cannot follow, and so they separated from each other more and more.

Gua Pi

"What is big goes away, farther and farther, what is small comes near, developing"; it is the symbolic image, Zheng Zi said, of the widening of the inferior man's way and the narrowing of the superior man's way. The Pi ideogram shows a plant underground, which illustrates the complete decadence and barrenness (since *gua* no. 12 expresses the absolute divorce), but

also the Being's absorption in non-manifestation.

Intriguingly, the hexagram for the month of October, Guan (no. 20), seems to have a different meaning. *Gua* Guan, with respect to the positivity's descendant series, suggests a slight revival, and we have to accept it as an illustration of the cycle's non-linearity; a cosmic cycle is never a straight, linear fall, but is composed of many secondary cycles, and from time to time retrieval occurs.

Gua Guan

Guan is built of Xun (wind) up and Kun (earth) down, which means only two continuous traits on top; since the broken lines extended, but did not conquer the fifth position, the position of the emperor in each *gua*, we may consider that the emperor succeeded, by personal example and with the support of sacred rites, to postpone the degradation of the world.[1] The cycle reached the moment when nobody else but the emperor himself could stop the disorder and indeed, when the fifth continuous line is replaced by a discontinuous one, we witness the "weariness," the "decay," the "fall," and the end of the cycle. "The deterioration – Zheng Zi made the comment – reached the emperor's position; it is the extreme limit of weariness." The hen sings instead of the rooster.

Gua Bo

The hexagram no. 23, Bo, corresponds to the month of November, and is called "weariness" or "fall"; it is built of Gen (mountain) up and Kun (earth) down. Zheng Zi affirmed: "There are five negativities – five broken traits, and only one positivity; the negativity commenced with one broken line at the bottom of the hexagram; it grew little by little until it reached perfect development and its extreme limit. The group of negativities wears at and destroys the positivity; it is the symbolic image of destruction. The multitude of inferior men

---

[1] "Emperor" also means an *avatâra*, or a redeemer like Christ or Buddha.

annihilates the sage; therefore, the sage must be humble in words and hide his traces to avoid the inferior men's insults."

If, in *gua* Guan, it was still possible for the two continuous lines to control the four broken traits, in this new situation the discontinuous lines are unleashed and the seer has to disappear, to hide, protecting and guarding the Lost Word, the Holy Grail, waiting for the new cycle to come. In different traditions a "hidden, subterranean center" is mentioned; when disorder and decadence have reached an exaggerate development, the world's spiritual center hides, disappears, and the sages – the inhabitants of this center – are the guardians of Tradition, which they guard like the serpents guarding the treasure, and they wait for the cyclic revival. For this reason the *Yi Jing*'s commentary describes how the superior man hides, which symbolizes in fact the hiding of the initiatory lore; of course, its disappearance takes place gradually, with its last reflection in the world being the exoteric rites supervised by the emperor in *gua* Guan.[1]

The sages melt into the crowd; they hide among the common people, disguised as inferior and humble men. Therefore, the winter solstice, which represents an extreme, is associated with the hexagram Kun, composed of six broken traits.

Gua Kun

"The full moon corresponds to the complete development of negativity" (*gua* Gui Mei, the fifth trait's commentary). At the winter solstice, the *Yi Jing* stated, the emperor, following Dao of Heaven, closes the kingdom's gates, and remains calm and in repose.

---

[1] Therefore the *Guan* ideogram presents a huge eye.

"The fifth discontinuous trait represents a young girl of noble and elevated condition:" she is the divine Maiden, the Emperor's daughter, which reminds us not to forget that the winter solstice is also *dêva-yâna*, "the gate of gods"; through this gate the *avatâra* descends to earth, ready to use his inner and initiatory work to straighten up the world.

The ascendant phase of the Year is also a symbol for the initiatory way of Man. It starts with the winter solstice, and the next hexagram, for the month of January, presents a continuous line at the bottom; this line, just born into the world, symbolizes the *avatâra* born through "the gate of gods," who inherits the Tradition from the hidden sages of the previous phase.[1] For this reason, Zheng Zi commented on the lone positivity, situated at the top of *gua* Bo: "The abolition and weariness of the continuous (positive) traits are total; only the superior continuous line remains, alone, still subsisting; it is like an enormous fruit, kept for reproduction." The continuous trait at the bottom of the hexagram for the month of January is the direct successor of the continuous trait at the top of *gua* Bo. The hexagram for the month of January is called Fu (no. 24), built of Kun up and Zhen (thunderbolt) down.

Gua Fu

Zheng Zi affirmed: "During the Year, the broken traits' (negativity's) development comes to a maximum; at the winter solstice a continuous line (a positivity) is reborn in the middle of earth [World Center], and therefore this *gua* is called Fu. The positivity is the way of the initiate. (...) Only one positivity starts to be born; of course, it cannot dominate yet the multitude of negativities, and, to produce the ten thousand

[1] Each cycle has its origin in the precedent cycle.

beings, it must, inevitably, await the arrival of the other positivities [which means the accomplishment of the initiatory way, of the ascendant and restoration phase]; after the positivities have arrived, this first one [*avatâra*] can produce the work of giving birth to beings, without error or irregularities."[1]

Gua no. 42, Yi, stresses the importance, for the prosperity of the world, of this positivity born at the bottom of the hexagram. Yi is called "increase" because "the continuous lowest line of the upper trigram has sunk down and taken its place under the lower trigram.

The Yi ideogram suggests not only increase but overabundance (it shows an overfilled vessel), which, on the one hand, points out what an extraordinary moment the birth of an *avatâra* is (the greatest entering the smallest) and, on the other hand, announces the restoration of the world.

The month of February has as token the hexagram Lin (no. 19), built of Kun up and Dui (marsh) down, and called "greatness."

Gua Lin

---

[1] We should note that the *avatâra*, born in the middle of earth, has the thunderbolt (Zhen) as emblem.

Zheng Zi continued his commentary: "The two positivities are new and just developed, and they obtained greatness; *gua* Lin means precisely growth, greatness. (…) The positivity's natural way becomes flourishing. The superior man, cautious, warns: even though positivity develops, after eight months the natural way will be exhausted."[1]

The spring equinox follows, with *gua* Tai (Kun up, Qian down).

Gua Tai

The hexagram Tai means "prosperity" and now, as we already know, the wedding of Heaven and Earth takes place, the dragon (capable of being invisible or visible, big or small, short or long) rises to heaven (as the fall equinox sinks into the abyss), the initiatory way finds completion, and the moment for the birth of a new cycle is close.[2] "What is small goes away, what is big comes. The superior man is inside [Heaven's trigram], the inferior man outside [Earth's trigram]; this is Dao of the sage."

The prosperity finds its continuation in the perfect blossoming and development of positivity, which is the meaning of *gua* no. 34, Da Zhuang, the hexagram for the month of April, built of Zhen up and Qian down.

---

[1] "After eight months" means *gua* Bo (for November), with only one positivity left. We note the number 8.

[2] This moment is described by an ideogram showing the sun reviving the vegetation as a cyclic event:

Gua Da Zhuang

Now the initiate defeats and transforms his ego, integrating it into the personality. Zheng Zi stated: "Any warrior can jump into boiling water or into fire, or can walk on the edge of a sword. But to defeat his ego and to return to the natural and ritual order is impossible without the greatness of the initiate's force."

Finally, the month of May is represented by *gua* Guai (no. 43), built of Dui up and Qian down, its symbolic image being the flood. Now, Zheng Zi said, Dao of the sage is accomplished.

Gua Guai

This allusion to the flood is very interesting. If the descendant phase illustrates the solidification of the world and the time changed into space, the birth of a new cycle is preceded by a cataclysm often described as flood. From this viewpoint, the ascendant cycle is *avatâra*'s work to redeem the world, to straighten it up, and thus, this phase is invisible and without duration, or we should say that it occurs simultaneously with the solidification of the world; so, when the sphere changed into a cube, when Qian changed into Kun, at the same time the flood takes place and Kun changes back into Qian: the "reversal of the poles" occurs and a new cycle begins.[1]

---

[1] The cycle of these 12 hexagrams, presented above, was used in some specific applications of the Chinese tradition. It showed in a logical and natural way

how, by changing in order one trait, each hexagram "started to function," in the same way as each cycle enter into operation, one after another, continuously, the end of a cycle being the beginning of the next one. In fact, there is only one hexagram that changes continuously, ending an operation and starting a new one.

SEVEN

THE RETURN OF MAN

THE ASCENDANT phase of the Year symbolizes, as we have
already mentioned, Man's initiatory way, the spiritual realization,
the conversion of the cube into a sphere. Of course, the two
phases are in direct relation to the double spiral and, in fact,
Man, as Emperor (*wang*), or Mediator, or Lord of the World,
complies with both branches of the spiral.[1]

The Emperor, as presented in the Far-Eastern tradition, is,
though, not any emperor, but a divine Man, who is in
possession of a complete spiritual realization; he is the median
term of the Great Triad. When we refer to the emperor, we
have in mind primarily the function ("Heaven's mandate"),
since – as we noticed in different quotations of the sacred texts
– the man exercising this function did not always have the
spiritual and initiatory capacity to be equal to the function. The
case of extreme harmony is when the function and the man

---

[1] The *wang* ideogram shows Man connecting the Three Worlds and identical to
Axis Mundi.

王 王

who exercises it are one and the same – a perfect situation, which implies that, first, the candidate covers the *complicative* branch of the double spiral (follows an initiatory path, a spiritual "quest"), actually realizing the "imperial" condition, reaching the spiral's center and finding liberation from the world's chains, uniting his Self with the Principle. Only in the second phase does he start to exercise his imperial prerogatives, in accord with the double spiral's *explicative* branch, and only now is he "invested" with Heaven's mandate, which is a true sacrifice forcing him to leave the beatific super-luminous night and descend in the changeable world. "He who takes upon himself the empire's disasters deserves to be emperor of the universe. The truth often seems paradoxical" (*Dao De Jing*, LXXVIII).

With the world's profanation and decadence, the men who were invested emperors obtained, it is true, a divine mandate, but, unfortunately, they did not have the needed qualifications; they were missing the initiatory journey upon the spiral's coagulant branch, and these emperors could not fructify their mandate[1]; they did not know what to do with it, or, in other words, they were in a situation similar to that of Ali Baba,[2] Icarus[3] or Epimetheus.[4]

Gua Jin   *Gua* Ming Yi

The commentary on *gua* no. 36, Ming Yi, is explicit with regard to this problem: "*Gua* Jin [no. 35] is the emblem of

---

[1] It is the case of the seed spread on a barren soil, as told in the Christian tradition.

[2] Ali Baba lost the key-word that opened the cave of treasure.

[3] Icarus was empowered with wings, but he was not qualified to use them.

[4] Epimetheus received the case with all worldly attributes, but he did not know how to administrate it.

perfect clarity; an intelligent emperor is in a superior rank; it is the moment when the sages advance with a steady pace.[1] *Gua* Ming Yi is the emblem of obscurity; an obtuse emperor is in a superior position; it is the moment when clarity diminishes. The sun hides underground, the light is altered." These are evident signs predicting the end of time. The dragon (*asura*, Titan) abducted and hid the sun, the spiritual center became subterranean and invisible for the world, and the emperor is a profane man. "*Gua* Ming Yi is built of simple *gua* Li (fire) down and simple *gua* Kun up; the sun disappears into the earth." It is the *Kali-yuga*, the tenebrous age when "clarity diminishes" and the darkness of ignorance governs.

"The emperor to govern should have intelligence and the perfect clarity of the sun lighting everywhere" (*gua* Feng, no. 55).

René Guénon calls the Emperor (*Wang*) the Lord of the World. The Emperor is the Principle's projection in manifestation, for a state of existence, for a cosmic cycle, or for the whole universal manifestation. The Emperor or Lord of the World is the cosmic Intelligence that reflects the pure spiritual Light and promulgates the Law (the Rule, *norma*)[2] for a specific cosmic, worldly, or earthly "formation," while the quality of "cosmic intelligence" (mentioned by Guénon in relation to the Hindu tradition) is somehow equivalent to *heng*, the intelligence, a "virtue" belonging to Wen Wang's formula.

The Emperor is the Principle's vicar; he is the regulator and *ordinator* of the World, of a cycle, or of a country; he resides in the center, in Ming-Tang, where Heaven's Activity shines; he is

---

[1] The Jin ideogram is:

We note the sun (underground) and two birds. Both images point out the celestial domain and the paradisiacal light, the perfect harmony (the two birds are in equilibrium); the sun could very well be the Midnight Sun.
[2] See Guénon, *Le Roi*, p. 13.

"the Pivot of the Rule," the one who, immutable and free, infallible and perfectly balanced, by his active and invisible presence, sustains the natural course of existence. The Emperor is the median void, the mediator between Heaven and Earth; he is the one who unites Heaven and Earth; he is the Universal Man, identical with Zhu Xi's tree, which means he is *Axis Mundi*, where *Wang Dao* ("the emperor's way") and *Tian Dao* ("Heaven's way") are one and the same. "Dao is great; Heaven is great; Earth is great; the Emperor is also great" (*Dao De Jing*, XXV).

The Emperor is the Sage,[1] the one who attained the spiritual realization and the perfection (*cheng*), who united his Self with the Middle Way (*Zhong Dao*); he is the King-Pontiff blessed with Heaven's mandate (*Tian ming*).[2] Zhuang Zi said: "The emperor's power is derived from Principles' power; Heaven chooses him." The Emperor is the Son of Heaven; he is the Orphan and even the Widow.[3] The Emperor represents the Principle completely and for a specific traditional society he is the Pivot or the Axis. If the axis is tilted, decadence follows; if the axis is broken (like the broken trait), the solidification of the world and the end of time are near.

Regardless of the individual qualities the emperor possesses as man, the *wang* state implies a divine nature, and Heaven's mandate invests the emperor with double power, sacerdotal and royal; the Lord of the World (or his substitutes) represents a sacred function maintained legitimate by the Heavenly Activity's influence. The emperor, for his people, was the Principle's delegate; he was, in a way, the Principle itself, and for this reason the emperors of China and Japan were seldom seen in public, as Dao is difficult to be seen. As Guénon said, the

---

[1] See Guénon, *La Grande Triade*, p. 125.

[2] See Guénon, *La Grande Triade*, p. 149.

[3] "Men hate to be 'orphaned,' 'widowed,' or 'worthless,' but this is how emperors and lords describe themselves. (*Dao De Jing*, XLII). There is a very interesting symbolism regarding the orphan and the widow. Jesus Christ said: "If any man come to me, and hate not his father, and mother, and wife, and children, and brethren, and sisters, yea, and his own life also, he cannot be my disciple" (*Luke* 14:26).

emperor was the "channel" through which the influences descended from Heaven to Earth.[1] But the emperor was also the people's delegate, and if the emperor obtained liberation, the people obtained salvation as well.[2] Therefore, the temples of Angkor (Cambodia), for example, are not the result of a painful labour done by slaves, but of people's energetic and fully aware activity, since the temple was the king's vehicle used for spiritual liberation and the king was identical not only with the temple but also with the people.[3]

There is another meaning with respect to the emperor and his temple. We have already mentioned the Chinese initiatory motto: "Destroy the darkness (*jing*) and restore the light (*ming*)," comparable to the Masonic initiatory task of spreading the light and gathering what was scattered. *Gua* Huan (no. 59) is built of Xun (wind) up and Kan (water) down, illustrating the dispersion: the wind blowing over water disperses it.

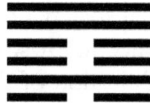

---

[1] *La Grande Triade*, p. 151.

[2] "The preeminence of Heaven, the richness of the four seas, the ten thousand beings, the greatness of Dao of the emperor, and Dao of the extreme greatness, is not everything gathered in the emperor?" (*Gua* Feng's commentary). *Gua* Feng (no. 55) is built of Zheng (thunderbolt) up and Li (fire) down; it is the emperor's *gua*.

"It is not given to every mortal to bring about a time of outstanding greatness and abundance. Only a born ruler of men is able to do it." "When the sun is in the middle, the light is complete, and the Pole Star is seen"; "at midday the Pole Star is seen."

[3] Similarly, the construction of any other ancient temple or pyramid was not an agonizing effort done by slaves, but a meaningful spiritual work.

Similarly, the man disperses his thoughts and heart, his attention and energy, tempted by details, and the world disperses its substance in multiplicity, forgetting the One. It is the emperor's duty as Pivot to gather what was scattered and the symbol of this gathering is the temple. The temple brings the people together, here the ancestors are venerated; the emperor institutes the cult of ancestors and so he gathers not only the people but also the dispersed ancestors. "In a time when the world is disunited and separated, the emperor assembles and unites the hearts, and builds a temple for the ancestors." "The adoration of the Lord and the building of temples to honour the ancestors always bring the hearts together and make the people obey." The Huan ideogram shows the water – symbol of dispersion and the emperor (the top position), correct oriented, invisibly reuniting the world (the two hands):[1]

In the sacred and initiatory tales, the hero aims at this imperial function and he strives to be invested *wang;* but this goal is not a materialistic one, incited by ambition and human desires; on the contrary, it is a natural accomplishment of the initiatory process, corresponding to Zhu Xi's ripened fruit and to the center of the double spiral's *complicative* branch, where the Principle resides.

The Emperor is the World Axis, which imposes on the man who is invested with this function to be a *shenren,* a transcendent or divine man, a *jivan-mukta* (in the Hindu tradition), since only then will he reside in the Center through which the World Axis passes, and only in this situation, is he *Pontis* (pontoon, bridge)

---

[1] "Huan; liberty, the king succeeds to have a temple for the ancestors; the advantage to cross a big river; the advantage of purity." The ideogram shows a man (identical to *wang* for *gua* no. 59) above "a space obtained by throwing away the stones and the soil" (Wieger 104), which suggests a cave as temple.

and *Pontifex* – the sacred link between Heaven and Earth and the artificer of it; otherwise, "the conformity with nature" would be missing and a serious disharmony would occur. Along the World Axis, the spiritual influences descend; along this Axis, the divine Activity operates; and in this mode Heaven directly invests the Lord of the World with *potestas clavis*, with the divine grace, and transmits to him a celestial mandate.

The Emperor is a synthesis of greatness, intelligence, liberty, goodness and perfection, which are precisely the "virtues" of Wen Wang's tetragram. Fu Xi is such an emperor; he is the Emperor, that is, a King-Pontiff, and not a king in the common sense of the word, as understood in the Occident. In comparison to the king, the genuine Emperor not only he governs, but he is the one who "coagulates" the society in the universe, leading the way to associate and organize the multitude.

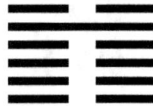

Gua Bi

In the *Yi Jing*, *gua* no. 8, Bi, means "association" and describes the crowd associating around the emperor to constitute countries, societies, or civilizations; the hexagram Bi is built of five broken traits and only one continuous line – the emperor's position.[1] The principle's absence, Zheng Zi stated, makes any association impossible, leading to disorder and anarchy, to a

---

[1] As René Guénon explained, the "universal will" is identical to Dharma. This Will manifests its activity in each cosmic cycle as Manu, which is a principle: the "cosmic intelligence." Manu is equivalent to the Islamic "Universal Man" and with Wang, the Daoist emperor. The "Law of Manu," for a cycle or humanity, is the submission to the natural hierarchy of the beings organized in a society (*Introduction générale à l'étude des doctrines hindoues*, Guy Trédaniel, 1987, p. 188). Gua Bi refers to this concept of Manu or Wang, and only in a secondary case to a historical society. The emperor, in his highest significance, is this cosmic principle, Manu.

disorganized throng, an inferior and turbulent herd, an amorphous mass; "In the universe, the inferior people are always assembled in crowds" (*gua* no. 40, Xie).

"The multitude of beings in the universe must have the assistance of a great man to receive the boons of a regulated governing. If the people get together, there is necessarily disorder and confusion; when people get together, there are necessarily fights and quarrels. (...) If there is no great man to make order reign, the crowd will be the source of disorder and fighting" (*gua* no. 45, Cui, "gathering together," "reunion").

Gua Cui

In comparison to *gua* Bi, Cui has two continuous traits. It is built of Dui, marsh, up, and Kun down, symbolizing the gathering of water over the earth. The fourth trait could unite the emperor (the fifth trait) with the crowd below, but this continuous line is in the wrong position (the fourth belongs to Earth, to negativity), which warns that, sometimes, even if the crowd follows the emperor and associates around him, the direction of governing may not be the right one; there are situations when the emperor is an usurper or an evil man who captivates the crowd for his unjust and criminal purposes.

The founding of societies or civilizations, similar to the production of the world – as *Ordo ab Chao*, draws its reality from the Principle, whose vicar is the Emperor. *Gua* no. 7, Shi, signifies also the gathering, but as an army, and in this case (in comparison to *gua* Bi) the only continuous trait is placed in the second position, mirroring the emperor's position from Bi: it represents the temporal power obeying the Emperor; it is the army general's position.

Gua Shi

In *gua* no. 20, Guan, the wind (Xun, the upper trigram) takes the place of *gua* Cui's marsh; the Emperor is compared with the wind, alluding to the fact that he has a great liberty.[1]

Gua Guan

Zheng Zi commented on it: "The wind runs over the earth, encompassing it, and touching all things,[2] which constitutes the symbolic image of overseeing, of the one who sees everything. Therefore, the first emperors accomplished this image by following the ritual rule of inspecting the provinces, supervising the peoples' customs and establishing social institutes and rules for instruction."

"The Son of Heaven covers and inspects the four regions, and observes (*guan*) the people; he establishes the instructions and plays the role of a mirror in which the people look (*guan*)"; at the same time, "the emperor looks (*guan*) at the spiritual way (*shen Dao*) above him,"[3] since from above he is invested with Heaven's mandate and the power to look after and down at the

---

[1] The marsh, due to its characteristics, is an emblem of the crowd; the wind illustrates the emperor. In the Christian tradition, the Holy Spirit is free like the wind, blowing wherever he wants.

[2] In the Hindu tradition, *bhûta* air or wind (*vâyu*) corresponds to the tactile sense.

[3] "This way, extremely intelligent, the most spiritual, *shen*, cannot be designated by a name."

people.[1] The Emperor's way of governing is the Principle's way; the Emperor's attributes are the Principle's attributes; the effects of the Emperor's activity are the effects of Heaven's Activity. The *Yi Jing* said: "Heaven's influence is activity; the initiate imitates it, striving without respite." The initiate, covering the Way, realizes Liberation and Illumination; he unites with the Principle and becomes at the same time Emperor, obtaining the Kingdom of Heaven; though, this Kingdom is not the exterior changeable empire.

If one has the curiosity to look at India's map, one will notice that various regions of the country are called *pradesh*. The word *pradesh*, in fact *paradesh*, in Sanskrit means "supreme region;" from this word is derived the well-known appellative "paradise," a remarkable thing suggesting that, for a traditional mentality, any country has the right and even the obligation to represent a land of prosperity and peace, based on the concord (*cum – cordia*, "the union of hearts") government – people,[2] on justice and natural laws (*dharma*).

---

[1] The *Guan* ideogram shows a huge eye:

[2] The government is the prince's mirror, as we can see in these two ideograms (Wieger 87):

In the same way, when the emperor invested someone with a function, he split a piece of jade in two and gave him half (Wieger 147); we notice that the two halves are symmetrical:

In the Judaic and Christian traditions, the legitimate leader of such an ideal *paradesh* is the mysterious Melkisedek, "the King of Justice" (Ebr. *melek* = "king," *tsedeq* = "justice"), the Lord of Salem, that is, the Lord of Peace.

In other words, in a traditional society, the king, obeying the cosmic Law, was seen as a warrantor of peace and justice, his residence being the core of the World Wheel, from where he regulates[1] its rotation, interfering as little as possible with the public activities,[2] striving to realize a perfect harmony between himself and the people,[3] establishing a prosperous and good government.[4]

"The emperor Yao strived to rule the people of the kingdom, and he thought he maintained a perfect government within the four seas. Having gone to see the four (Perfect) Ones [the Guardians of the Rule] on the distant island [the World Center, the Pivot], when (he returned to his capital) he admitted

---

[1] In the Hindu tradition, the king was Chakravarti, "the one who turns the wheel," and Dharmachakra, "The Wheel of Law," symbolized the World; the king was the Latin *rex*, who regulates and guards the rules (the words rex, regulate and rule are related).

[2] The traditional leader had the duty to oversee that the natural regulations were observed; the less artificial decrees he promulgated, the less he interfered in the public details, the more the country prospered.

[3] Tit Livy affirmed: *Multitudo semper ferme regenti est similis* ("the populace always is similar to its leader"). Yet Joseph de Maistre said: "No nation owes its character to the government; on the contrary, the nation owes its government to its character," that is, "each nation has the leader it deserves." Therefore, the populace must contribute, in the same proportion as its leader, to the realization of "paradise," obeying the Law (in the Islamic tradition, each member of the society is a Muslim, that is, "complying with the divine Will"). The *Yi Jing* stated: "The Dao of emperor signifies to supervise, from the height of his exceptional rank, the plan of Providence, while everything contained inside the four cardinal points follows his government and obeys him; if the emperor realizes and operates the celestial Way (Dao), all the provinces enjoy peace."

[4] A good government means to respect and understand the *principial* Rule (in Daoism), the supreme Law (Dharma, in the Hindu tradition), which means *eynomia*, the good legislation (see Plato). If the Law is tarnished and desecrated by ignorant, arrogant, and fake translators, who deceive the people, there are in that country no more "Muslims" but "anti-Muslims," and this truth applies to any nation, including the Islamic countries.

to have ruined his government [with his artificial endeavor]" (*Zhuang-zi*, 1, 6/D). The traditional perspective[1] is so different that probably the modern mentality is completely obtuse to it. No profane individual would understand today that a leader of a country, region, company, organization, or group must do nothing in disaccord with the natural law and with the welfare of people, that he must forbid completely his individual impulses, and repress his desire to express his power by inventing all types of rules.

"Therefore the superior man, who feels himself constrained to engage in the administration of the world will find it his best way to do nothing. In (that policy of) doing nothing, he can rest in the instincts of the nature with which he is endowed. Hence he who will administer (the government of) the world, honouring it as he honours his own person, may have that government committed to him, and he who will administer it, loving it as he loves his own person, may have it entrusted to him" (*Zhuang-zi*, 11, 2/A).

In our modern world, the individual initiative is the most praised characteristic. It is the characteristic of a revolted Shûdra, of course.[2] Even if various leaders will try to hide their initiatives under the cover of stentorian words such as "in the name of the people" or "it is God's Will," make no mistake: it is all about their own limited, pitiful and ignorant desires and ideas; it is about their own greed and arrogance. It is amazing how such people cannot learn from the natural laws; how they

---

[1] We always have to keep in mind the difference between "religion" and Tradition; too often the modern people confuse, purposely or not, these two domains, and we witness the inanity of blaming Tradition for today's contradictions. The Shaikh al-'Arabî ad-Darqâwî said in his *Letters*: "I understood the prophetic saying: 'Better an hour of meditation than seventy years of religious practice.'"

[2] We must insist: when we talk about the modern or revolted Shûdras, we don't have in mind the normal and natural Shûdras, who have as their main characteristic obedience, a very important trait in any initiatory and spiritual process. We refer to the ages of disorder when the Shûdras usurped the place of Brahmanas and Kshatriyas, becoming pseudo-Shûdras.

cannot see that a simple storm is impossible to stop, how they, like puppets on strings, play their dissolvent roles.

"Therefore, if the superior man will keep (the faculties lodged in) his five viscera unemployed, and not display his powers of seeing and hearing, while he is motionless as a representative of the dead, his dragon-like presence will be seen; while he is profoundly silent, the thunder (of his words) will resound; while his movements are (unseen) like those of a spirit, all heavenly influences will follow them; while he is (thus) unconcerned and does nothing, his genial influence will attract and gather all things round him: what leisure has he to do anything more for the government of the world?" (*Zhuang-zi*, 11, 2/A).[1]

What Zhuang Zi described here was, of course, an ideal case, difficult to follow in the "Iron Age," and we have to keep in mind that in Zhuang Zi's times the tenebrous age was fully evolved. The following anecdote will stress why today's endeavour to "subdue the nature in favour of humankind" and "for a better life" is, in fact, a lethal peril, even if it is truly desired, and, again, only a profane individual could believe that such an enterprise would have an auspicious ending. *Quidquid agis prudenter agas et respice finem.* But what we see today in the whole world is a tremendous appetite to act without any intellectual thinking, without any providential intuition, without any vision of the ending.

"Huang-di had been on the throne for nineteen years, and his ordinances were in operation all through the kingdom, when he heard that Guang cheng was living on the summit of Kung-tung, and went to see him. 'I have heard,' he said, 'that you, Sir, are well acquainted with the perfect Dao. I venture to ask you what is the essential thing in it. I wish to take the subtlest influences of heaven and earth, and assist with them the (growth of the) five cereals for the (better) nourishment of the people. I also wish to direct the (operation of the) Yin and Yang, so as to secure the comfort of all living beings. How shall

---

[1] This is what Guénon called "the activity of presence."

I proceed to accomplish those objects?' Guang cheng replied, 'You push your ambition to the limit, wanting to govern nature. If you receive such a power, you will ruin all the beings. According to your government of the world, the vapours of the clouds, before they were collected, would descend in rain; the herbs and trees would shed their leaves before they became yellow; and the light of the sun and moon would hasten to extinction. Your mind is that of a flatterer with his plausible words; it is not fit that I should tell you the perfect Dao.' Huang-di withdrew and gave up (his government of) the kingdom" (*Zhuang-zi*, 11, 4/C).

The next anecdote will elaborate on the difference between a real king and a profane leader, between a traditional government and a government of usurpers, if not worse. The major element of governing is, we must stress, the concordant government – people, the peace of the kingdom and the welfare of the society.

"Yao asked Hu Yu, saying, 'Is Nie Kue fit to be the correlate of Heaven? (If you think he is), I will avail myself of the services of Wang Yi to constrain him (to take my place).' Hu Yu replied, 'Such a measure would be hazardous, and full of peril to the kingdom! The character of Nie Kue is this; he is acute, perspicacious, shrewd and knowing, ready in reply, sharp in retort, and hasty; his natural (endowments) surpass those of other men, but by his human qualities he prevents the Heaven, the Principle from governing; he exercises his discrimination in suppressing his errors, but he does not know what is the source from which his errors arise. Make him the correlate of Heaven! He would employ the human qualities, so that no regard would be paid to the Heavenly gift. Moreover, he would assign different functions to the different parts of the one person. Moreover, honour would be given to erudition, and he would have his plans take effect with the speed of fire. Moreover, he would be the slave of everything he initiated. Moreover, he would be embarrassed by things. Moreover, he would be looking all around for the response of things (to his measures). Moreover, he would be responding to the opinion of the multitude as to what was right. Moreover, he would be changing as things change, and would not begin to have any principle of constancy. How can such a man be fit to be the correlate of Heaven? Nevertheless, as there are the smaller branches of a family and the common ancestor of all its branches, he might be the father of a branch, but not the father of the fathers of all the branches. Such government (as he would conduct) would lead to disorder. It would be calamity in the position of a minister, and ruin if he were in the position of the sovereign" (*Zhuang-zi*, 12, 5/E).

Various traditions dealt with the way of governing. In the *Dao De Jing*, Lao Zi stated: "In the highest antiquity, everything was in accordance with the Principle; (the people) did not know that there were (rulers). In the next age, they loved them and praised them (because of their benevolence). In the next, they feared them (because of their laws); in the next, they despised them (because of their injustice). Thus it was that when faith (in the Dao) was deficient (in the rulers) a want of faith in them ensued (in the people) (XVII). "Governing a large country is like frying a small fish. You spoil it with too much poking" (LX). "Why are the people starving? Because the rulers eat up the money in taxes. Therefore the people are starving. Why are the people rebellious? Because the rulers interfere too much. Therefore they are rebellious. Why do the people think so little of death? Because the rulers demand too much of life. Therefore the people take death lightly. Having little to live on, one knows better than to value life too much" (LXXV).

Lama Rajah of Dugyul affirmed: "The king who became rich by robbing his subjects, who rejects the white umbrella of the ten virtues, who does not reward or punish the good and bad deeds, such a king runs to his own end."

Finally, in the Hindu tradition, the *Mânava-Dharma-Shastra* stated: "For, when these creatures, being without a king, through fear dispersed in all directions, the Lord created a king for the protection of this whole (creation)" (7.3). "Let him act with justice in his own domain, with rigour chastise his enemies, behave without duplicity towards his friends, and be lenient towards Brahmanas. The fame of a king who behaves thus, even though he subsists by gleaning, is spread in the world, like a drop of oil on water" (7.32-33). "The king has been created (to be) the protector of the castes (*varna*) and orders, who, all according to their rank, discharge their several duties" (7.35). "Not to turn back in battle, to protect the people, to honour the Brahmanas, is the best means for a king to secure happiness" (7.88). "That king who through folly rashly oppresses his kingdom, (will), together with his relatives, ere long be deprived of his life and of his kingdom" (7.111).

With regard to the Shûdras, the *Mânava-Dharma-Shastra* declared: "A Brahmana who subsists only by the name of his caste (*gati*), or one who merely calls himself a Brahmana (though his origin be uncertain), may, at the king's pleasure, interpret the law to him, but never a Shûdra. The kingdom of that monarch, who looks on while a Shûdra settles the law, will sink (low), like a cow in a morass. That kingdom where Shûdras are very numerous, which is infested by atheists and destitute of twice-born (inhabitants), soon entirely perishes, afflicted by famine and disease" (8.20-22).

The *Mânava-Dharma-Shastra* also stated an apparently curious rule: "Day and night the king must strenuously exert himself to conquer his senses; for he (alone) who has conquered his own senses, can keep his subjects in obedience (7.44). Zhuang Zi said too: "Jian Wu went to see the fool (recluse), Ji-yu, who said to him, 'What did Ru-Zhung-Shu tell you?' The reply was, 'He told me that when rulers gave forth their regulations according to their own views and enacted righteous measures, no one would venture not to obey them, and all would be transformed.' Ji-yu said, 'That is but the hypocrisy of virtue. For the right ordering of the world it would be like trying to wade through the sea and dig through the Yellow River, or employing a mosquito to carry a mountain on its back. And when a sage is governing, does he govern men's outward actions? He gives example of virtue [rectitude, De], which people, if they want, will follow" (*Zhuang-zi*, 7, 2/B). And Zheng Zi made this comment in connection with the *Yi Jing*: "The family is the reduced image of the empire. (...) Dao of emperor means that the emperor reforms his own person, to regulate the family, and if the family is correctly organized, the universe is in order."

There is, in accordance with the traditional lore, a perfect analogy between macrocosm and microcosm, and also between a human being and the social organism. Therefore, the traditional leader, instead of governing the outside, will strive first to control his own being, realizing the inner kingdom,[1] the castle inside the heart, the Hindu Brahma-pura. As Plato showed in *Politeia*, the Cosmos (Gr. "order")[2] is reflected accordingly in universe, city (or society), and in the individual's soul, the royal man being the one who realizes, by the way of wisdom, "the inner republic," this realization being precisely the *politeia*![3]

As Yoga or Dao means both the way toward the target, and the target itself, so Politeia designates not only the city or the kingdom itself, but also the realization of it; it represents the policy of the traditional leader, who, in order to establish a social and exterior *paradesh*, must first realize and accomplish an inner paradise, where Peace will reign, the real Salem (identical to Brahma-pura and the Heavenly Jerusalem) residing in the heart, where *mishkat al-anwâr*, the tabernacle of Light, is placed.[4]

Such a *politeia*, for a traditional society, is the warrantor of a good government, but it appears nowadays as an ideal policy,

---

[1] It is said in the Christian tradition: *Regnum Dei intra vos est.*

[2] The Cosmos is, of course, not the "cosmos" of the modern scientists, who are completely sunk in the domain of quantity.

[3] The monarch, through his orders, realizes Order; placed in the center of the wheel, as Chakravarti, he, in a ritual mode, produces and regulates the Cosmos. In the Judaic tradition and also in the Christian one, the first order was *Fiat Lux*. In the Hindu tradition, the king is *antaryami*, "the inner ruler." In the Islamic tradition, the realization of the "inner kingdom" means *el-jihâdul-akbar.*

[4] Ghazali stressed that the true Light corresponds to the "eye of the heart": "There is truly in the man's heart (*qalb*) an eye (*ayn*), which possesses the perfection [to see the absolute Light]. (...) This inner eye belongs to another world that is the heavenly kingdom (*Malakût*)." The light that shines in Malkût, the inner kingdom, is Dante's "silent light" and the Hesychastic "perfumed light."

much too different and incomprehensible for the modern mentality[1]; since it is clear enough that a *politeia*, to be successful today, requires a wisdom (*khawashsh al-khawashsh*) that facilitates avoiding errors (*Al-Munqidh min al-Dalâl*), and that seems nowhere to be found in our profane world; the Buddhist adage *dharmam saranam gacchâmi* ("I seek refuge in order and laws") is, in the present days, more neglected than ever.

Let us offer one more quotation, even if we know that so many modern minds prefer a plain, simple text, exempted of footnotes and quotations.

"A time arrived when a great disorder ensued in the world, and sages and worthies no longer shed their light on it. The Principle and its characteristics ceased to be regarded as uniform; other principles were invented, the discussions commenced, and everyone considered his opinion the right one. Many in different places got one glimpse of it, and plumed themselves on possessing it as a whole. They might be compared to the discussions among an ear, eye, nose, and mouth. Each sense had its own faculty and was right, but their different faculties cannot be interchanged. So it was with the many branches of the various schools. Each had its peculiar excellence, and there was the time for the use of it; but notwithstanding no one covered or extended over the whole (range of truth). The case was that of the narrow-minded scholar who passes his judgment on all the beautiful in heaven and earth, discriminates the principles that underlie all things, and attempts to estimate the success arrived at by the ancients. Seldom is it that such an one can embrace all the beautiful in heaven and earth, or rightly estimate the ways of the spiritual and intelligent; and thus it was that the Dao, which inwardly forms the sage and externally the king, became obscured and

---

[1] Without details, we should mention the immense difference between the traditional civilizations of the so-called "native" people of the world, which were based on harmony and a complete accord with nature, and the modern civilization that destroyed them, in the name of "civilization." The *politeia* of the native peoples meant a conformity to order that brought happiness, music and light.

185

lost its clearness, became repressed and lost its development. Everyone in the world did whatever he wished, and was the rule unto himself. Alas! The various schools held to their several ways, and could not come back to the same point, nor agree together. The students of that later age unfortunately did not see the undivided purity of heaven and earth, and the great scheme of truth held by the ancients. The system of the Dao was about to be torn into fragments all under the sky" (*Zhuang Zi*, 33, 1/A).

Zhuang Zi describes nothing less than the reign of the revolted Shûdras; and, all the more, his sayings match the actual situation of the world. Each modern Shûdra is so conceited, so arrogant of his pseudo-knowledge, so final with respect to his opinion, so thirsty for gossip, so ready and inflexible in criticizing any detail, any trivial mistake, but so totally ignores the essence and whole, that even the suggestion of such a notion like *Politeia* would be an insult for him.

The modern Shûdras have no clue how important the spiritual activity is[1] and how this occurs. They, who are the personification of selfishness, think that the salvation of the world can be accomplished with common, individual and inferior means. They don't understand what the Liberation signifies, as a result of an initiatory process, which is regarded as a selfish enterprise, a non-action; they don't understand that the sage in his non-action develops a tremendous spiritual activity and this activity is not egoistic but regards the welfare of the whole world. Such an activity, like meditating upon a sacred text, during the initiatory realization, and plunging deeply into its real significance, represents enormously more than any humanitarian or militant actions.[2] The modern Shûdras have no idea that there are other ways, besides the corporeal ones, that

---

[1] To prevent any misunderstanding, we must insist that "spiritual" has nothing to do with what the modern world tries to suggest it represents, and is not connected with religious notions like "faith" and "belief."

[2] The Shaikh al-'Arabî ad-Darqâwî said in his *Letters*: "Strike neither Jew nor Christian nor Moslem, but strike your own soul *(nafs)* and do not cease to strike it until it dies!"

are much more efficient, which lead to Salem. In Paradise, in Salem, everything is in accordance with natural laws, from both viewpoints, of Man and Cosmos. It is impossible today for the modern mentality to comprehend the situation of a profound concord between man, water, fire, sky, animals, plants and earth, as stated in Daoist texts, since the profane man, instead of standing as a central being, as a pivot, behaves often and persistently in an inferior way, below the animal reign.[1]

There is no other reason for the origin of "zoological gardens." In the ancient civilizations, the emperor's residence included such a garden, not only to illustrate the absolute and central power, as well as the emperor's heavenly mandate, but to stress that his residence symbolized the paradise, the Salem.[2] The animal's natural state was at the beginning a "domestic" and not a "wild" one. As the tradition affirms, there was a great familiarity between men and animals, their understanding being "mutual." The Far-Eastern tradition considered that "in paradise, the genies lived together with animals and the saints looked to obtain animals' familiarity." In fairy tales, the hero understood the animal speech, and sages, like Francis of Assisi, Ramana Maharshi or the Daoist seers, tamed the animals with their look. Plato mentioned, in his *Politeia*, the conversation with the animals in the times of Kronos; and in the Hesychastic work, *Récits d'un Pèlerin russe*, it is said that all the animals obeyed Adam.

Lie Zi talked about Liang Yang, the guard of the king's zoological garden, who was skillful in rearing wild beasts and birds. Different species lived in peace together, and the king wanted to know Yang's secret. But Liang Yang replied: "There is no secret; I have no art to teach you. Each animal has its own nature and if you are in accord with it, the animals are happy, if not, they are offended. Although tigers are a different species from man, when they fawn on the man who rears them it is

---

[1] It is not our purpose, but a comparison between today's behaviour of man and wolf, for example, would bring surprising results.
[2] The name "garden" associated to animals refers to the garden of Paradise.

because he lets them have their way and is in conformity with their nature; and likewise, when they kill him, it is because he opposes their nature" (*Lie-zi*, *The Yellow Emperor*, 7). Such a pacific state was the primordial state, when the animals lived in peace with men, in accordance with natural laws, and the important thing was the concord, "the harmony of hearts," the mutual wisdom, and not the external differences.[1]

The sage, *shengren*,[2] Lie Zi explained (*Lie-zi*, *The Yellow Emperor*, 18), prefers those who share his wisdom, demanding an identity on wisdom and not on form, but the ordinary man feels closer to those who look like himself; a man, although he has the form of a man, may well have the soul of a beast. On the other hand, Fu Xi, Niu Wa, Sheng-nong, and Xia Hu had, some of them, dragon bodies, others, bull heads or tiger jaws. These beings did not have human forms, but they were in possession of the great sages' Rectitude. Lie Zi also mentioned Kui, the music master, similar to Orpheus, whose music tamed and attracted the animals and so, how could the beasts' souls be different from men's? The sages, *shengren*, knew everything and possessed the wisdom and therefore they could attract and control. "In the most ancient times," Lie Zi concluded, "men and animals lived together and walked side by side. In the time of the Five Emperors and the Three Kings, the animals were frightened away and scattered for the first time. In our own degenerate times, they crouch in hiding and flee to their lairs to avoid harm. Even now, in the East, there are many people who understand the speech of domestic animals. The divine sages of the most ancient times knew the habits of all the myriad of things, and interpreted the sounds of all the different species."

There should be no distinction between the Emperor and Man (transcendent, perfect, veritable or wise), but with the decadence of the world and of the emperors (when animals

---

[1] This very important Daoist statement has many consequences in our world.

[2] René Guénon considered *zhenren*, "the veritable man," to be related to Lesser Mysteries, and *shenren*, "the transcendent man," to be related to Greater Mysteries. In this spiritual hierarchy, *shengren*, the sage, Guénon said, is at the bottom, identical to the Confucianist sage (the top of Confucianist hierarchy).

"crouch in hiding and flee to their lairs to avoid harm"), the Far-Eastern tradition preferred to describe the divine or perfect sage as a role model. In the primordial state, when the animals and men were in concord, *principial* unity and immutability reigned, and there were no oppositions caused by form or colour. The oppositions appeared due to the universal rotation (the whirl of changes) and multiplicity; if the rotation stopped, the oppositions would cease to exist.

The perfect man pervades all substances, metal or stone, without resistance; the perfect man walks under water without encountering any obstruction, treads on fire without being burned, and walks on high above all things without any fear. The perfect man is established in the center of the wheel, beyond changes and multiplicity, and he opposes nothing and no one. If a man is crossing a river in a boat, and another empty vessel comes into collision with it, he will not be angry with it, since no other man opposes him; yet, if there is somebody in the other boat, he will bawl out to him and shout and curse him. Formerly, he thought the boat was empty, but now there is a person in it. If a man can empty himself of his individuality, during his time in the world, who can harm him? (*Zhuang-zi*, 19, 2/B; 20, 2B).

The transcendent man is Heaven in a human form. Void of any contingencies, he hides inside the transcendence. With all his purity, he is forbearing to others; where they are without Dao, he rectifies in silence their demeanour. The common or exterior sage sustains all things, following the current of beings. The transcendent man sustains and is beneficent to the current of beings, but he is established in Dao, outside the current (*Zhuang-zi*, 21, 1/A; 22, 5/E).

The transcendent man is like a child, and all the traditions agree in describing this divine state as that of a child-like one. Lao Zi stated: "Can you become a little child? The child will cry all day, without its throat becoming hoarse; so perfect is his new nature. He will keep his fingers closed all day without relaxing their grasp; such is the concentration of his powers. He will keep his eyes fixed all day; so is he unaffected by the external things. He walks without target; he rests without reason; he is calmly indifferent to things, and follows nature. These are what I call the breaking of the ice, and the dissolving of the cold, the commencing of the transcendent man's way. I asked whether you could become a little child. The little child moves unconscious of what he is doing, and walks unconscious of whither he is going. His body is like the branch of a rotten tree, and his mind is like slaked lime. Being such, misery does not come to him, nor happiness. He has neither misery nor happiness, how can he suffer from the calamities incident to men?" (*Zhuang-zi*, 23, 5-6/C).

The transcendent man, even though the lesser, knows the Greater. He knows it as The Great Unity; The Great Mystery; The Great Illuminator; The Great Framer; The Great Boundlessness; The Great Truth; The Great Determiner. This makes his knowledge complete (*Zhuang-zi*, 24, 14/M).

There is, though, an important difference between the Emperor and the transcendent man. In the case of the latter, the sage does not have the sacrificial mission to come back into the world as a public figure. The Emperor, on the other hand, is the one who has accomplished not only the ascendant spiritual realization, but also the descendant one. He suffers the sacrifice to come back into the world, to reveal himself, and govern a new cycle. In comparison to the transcendent man, who "comes alone and goes alone, comes out alone and goes in alone" (*Lie-zi*, *Endeavour and Destiny*, 9), the Emperor is not alone. Fu Xi is represented as having his dragon tail interlaced with Niu Wa's dragon tail; Fu Xi even changed his attribute with Niu Wa's.

Niu Wa is the Emperor's sister and wife, which brings us to another important symbol of the Far-Eastern tradition, related to Man's way: the family symbol.

In the traditional China, the family was the fundament of the social organization, but it also represented the Whole, from a *principial* viewpoint: Heaven – the active Perfection is the Father, Earth – the passive Perfection is the Mother of ten thousand beings, and the Man is the World or the universal

Existence. We observe here the Great Triad, Tian – Di – Ren, but this sacred triad is necessary only for our worldly benefit. When the jaws are closed, Tian, Di, and Ren unite and the Wedding takes place within the Void, in non-manifestation.[1]

If we reverse the Sun's trigrams (*gua* no. 41), Dui (marsh) will be up and Gen (mountain) down, which represents *gua* no. 31, Xian. Xian illustrates precisely the Wedding, the divine union, *hierogamos*.

gua Sun   *gua* Xian

Marsh up and mountain down describes the reversal of normal hierarchy, associated with the hierogamic exchange that seals the union.[2] In the Far-Eastern tradition, as we have already noted a few times, Fu Xi has the square and Niu Wa the compass. The *Yi Jing*, when it presents in its hexagrams the symbolic image of union, harmony, or wedding, also underlines the hierogamic exchange.[3]

The commentaries on *gua* Xian affirmed: "The male tendencies are firmness and sincerity, and they cause the masculine being to descend for the union; the female heart is satisfied and the feminine being ascends, sympathetic, toward

---

[1] However, the ideogram for "union" is a triad, a triangle:

[2] In the Christian tradition, for example, the groom and the bride exchange rings. The symbol of Yin-Yang, from this point of view, suggests the same union and exchange.

[3] "When you make male and female into a single one, so that the male will not be male and the female will not be female, (...) then you will enter the kingdom of heaven" (*The Gospel of Thomas*, 22).

the masculine. (…) Masculine and feminine unite and influence each other. Emperor and vassal, superior and inferior, all obey the law of reciprocal influences. (…) If the emperor and vassal influence each other, then emperor's Dao and vassal's Dao are free and open; if superior and inferior influence each other, then their tendencies freely develop. And it similarly happens to father and son, husband and wife, friends and companions; if there are in each case reciprocal influences, then peace and harmony freely reign."

The hierogamic exchange imposes the man to kneel in front of the woman, a symbolic gesture cultivated by Chivalry. *Gua* Xian's commentaries stated: "The malleable sweetness up, the energy down, they influence each other and unite; joy and halt. Masculine bows in front of feminine; this means to enjoy freedom and the advantage of perfection." Zheng Zi explained: "Negativity and positivity united, the boy and girl join together and exchange their influences. Moreover, *gua* Dui, the girl, is up; simple *gua* Gen, the boy, is down. (…) When the man bows in front of the woman, the highest concord takes place. (…) Heaven and Earth unite and influence each other; they transform and produce all ten thousand beings." And the symbolic formula said: "Above the mountain, the marsh: union."

Nevertheless, the *Yi Jing* does not forget the importance of maintaining, at the same time, a normal hierarchy. "In *gua* Heng, the boy is situated above the girl; the man has the privileged position, the girl has the inferior rank; it is Dao of husband and wife inside the home;" *Gua* no. 32, Heng, is built of Zhen, the eldest son (thunderbolt), up and of Xun, the eldest daughter (wind), down.

Gua Heng

The hierogamic union has the Great Triad as immediate effect, with the birth of Man, and so, the commentary on hexagram Xian continued in this mode: "What makes all the hearts of the universe enjoy respite and peace is the saintly man's influence upon them. Scrutinizing the reason for Heaven and Earth to unite and influence each other, and to produce all ten thousand beings, and examining how the saintly man, in accordance with Dao, influences the people's hearts, bringing harmony and concord, the nature of Heaven, and Earth, and of all the beings becomes clear" and "only extreme sincerity can influence the people." With regard to "extreme sincerity," we note *gua* no. 61, Zhong Fu, which has in the middle (*zhong*) two broken traits (and at its each extreme two continuous lines), associated with this commentary: "The two malleabilities inside this *gua*: it is the symbolic image of the inner void, which represents the good faith and perfect sincerity." Zheng Zi added: "Inner sincerity and purity; in this situation, there is sympathetic correspondence with Heaven. Dao of Heaven is nothing else but perfect sincerity."

Gua Zhong Fu

Gua Xian could be derived from the fall equinox's *gua* (Pi, no. 12), with Qian up and Kun down, by exchanging between them the superior traits of the two simple *guas* (negativity takes the place of positivity in the sixth position, and positivity takes the place of negativity in the third position). The hexagram Pi indicates the divorce, and now, the hexagram Xian announces the wedding as a result of the hierogamic exchange, yet this exchange is not perfect, not complete, like in *gua* Tai (no. 11), because it suggests also the natural hierarchy in the family. Zheng Zi made these comments: "Heaven and Earth existing, the existence of all ten thousand beings occurs immediately, as a result; consequently, the distinction of sexes[1] and the relation husband-wife occur. The relation husband-wife produces, necessarily, the relation father-child, and from here, the relation emperor-vassal. From this last one, the relation superior-inferior results; this produces, in its turn, the ritual rules and the reciprocal duties. Heaven and Earth are the origins of the ten thousand beings, and the relation husband-wife is the origin of all the social relations. The wedding is the origin of everything, and family is the fundament of Cosmos and, in particular, of the society." And Zheng Zi added: "The family is the reduced image of the empire. (…) Dao of emperor means that the emperor reforms his own person, to regulate the family, and if the family is correctly organized, the universe is in order."

The hexagrams are symbols of everything that exists in the universe; but even more, they are symbols of what does not exist, and therefore, the hexagram can also be the reduced model of the family. *Gua* no. 37, Jia Ren, symbolizes Dao within the family,[2] with Xun (wind) up and Li (fire) down, the fire situated inside (the inner trigram) signifying the home's hearth.

Gua Jia Ren

Zhu Xi commented on this *gua*: "The superior trait represents the father, the first trait represents the son, the fifth and third the husband, the fourth and second – the wife." Moreover, the *ba* (eight) *guas* compose a family, as we have already seen: "Qian, Heaven is also called father; Kun, Earth is also the mother; Zhen (thunderbolt) expresses a quake, an agitation, and it represents the masculine principle, being called the eldest son;

---

[1] Etymologically, this word means "distinction."
[2] The ideogram shows a "boar" inside the house. "The family is the image of the empire," the traditional commentary said.

Xun (wind) expresses an agitation too and it is called the eldest daughter; Kan (water), a new shakeup, resulting in the masculine, and therefore it is the middle son; Li (fire), another quake, resulting a girl, and therefore it is called the middle daughter; Gen (mountain), a third quake, resulting in a masculine principle, and so it is called the youngest son; Dui (marsh), the third shakeup and feminine principle, therefore it is called the youngest daughter."

This commentary presents a large numbered family,[1] nothing unusual for the Far-Eastern traditional society; but we discover here primarily a sacred meaning, the three sons and three daughters referring to the three lights and three *gunas*, to the heavenly and earthly influences and tendencies. Nevertheless, this family can be reduced to a Triad, Father – Mother – Son, as reflected in the social rules where the eldest son had preponderance.

The fall equinox's hexagram, Pi, from which *gua* Xian derived, could be an emblem of the family as essential triad, illustrating the following commentary: "Among the six traits, first and second (two broken lines) represent Earth (the Mother); third and fourth (broken and continuous lines) represent the Man (the Son uniting Heaven's positivity and Earth's negativity); fifth and the superior one (continuous traits) represent Heaven (the Father)."

Gua Pi

In the *Book of Rituals* it was stated: "In Man's composition Heaven's and Earth's strength are united, due to the encounter

---

[1] We have here in mind the traditional family, of course, where the hierogamic exchange and the normal hierarchy were natural ways of life. The modern family is an image of worldly disarray and disorder – no hierarchy, the young not listen to the elder, the elder is not wiser than the younger, and so on.

of *yang* and *yin*, and to the union of inferior and superior spirits, *shen*"; and Huai Nan Zi affirmed: "The sages make Heaven their father and Earth their mother, and *yin* and *yang* their reliable string."

The Great Triad, Tian – Di – Ren, the *principial* family, is highlighted here. "What constitutes the *Yi Jing*, what makes it perfect and immense, is the fact that it contains Dao of Heaven, Dao of Man, and Dao of Earth. The *Yi Jing* reunites the three great efficient causes and each one is doubled, which means six."

This triad, found in various other traditions, cannot be an equivalent of the Christian Holy Trinity. René Guénon explained that, if in the Great Triad the first and the last terms are somehow symmetrical and complementary, in the Holy Trinity, the second term derives from the first one and the third (corresponding to the second term of the Great Triad) is not the son of the other two. In fact, Guénon wrote: "'the operations of the Holy Spirit' with regard to Christ's birth correspond to the Heavenly Father's activity of presence (in the Hindu tradition Purusha)[1]; the Virgin, on the other hand, is a perfect image of Prakriti, designated by the Hindu tradition as Earth; with regard to Christ himself, he obviously is identical to the Universal Man.[2] Hence, if we want to find a concordance, we should say, using Christian theology's terms, that Triad does not concern the generation of the Word *ad intra*, which is included in the concept of the Trinity, but the generation *ad*

---

[1] The Holy Spirit corresponds to the stork that brings the new-born. The stork, like the swan, heron, etc., is the "feathered serpent," unifying Heaven and Earth, and alluding to *avatâra* as Universal Man and Mediator. In the Christian tradition it is said: "Therefore be as shrewd as snakes and as innocent as doves" (*Matthew* 10:16), and Clement of Alexandria wrote about the Gnostic that he unifies the serpent and the dove (VII, 13); the dove is an emblem of the Holy Spirit.

[2] René Guénon wrote in the footnote: "We stress again, related to this, that we do not want to deny the 'historical' aspect of some events as such, but, on the contrary, we consider the historical facts as symbols of a superior reality, and only for this reason are they interesting for us."

extra, that is, in conformity with the Hindu tradition, the birth of Avatâra in the manifested world."[1] The Blessed Virgin, as mother of *avatâra*, Guénon stated,[2] corresponds rather to Shakti of the Hindu tradition, Prakriti being her "terrestrial" projection; Shakti, like Shekinah of the Judaic Kabbalah, is the divine Maiden. *Mâyâ-Shakti* is the superior aspect of the Virgin, woman and mother within the Principle, and "she is first of all, the Principle's Shakti, the same and one with the Principle, its 'maternal' aspect"[3]; *Mâyâ-Prakriti* is the inferior aspect, woman and mother within the world, "and she is also, with regard to her birth in the manifested world, Prakriti."

If we however try to find a triad similar to the Far-Eastern one, that is, a Holy Family, we have to heed the trio Joseph, Mary and Jesus. Saint Mary represents in this case passive Perfection, Kun in the Far-Eastern tradition, the feminine principle as Shakti, the divine Maiden, symbol of Gnosis and Sophia, of (divine) Love and Mercy, mother of *avatâra*. Christ is obviously the Universal Man, the Son of Heaven, and the Emperor. And Joseph should correspond to the celestial Father; yet he is the earthly mortal father, he is what the initiatory scenario calls "the inferior (or unworthy) husband," token of the ego, of the psycho-corporeal individuality, which must be transformed, destroyed and recovered during the initiatory process, the real, immortal husband, token of the Self, of the Spirit, being the Holy Spirit, the lightning of the Far-Eastern tradition, who produces the miracle of the virgin becoming mother.[4] Consequently, we find another triad, "the family triangle" (Holy Spirit, Mary, Joseph), which, in fact, can be

---

[1] Guénon, *Grande Triade*, pp. 20-22.

[2] See, for example, *Mâyâ* (*Études sur l'hindouisme*, Éd. Trad., 1979, p. 101).

[3] Guénon, *Études sur l'hindouisme*, p. 102.

[4] Of course the Holy Spirit is not the celestial Father, but His Activity, therefore the equivalent of the lightning. We should stress that our hermeneutical endeavour does not want to insult Joseph's status (as defined inside the Christian religion), but to bring it to a "mythical" level.

reduced to a couple, the duality Holy Spirit – Saint Mary, at the very moment when the "unworthy husband" is annihilated.

The theme of a "family triangle" is typically initiatory. In the tradition of the ancient Greeks, for example, Hercules, one of the greatest initiatory heroes, has as parents a triad composed by Zeus and Alcmene, plus the "inferior husband," Amphitryon; the "triangle" is obvious since Zeus took Amphitryon's appearance.[1] Zeus took Amphitryon's place; the Holy Spirit took Joseph's place; in this mode *avatâra*, the Son of Heaven can be incorporated into the world. In the Far-Eastern tradition, the emperor is "the Son of Heaven" and there are legends explaining his divine birth and celestial paternity.[2]

In the *Yi Jing*, of hexagram no. 41, Sun, it is said: "When three people journey together, their number decreases by one and then each man finds a companion. Indeed, in the universe everything exists as couples; one and two, by their contrast, they are the origin of all ten thousand beings' birth; three is therefore too much and must decrease: this is the elevated meaning of *guas* Sun (decrease) and Yi (increase)."

Sun – Yi: decrease – increase; in the *Dao De Jing* (XLVIII), this pair is applied to knowledge: the discursive knowledge means an increase in erudition (to intellectual activity's

---

[1] The superior and the inferior "husbands" appear as twins: the immortal-mortal pair. Another famous example is the pair Ulysses – Penelope. Penelope is not only the patron of spiritual realization, but she is also the cosmological activity of God. It is said that Penelope was weaving a shroud for Laertes (*Odyssey* II, 95). Each night she was undoing the work she did during the day. Weaving the web symbolizes the production of the World, the *Fiat Lux*, while dissolving the web during the night means the absorption of the Cosmos back into the Principle. Penelope is the divine Maiden and the suitors represent our lowest passions and appetites, the "inferior husband."

[2] See, for example, Granet, *La religion*, pp. 84-85. We have already talked about the emperor Diku's first wife who stepped into a gigantic footprint (a trace of the One-Footed Principle in manifestation) and therefore she gave birth to Qi, or, how a maiden called Huaxushi stepped on the gigantic footprint and gave birth to Fu Xi. We may note that the emperor himself, at the spring equinox, used to trace three furrows on the soil (Granet, *La religion*, p. 59), which should be compared with the three footprints of some important ideograms.

detriment); the metaphysic knowledge means a gradual decrease of external agitation, of mental actions.

 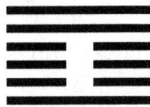

Gua Sun   *Gua* Yi

Pu Zi, in the annexed formulas, added: "Heaven and Earth, by their mysterious union, produce and develop all ten thousand beings; the masculine and feminine principles, by their intimate union, produce all ten thousand beings. The *Yi Jing* says: three people journey together, therefore, one diminishes; a man walks, therefore he has a friend; this expresses the exclusive unity."

The commentary on the *Yi Jing* affirmed: "the masculine and feminine principles' essences unite and produce all ten thousand beings; only the Principle's absolute unity makes the production possible. How could the unique negativity and unique positivity constitute the duality? Thus, when the number becomes three, the decrease is convenient, that is, the exclusive keeping of absolute unity [non-duality]."

Consequently, even though the dragon's beheading means to determine the primordial duality, Heaven – Earth, without which the universal manifestation couldn't be produced, the cosmogony implies also the Wedding, the union Heaven – Earth in non-duality. "The gods say: it is not enough to dismember into pieces the Sacrifice; we must reunite it" (*Aitarêya Brahmana*, I, 18); "dismember Ahi, but then reunite it" (*Atharva Vêda Samhitâ*, 139, 6). In the Hermetic tradition, this double operation is: *separabis terra ab igne, subtile a spisso, suaviter magno cum igenio.*

The supreme Principle, primordial and initial cause of universal manifestation, was in various traditions described as a dragon, without feet, sometimes biting his tail (without head and tail), centrally established in *wu-wei* (that is, lame or without

199

feet or hands), barren (without manifestation) and blind (suggesting the super-luminous night). "The sage knows Dao. He knows without traveling; he understands without seeing; he accomplishes without doing (*wu-wei*)" (*Dao De Jing*, XLVII).

The Great Hero brings back the night and *wu-wei*, and the non-manifestation, by blinding, emasculating or crippling the Dragon, and so the end of time occurs; simultaneously, the Hero accomplishes the restoration of the primordial Dragon; hence, the dragon's reunion is realized not only at the beginning of the world, when the Wedding takes place, but also at the end of the world, a natural symbolism indicating the *principial* identity of the two ends. "The union of man with the woman is called One, and only when the feminine and masculine are united we can use the word One" (*Zohar* III, 7 b).

Moreover, the Wedding, the mysterious and exclusive union, is associated with the dragon's beheading, when Heaven and Earth emerge as duality. This primordial sacrifice is mentioned in *gua* Xie (no. 40): "Heaven and Earth separated, thunderbolt and rain operate; thunderbolt and rain operating, the one hundred fruit, plants and trees break the shell. This moment is great!" The World Egg's shell is broken, the superior hemisphere – Heaven, and the inferior hemisphere – Earth have split the One and produced, using the thunderbolt's operation – the masculine *principial* instrument, and rain's influence – the spiritual influence, the World.

Gua Xie

Gua Xie, built of Zhen (thunderbolt) up and Kan (water, rain) down, "expresses the activity of thunderbolt and rain. Indeed, positivity and negativity unite and mutually influence each other; harmony pervades and gradually spreads. (...) The calamities are straightened out and disappear." This scenario, when the thunderbolt operates, is as well attached with other *guas*, the difference being the "straightening out," a special symbolic operation, which suggests the emptiness of forms (the omniform dragon), and the restoration of the primordial state. The commentary on *gua* Xie said: "*Gua* Kun's substance is immensity, straightened out and uniform. (...) When the sages have straightened out the universe's difficulties, restoring peace and imposing the reign of calmness, then nothing else is to be done." In the primordial state, "Dao of Heaven regulates the emperors; they reign with mercy and charity, spread their benefits and grace, take care of people, even of vegetation and insects. It means conformity with the moment of separation, and union of the emperor's nature with the natures of Heaven and Earth."

It means the Great Triad; yet, the Great Triad could not exist if what was separated, Heaven and Earth do not reunite: "If Heaven and Earth did not meet, the beings would not be born" (*gua* no. 44, Gou). Matgioi commented on Lao Zi's fifth apothegm: "If Heaven and Earth did not unite, the universe would not exist. If the perfect man did not exist, humanity would not have any example to follow; it would be inert, as good as non-existent." And this union takes place both at the beginning and the end of the cycle: "the girl's wedding means the beginning and the end of man" (*gua* no. 54, Gui Mei), the wedding and divorce occurring simultaneously, in the eternal present. "'If at the beginning there were no beings, how come there are beings now?' 'The men who live after us could say there are no beings now.' (...) 'In this case, there is no temporal succession for beings?' (...) 'The starting and ending of beings are not absolute concepts. The start of one is the end of another, the end of one is the start of another. Who knows which came first?'" (*Lie-zi*, *The Questions of Tang*, 1).

EIGHT

EPILOGUE: THE JAWS

EVERYTHING changes in the world, yet the Man embarked on a spiritual journey ennobles the change, since he aims at transformation, and the *Yi Jing*'s old commentaries affirmed: "Dao of Heaven means change and transformation; modification means progressive transformation; transformation is the perfect accomplishment of change; change is the process of producing the ten thousand beings. (...) Transformation is the process of absorbing the beings; it is the good and the perfection."

We observe the descendant way, from Qian to Kun, and the ascendant way, from Kun to Qian, the two ways reflecting the two Hermetic serpents coiled on the Caduceus (*Axis Mundi, Zhong Dao* – the Middle Way): the descendant serpent – celestial influence – follows *Tian Dao*, and the ascendant serpent – terrestrial influence – follows *Di Dao*, which represents the beneficial situation when Heaven and Earth advance towards each other, their influences unite and interlace, the spiritual Wedding takes place – the perfect union, active and passive Perfections melt into the non-dual and absolute Perfection, and now the quadrature of the circle is realized. On the contrary, if what belongs to Heaven ascends and what belongs to Earth descends, divorce or separation is in view, the jaws cannot chew ambrosia anymore, being separated by "Adam's apple" stuck between the maxillaries.

The closed Mouth is the sign of silence, of non-manifestation, and also the Wedding's token, illustrating the Principle enclosing the whole universal manifestation, reminding us of the closed mouth containing the nourishment.[1] To open the mouth implies to drop the nourishment out, which means to produce the world by uttering the word *bhu* (Sanscr. "to be"). We may note how the absorption and swallowing of the worlds and cycles, that is, their death, correspond to pronouncing the sound M (the *mortuary* emblem), with the mouth closed, while B (the *being* emblem) is pronounced explosively, opening the mouth – it is the explosion of the primordial sound. The opened mouth, with Heaven and Earth separated, bangs the initial whirl or tornado; from this whirl, which represents the World Wheel, the worlds will become distinct as spires of the rotational helix, and the whole universal Existence will appear impregnated by this vortex; even the *Yi Jing* is called "The Changes in Circular Rotation."

The *Yi Jing* obstinately repeats that everything in the world of changes follows the way of rotation, the cyclic way – seasons, increase and decrease, life and death succeed one after another, as a wild whirl, controlled by the Principle's endless mill, a mill which, like the mouth, chews the worldly nourishment. "Decrease and increase, plenitude and void succeed and alternate continuously with time" (*gua* no. 41, Sun). "Perfection and decadence, decrease and increase follow like in a circle: it is the very nature of things" (*gua* no. 42, Yi). "When the sun disappears, the moon appears; when the moon disappears, the

---

[1] The ideogram of *gua* Xian (no. 31) shows a mouth closed and a halberd. The halberd destroys the obstacle found between the jaws and the mouth closes: the Wedding and the hierogamic union are accomplished, which is the meaning of this hexagram.

sun appears; sun and moon support each other and the light is born.[1] When cold weather goes away, warm weather comes; when warm weather goes, the cold weather appears. To go away – it is the contraction; to come – it is the expansion; contraction and expansion mutually support each other and the good results. If there is contraction, there will also be expansion; if there is expansion, there will also be contraction: this is called 'influence and sympathy.' Any movement is caused by an influence and any influence has to have a correspondent sympathetic effect; what is a sympathetic effect becomes, in its turn, influence and cause, and any influence and cause become again effect, and so, the succession has no end. The caterpillar's movement has a contraction, followed by an extension, and then another contraction" (*gua* no. 31, Xian). "What diminishes will increase and what increases will diminish" (*Dao De Jing*, XLII).

René Guénon and Matgioi were very explicit about the universal vortex. The primeval whirl is the thunderbolt's effect, illustrated by *gua* no. 42, Yi, with Xun (wind) up and Zhen (thunderbolt) down, where Xun (wind) represents the whirl which accompanies the thunderbolt, and Zhen (thunderbolt), Zheng Zi said, is the symbolic image of the masculine principle. The thunderbolt, found also in the symbol of the mouth (*gua* no. 21, Shi He, and *gua* Yi), is associated with the big bang, quake, sudden shakeup, noise of thunder, light of lightning, and it is the movement's principle; hence, Zhen (thunderbolt) possesses three characteristics typical of the Principle: sound, light and activity.[2]

---

[1] The ancient ideogram *ming* (light), and also the modern one, presents this association.

[2] The Tradition was transmitted using sound and light. The thunderbolt's "fire" facilitates a clear audition and vision: "the clarity of simple *gua* Li, with inner void (middle broken trait), represents the symbolic image of ears and eyes, hearing and seeing with clarity" (*gua* no. 50, Ding).

Epilogue: the Jaws

"The trigram Zhen is considered to express the adult male principle. Its symbolic image is the thunderbolt." *Gua* Zhen (no. 51) is built of Zhen up and Zhen down, and its ideogram is the same as the one for the trigram.

The thunderbolt is *Primum Movens*,[1] which produces the initial impulse, starting the *Circle of changes'* rotation; it liberates the light and illuminates the seers (who know how to see); it

---

The activity sustains the world's whirl. Djalâl ad-Dîn Rûmi chanted: "In the night of my soul/ Along a narrow way/ I digged; and the light burst out;/ An endless world of light"; it is the light from the heart's cave, the light accompanying the thunderbolt. "Many ways lead to Allâh, but I chose the way of dance and music"; "The rhythm of music hides a mystery; if I reveal it, the world would be confused"; the thunderbolt bursting out in the Center is the symbolic image of music and sound. Also, the sacred dance of the whirling dervishes imitates the cosmic vortex, while the music suggests the primordial vibration loaded with harmony and order. "When Pao Ba played the lute (*qin*), the birds danced and the fish bounded." Shi Wen of Zheng obtained perfection in this art. "During the spring, he touched the *shang* string [corresponding to fall and metal] and called up the note of the eighth month; a cool wind came suddenly, and fruit ripened on the bushes and trees. When autumn came he touched the *jiao* string [corresponding to spring-summer and wood] and aroused the note of the second month; a warm breeze whirled gently, and the bushes and trees burst into flower. During the summer he touched the *yu* string [corresponding to winter and water] and called up the note of the eleventh month; frost and snow fell together and the rivers and lakes abruptly froze. When winter came he touched the *zi* string [corresponding to summer and fire], and aroused the note of the fifth month; the sunshine burned fiercely and the hard ice melted at once. When he was coming to the end he announced the *gong* string [corresponding to spring and wind] and played the other four together; a fortunate wind soared, auspicious clouds drifted, the sweet dew fell, the fresh springs bubbled" (*Lie-zi*, *The Questions of Tang*, 11).

[1] It corresponds symbolically to *vajra* of the Hindu tradition. Kaltenmark related *shen* (divine, spiritual) to thunderbolt and fecundity (*Lao tseu*, p. 53), and Grison stated that the thunderbolt corresponds to cosmic fecundity and to the dragon.

205

produces the primordial sound[1] and transmits the *Shruti* to those who know how to listen; finally, it is the *Avatâra*.[2] The thunderbolt's ideogram deserves special attention, since it contains a very rich and spiritual symbolism, which we can only point out without properly exploring it.[3]

---

[1] When the thunder starts its activity, a new cycle begins and the animals end their hibernation; at the spring equinox, the thunder is liberated from its subterranean retreat (Granet, *La pensée chinoise*, pp. 111, 129).

[2] In the Greek Mysteries, this identity thunderbolt = *avatâra* was well represented. This identity appears, for example, in the case of Zeus and of Zagreus. About the thunderbolt, see Jane Ellen Harrison, *Themis*, Merlin Press, 1989, pp. 56-59.

[3] The thunderbolt's ideogram is:

The commentary says that the influence *yang* descends to earth and fights the influence *yin*, which produces the light (Wieger 138). The ideogram for the descending influences shows the horizontal superior trait and the vertical trait; the thunderbolt's ideogram adds the cloud and the rain, but we notice two hands as well, which are in connection with the idea of the alternate expansion of *yang* and *yin* (the two hands are extending a cord), as in the following ideogram:

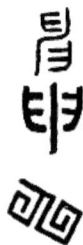

We note the double spiral and also the two "hands" and these hands reappear in the ideogram representing the immortal Daoist, where the hands suggest the ascending to heaven (Wieger 74, 140):

The ideogram for learning shows again the two hands (Wieger 139):

Gua Yi, which contains the thunderbolt, has a special quality: it represents the Mouth swallowing an obstacle that forces it to stay opened. We can organize in a symbolic group all the hexagrams that describe the mouth, hexagrams that have continuous lines in the extreme positions, while the broken traits are in the middle positions; a migratory continuous trait signifies the obstacle, which takes odd or even positions, and, consequently, fills the hexagram with a benefic or malefic meaning.

We should mention first the two *guas*, Sun (no. 41) and Shi He (no. 21), where the interior continuous trait has respectively the second and the fourth place, the even numbers belonging to Earth, to passivity and feminine.

Gua Sun   *Gua* Shi He

Gua Sun represents the decrease, and, in a way, the disadvantage, the decay. *Gua* Shi He indicates the obstacle that separates, divides and creates dissensions, and the misfortune this obstacle could cause. The only way to salvation is to destroy the obstacle and realize the union, which means the

and these hands, Wieger said, dissipate the darkness of ignorance (Wieger 109). This double activity of the two hands has a hidden meaning and we should mention here that Dionysius the Areopagite (*The Divine Names* III.1) gave us the best illustration when he spoke about God's "chain of lights." The neophyte will try to pull the chain to bring God to his heart. But God is like a rock, immutable. If we are on a boat and a rope is tied to the rock, when we pull the rope to bring the rock to us, actually the boat will be pulled to the rock. In the same way God will pull the neophyte to Heavens. The cord plays an important role in the Scottish Rite. Also, we may note that the two hands and the cord are present in the Kun ideogram.

obstacle has to be bitten (*shi*), and so the jaws are reunited (*he*); Zheng Zi said: "*Gua* Shi He expresses the great modality of governing the universe," which suggests the Wedding or the Union as warrantor of harmony and perfection.[1]

Gua no. 22, Bi, has a continuous trait in the third position (the odd numbers belong to Heaven) and signifies organizing the Cosmos, while *gua* Yi (no. 42), with the positivity in the fifth (odd) position (emperor's place), means increase and advantage.

     Gua Bi   *Gua* Yi

To understand these *guas*, from such a specific viewpoint, we should refer to the Wedding and equinoxes. *Gua* Tai, the spring equinox's hexagram, symbolizes the divine Wedding,[2] with Kun

---

[1] The Shi He ideogram presents not only the mouth but also two men between Heaven and Earth separated by a wall: it is the obstacle that separates wisdom from ignorance:

The second part of the *gua*, He, illustrates also the mouth, but now the union occurred and the beverage of immortality is enjoyed from the sacred cup. The ideogram for the sacred cup filled with the sacrificial blood is (Wieger 27):

[2] In the Far-Eastern tradition, marriage was negotiated by a mediator. At the spring equinox, the emperor offered a sacrifice to the divine Mediator, and the

208

up and Qian down, "the negativity and positivity interpenetrate in harmony" exchanging their attributes, "it is the prosperity of Heaven and Earth."

Gua Tai

From a transcendent and polar point of view, Kun is in the superior position, and Qian in the inferior position, underscoring the Union, the Wedding, and the hierogamic exchange, when "the positive influence descends and bows, the negative influence ascends and unites with the positive one," "Heaven's and Earth's influences unite and harmonize," while, from an immanent, central viewpoint, Qian is inside (in a central, essential position), and Kun is outside (in a peripheral, substantial position). "Tai, prosperity; what is small goes away; what is great comes; joyous liberty"; "negativity goes outwards, positivity comes inwards."

We note two perspectives, immanent and transcendent, both valid, beside others: the former designates the natural hierarchy active – passive, masculine – feminine, superior – inferior, and emperor – vassal; the latter depicts *coincidentia oppositorum*, peace, the union within the Principle, since nothing can exist without it, the separation or divorce – as described in the fall equinox's *gua*, Pi – heading to decadence, agony and chaos, to losing the reality by breaking the link with the Principle.

For a prosperous existence and accord with natural laws, both the hierarchy and the union (hierogamic exchange) must be observed; husband and wife, emperor and people will live in peace and harmony if they work together and "co-operate," seeing and listening to each other, assimilating each other's

---

human (marriage) mediator, after that, covered the empire announcing the order "to gather together men and women."

influences, and, at the same time, observing the hierarchy and order.[1] The husband is hierarchically superior to his wife, but they participate together at the ritual regarding the ancestors; and it was Niu Wa, the sister and wife, who received the compass and mended the Cosmos.[2] The emperor is superior to his people, he organizes the crowd into a civilized society, but if he does not allow the people to follow its natural needs, he will not govern in peace.[3]

Gua Sun derives from *gua* Tai, by diminishing Qian and increasing Kun, the third trait becoming a broken line (Qian changes in Dui), which represents a decrease, and the sixth trait becoming a continuous line (Kun changes in Gen), which represents an increase. "The mountain (Gen) is tall, the marsh (Dui) is wet and deep [like the Valley]. The deeper the low down, the higher the tall, which gives the meaning of decrease to the low down and increase to the up." It is a mouth that opens wide, with an obstacle – the continuous line in the second position, and this obstacle could be regarded as the tongue "tied" to the inferior jaw (the inferior continuous trait). This triplet (jaws and tongue) can be diminished to the primordial dyad, to the duality that fundaments the worlds,[4] when the tongue retreats and superposes over the inferior jaw; the mouth can close now and duality regains Unity.[5]

---

[1] "Even as the Son of man came not to be served, but to serve" (*Matthew* 20:28); "The disciple is not above his master, nor the servant above his lord" (*Matthew* 10:24).

[2] The hierogamic exchange makes sun feminine and moon masculine in the Norse myths; in ancient Egypt, the goddess Nut (described as a semicircle) is Heaven that covers and the god Geb (presented as a square) is Earth that supports.

[3] Even though the emperor has the supreme position, he will not intervene with artificial decrees and will accept the people's natural needs.

[4] Mountain: masculine, superior, plenitude, Purusha; marsh or valley: feminine, inferior, emptiness, Prakriti, the plastic substance.

[5] There is an ideogram showing the movement of the tongue, out and in (Wieger 149):

Epilogue: the Jaws

Diminishing or decrease is disadvantageous, since it weakens the interior, the kernel, and dangerously loads the exterior, the shell; on the other hand, it suggests the need for hierarchy: from the transcendent point of view, increasing the up and diminishing the low down means to organize and regulate the universal manifestation using as model the positivity up and the negativity down. This order is better seen in *gua* no. 22, Bi, where the median continuous trait is in the third position. *Gua* Bi, built of Gen up and Li down, derives from *gua* Tai as a result of "castling" between the second and sixth positions; apparently, also here it is possible to consider the decrease of interior, of low down, but what diminishes is an even position (the second) and not an odd one (like in *gua* Sun), which explains the accent on hierarchy, order and regulation with regard to superior – inferior, positive – negative.

Zheng Zi made the following comment: "The essential nature of inferior simple *gua* was activity (*qian*); the malleable sweetness (the broken trait in second position) comes to give its appearance to trigram's middle trait, constituting simple *gua* Li (fire). The primitive substantial nature of superior simple *gua* was passivity (*kun*); the energetic firmness gives its appearance to superior trait, constituting simple *gua* Gen (mountain); thus, Bi is obtained or the realization of established order."

Both *guas*, Sun and Bi, have the mountain outside and respectively wetness and fire inside. The fire is masculine, the water feminine, and both find shelter inside the mountain. The former is the thunderbolt descended to the center of the Earth (the light ordering the Cosmos); the latter is the plastic substance sustaining the order (the formative marsh or mud). Fire and water are a well-known pair of complementaries, related here with the obstacle – the second position in *gua* Sun and the third position in *gua* Bi.[1]

The mountain is *Axis Mundi*, the Pivot of the Rule, and its peak is the "transcendent" Principle, the Pole; inside the

---

[1] "For as Jonas was three days and three nights in the whale's belly; so shall the Son of man be three days and three nights in the heart of the earth" (*Matthew* 12:40).

mountain, there is the cave of Horeb, the median void, the World Heart, and the "immanent" Principle, hidden like the dragon in the first hexagram Qian. They are two representations, two different garments for one and the same truth: the mountain's peak, The Most High, is associated with the heavenly thunderbolt and rain; the cave, *Zhong Yong* (the Invariable Middle), is associated with water and fire hiding in the depth of Earth.

Zhun, the third hexagram, built of Kan (water) up and Zhen (thunderbolt) down, designates the thunderbolt and rain, light and water, both symbolizing, as René Guénon said, the spiritual influences.[1]

Gua Zhun

"Light and rain, both have a vivifying power, which represents precisely the action of [celestial or spiritual] influences"[2]; and Guénon noted that thunderbolt or lightning, acting upon the clouds, liberates the rain.

The celestial influences, masculine (thunderbolt) and feminine (rain), descend to vivify the Earth[3]; but first, a Wedding takes place in Heavens, this Wedding giving birth to thunderbolt and rain; for this reason, there are representations

[1] "*Yin* and *yang*, rain and dew, have to be in accord"; rain is *yin* and dew *yang* (Granet, *La pensée chinoise*, pp. 108, 490). As Guénon explained, the dew is another symbol for the spiritual influences, a symbol found in many traditions, like Hermeticism, Rosicrucianism and Kabbalah (*Symboles fondamentaux*, p. 361, *Le Roi du Monde*, p. 28). "Heaven and Earth will unite and sweet dew will fall" (*Dao De Jing*, XXXII).
[2] Guénon, *Symboles fondamentaux*, p. 361.
[3] As Harrison said, with regard to the ancient Crete: "The Earth is barren till the Thunder and the Rainstorm smite her in the springtime – till in his Epiphany of Thunder and Lightning Keraunos comes to Keraunia, the Sky-god weds Semele the Earth, the *Bride of the bladed Thunder*" (*Themis*, p. 168).

of the sun with two types of rays, straight and undulate lines, which symbolize – Guénon stated – the light and rain. Here the sun is not so much the physical sun, but the Principle as Light resulted from the Sun's marriage with the Moon,[1] or from the gathering of ten suns.

Gua Zhun illustrates this wedding supported by the hierogamic exchange, and therefore water is up and thunderbolt down. It also means that, first, *avatâra* (thunderbolt) descends into the center of the world, and the celestial influences are not yet liberated to pour down. Zheng Zi said: "Zhun expresses the beginning of life [of 'vivification']; it is the cloud's and thunderbolt's formation. Negativity and positivity unite and produce the cloud and the thunderbolt, but the benefits of this union are not yet completed. (…) *Gua* Xie illustrates how the benefits of this union are produced."

Gua no. 40, Xie, built of Zhen up and Kan down, "expresses thunderbolt's and rain's action," and it is *gua* Zhun reversed. Now we notice the normal hierarchy, thunderbolt up, operating

---

[1] This marriage is seen in the ideogram *ming* (light) (see Guénon, *La Grande Triade*, p. 140). The ancient sun's ideogram was a circle with a central point or with a horizontal diameter (Lionnet 255). The ideogram for light is (Wieger 119):

We notice the old ideogram (but not the oldest) showing the moon and a window. The modern ideogram replaced the window with the sun. Lionnet considered the change from sun to window a result of decay and then, the return to sun, a restoration of the ancient Tradition (p. 258); but, from another viewpoint, as we have already said, the pair sun – moon is an image of the Principle and for the world to exist the light must be crippled, that is why the window takes the sun's place. We may add the Chinese traditional data, which regard the character Yi (found in the *Yi Jing*'s name) composed of two other ideograms, sun and moon (Philastre's note, *Le Yi: King*, Adrien Maisonneuve, 1975, I, p. 11).

upon the clouds, and rain descending down and vivifying the Earth.[1]

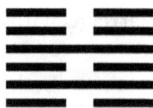

Gua Xie

Light and rain are also to be found inside the mountain, in the center, with the same vivifying action, as illustrated in *guas* Sun and Bi. In these hexagrams the idea of the "immanent" Principle is stressed, but we must understand the thunderbolt's twin activity: it unchains the celestial waters, which vivify the Earth, but also shakes the Earth and unchains the terrestrial waters, which vivify the beings.[2]

There is a hexagram which places the thunderbolt, namely the *principial* activity, inside the mountain, and it signifies "producing and vivifying all ten thousand beings," "the happy prediction of perfection:" it is *gua* Yi (no. 27), Gen up and Zhen down, which means the symbolic image of the Mouth, with continuous traits at extremities, and four broken traits inside.

Gua Yi   *Gua* Fu

---

[1] In the Christian tradition, *gua* Zhun corresponds to Christ's descending to earth, as man, and suffering the sacrifice; *gua* Xie corresponds to Christ rising to Heaven, while the Holy Spirit comes upon the Apostles and the baptizing water upon the believers.

[2] In fairy-tales these are the "mortal" and "immortal" waters, or the "dead" and "alive" waters; they correspond to Christ's double nature and to Daoist methods regarding the immortality of body and spirit.

Epilogue: the Jaws

It is the image of the dragon's mouth, without any obstacle, the mouth itself, depicted by the signs of thunderbolt and mountain, with the thunderbolt descended into the mountain's cave. In another hexagram, *gua* no. 24, Fu, built of Kun up and Zhen down, the thunderbolt is in the middle of the Earth; "positivity revives from the bottom [as *avatâra*], the sage's way blossoms. (...) Little by little positivity develops and produces the ten thousand beings. (...) When positivity is born, it appears from the interior [the bottom], it enters, and then grows and advances outwards, that is, exits" (Zheng Zi's commentary).

The thunderbolt, as *avatâra*, or as celestial influence, activates in the center of manifestation; it comes into the world, descending from Heaven along the Axis, and then it bursts outwards.[1] The thunderbolt is light and fire, yet it is accompanied by rain and clouds, and therefore, we find inside the mountain not only fire, but also water. *Gua* Sun, the Mouth with a wet tongue fixed to the inferior jaw (the passive Perfection), represents "the marsh [which] is down, under the mountain, and its influence rises freely; the humidity reaches plants and trees, and also all ten thousand beings." This humidity vivifies the world; it is the rain as celestial influence regarded upside down, from the "immanent" point of view. Similarly, *gua* Bi "represents the fire under the mountain. The

---

[1] The origin of jade, the tradition affirmed, is the activity of the thunderbolt inside the earth (Grison, p. 66). Thus, the jade, the most precious stone of the Far-Eastern tradition, symbolizes the divine Knowledge and the Tradition; and corresponds to the *avatâra* as well. "Those that know me are few; those that abuse me are honoured. Therefore the sage wears rough clothing and conceals in his heart a priceless piece of jade" (*Dao De Jing*, LXX); as we see, the jade is also the immortal Self and the inner Kingdom. The jade, combined with drops of dew (spiritual influence, *yang*), was the beverage of immortality (Grison, p. 67). Yet, even more interesting is the fact that the ideogram for jade and the one for *wang* (emperor) are very similar, which allows us to consider the emperor an *avatâra* and an effect of the divine thunderbolt. The ideogram for jade stresses the subterranean birth:

玉 王

mountain is the place where are gathered plants and trees and all ten thousand beings. Below is the fire, which brings light and makes the peak visible; plants, trees, and all kinds of beings are lighted by the fire's brightness and light; this gives the symbolic image of order and regulation." Plants, trees, and all the beings symbolize the universal Existence existing as seed in *Axis Mundi*; the fire inside the mountain is the Light of *Fiat Lux* and not the lethal fire of Ragnarok.

Gua Bi is the Mouth with an obstacle – positivity in the third position. This positivity is the dragon's "tongue of fire," which burns the world, but in this case the symbolism refers to the world's "vivification." There is here another symbolism, related to the dragon. In different traditions, the dragon hides in the cave, in the heart of the mountain, after abducting the waters and the light, which symbolizes the end of time; in the Hindu tradition, Vala, the dragon, guards the luminous cows in a cave, and Shri Aurobindo noted that these cows are identical to the seven rivers and the seven lights.[1] The hero (Indra) sacrifices the dragon[2] and liberates the waters, and the waters will burst outside the mountain. But these waters are blind and confused, passive and indecisive, not knowing the way to follow.

Gua no. 4, Meng, describes this situation. Zhu Xi said: "Meng means sun at the horizon, without clarity. At the beginning of life, the beings, blind and without clear judgment, are not yet illuminated or clarified."

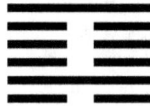

Gua Meng

Meng is composed of Kan, water, under the mountain (Gen): "at the foot of the mountain a spring surfaces; this water does

---

[1] Sanskrit *go* means both cow and light.
[2] The weapon used is an equivalent of the thunderbolt.

not yet have bed and direction."[1] The clarification comes from the fire's light; the sun, which sent a hazy light at the horizon, shines now and illuminates the beings, dissipating blindness and uncertainty, and, in fact, activating and organizing the plastic, substantial element – the waters. The midnight sun, hiding in the cave, liberates itself and shines as the noon sun, first with undulated rays, then with straight rays (in reality, simultaneously).[2]

Zheng Zi commented on *gua* no. 22, Bi: "Bi, to organize and regulate. For the beings' reunion a plan must be drawn; this plan means to organize, and put in order, and regulate. It must be authority, and principles, inferior and superior, classifications and hierarchy." Zhu Xi added: "Each one is placed in accord with his condition"; Zheng Zi also said: "*gua* Bi means realization of the established order," and it corresponds to *Fiat Lux*, in which case the continuous trait in the third position is equivalent to the Logos – also a "tongue of fire." On the other hand, *gua* Shi He symbolizes the Mouth with an obstacle in the fourth position and corresponds to the situation "and there was light." The hexagram Shi He is built of Li (fire) up and Zhen (thunderbolt) down, unifying the light of fire with the light of thunderbolt; "the shaking of thunderbolt and the lightning unite," "it is the symbolic image of discrimination with intelligence and clarity."[3]

From a point of view, *gua* Shi He, uniting thunder and lightning, designates the cosmic Intelligence that comes as Lord of a World just produced from light, the Lord who will promulgate the Rule; therefore, the first emperors, Zheng Zi

---

[1] In the traditional art of painting, the brush represents the mountain and the ink is the water.

[2] Similarly, the master, transmitting his sacred influence, dissipates the disciple's ignorance (Wieger 109):

禾 夆

[3] *Gua* Shi He is related to *gua* Feng, which is built of Zhen and Li as well.

affirmed, regarded the symbolic image of the union between thunder and lightning, and took the clarity and power of action (intelligence and authority) as rules to produce laws and regulations. On the other hand, *gua* Shi He represents the Mouth with an excessively strong obstacle, which creates separation and, consequently, disorder; of course, at the beginning, separation and disorder are not visible, but later, simultaneously with the Word scattered in more and more words, and with the initial light of thunder and lightning creating a more and more accentuated distinction and quantification (an analytical clarity), the disorder and separation between Heaven and Earth increase, the Mouth opens wider and wider.

The obstacle occupies an even position and, in comparison with *gua* Sun, it cannot be easily annihilated; the world started to exist and decay, and the only way to stop this fall would be to bite and smash the obstacle, reuniting the jaws and closing the Mouth (which means silence). It is the way indicated by *gua* Shi He's name.

In the end, the world must be destroyed and another one produced, which implies an *avatâra* that has to replace the malefic obstacle. *Gua* no. 42, Yi, built of Xun (wind) up and Zhen (thunderbolt) down, illustrates precisely this statement. The hexagram symbolizes increase and perfection: "The two simple *guas* Xun and Zhen start to reach accomplishment, both by transforming the inferior trait," Qian up becomes Xun, by diminishing, Kun down becomes Zhen, by increasing, which means that the kernel, the interior, becomes stronger, and the outside becomes weaker: it is good news, because it announces the union, the wedding with its hierogamic exchange. *Gua* Yi is the image of the Mouth with an obstacle in the fifth position, the emperor's position; this obstacle is the *avatâra*, the future emperor who covers the initiatory journey.

In some traditions, the initiate appears between the dragon's jaws, and we note the Great Triad: the upper jaw – Tian, the

Epilogue: the Jaws

obstacle (*avatâra*, neophyte) – Ren (Jen), the inferior jaw – Di.[1] The initiate, half-swallowed by the dragon, is embarked on the Middle Way, *Zhong Dao*[2]; he is in the middle: half in non-manifestation (inside the dragon) and half in manifestation, but also in the middle of the Mouth. This dragon is the equivalent of Tao-tie,[3] which sometimes does not have the inferior jaw, which stresses that it represents the Principle. As Guénon explained, Tao-tie refers to supernal darkness (the non-manifestation) and its mouth is comparable to *Kâla-mukha*, the Mouth of the Principle as "transformer."

The initiate who passes through the Jaws obtains Dao. Even if *dedao* means at the same time "to obtain Dao" and "to possess Dao," only completing a difficult initiatory journey and, especially, only after the Mouth swallowed the initiate, does *dedao* become *dedao*. Moreover, the initiate, born again, will descend into the center of the new cycle (the descending spiritual realization) as emperor invested with the heavenly mandate and he will shine and illuminate everything like a lamp.

There is an ideogram representing a lamp and meaning "prince, lord," and we may remember the metaphysical meaning of the "three lights" from other traditions:[4]

主 主

---

[1] The Sforzesco Castle in Milan preserves the Visconti family's coat of arms representing the dragon half-swallowing a young person. For the modern visitor this picture depicts, without a doubt, the vicious beast, the devil, devouring the poor human being. It is hard to believe that a coat of arms would illustrate evil. That is the error when deciphering the heraldic symbolism. The dragon is here, on the contrary, the sign of the divine Principle, the spiritual Sun liberating the neophyte (see our *The Everlasting Sacred Kernel*, Rose-Cross Books, 2002, p. 51). Ananda K. Coomaraswamy stated that, sometimes, in the Hindu tradition, the superior and inferior lips are symbols for Heaven and Earth (*Autorité Spirituelle et Pouvoir Temporel*, Archè, Milano, 1985, p. 55).

[2] About the Middle Way see Guénon, *Grande Triade*, p. 209.

[3] Guénon, *Symboles fondamentaux*, p. 357.

[4] See our work *The Wrath of Gods*, Rose-Cross Books, 2004, pp. 231-232.

The emperor, like the lamp's flame, is above the Three Worlds, and from his height he illuminates the whole manifestation. *Gua* no. 14, Da You, marks this unique moment.

Da You is built of Li (fire) up and Qian (heaven) down. It represents the "absolute liberty" and the "great possession." The fire is above heaven and shines far; everybody can see it and can receive its light. The hexagram has just one broken trait, the fifth (the emperor's place), which in this case illustrates the inner Void; it is the same Void we presented at the beginning of this work, without words, like this:

www.ingramcontent.com/pod-product-compliance
Lightning Source LLC
Chambersburg PA
CBHW062222270326
41930CB00009B/1825